# The Clientelistic Turn in Welfare State Policy-Making

## ECPR Press

ECPR Press is an imprint of the European Consortium for Political Research. It publishes original research from leading political scientists and the best among early career researchers in the discipline. Its scope extends to all fields of political science, international relations and political thought, without restriction in either approach or regional focus. It is also open to interdisciplinary work with a predominant political dimension.

# The Clientelistic Turn in Welfare State Policy-Making

## Party Politics in Times of Austerity

Evelyne Hübscher

ecpr PRESS

Published by the European Consortium for Political Research, Harbour House, 6-8 Hythe Quay, Colchester, CO2 8JF, United Kingdom



**British Library Cataloguing in Publication Data Available**

A catalogue record for this book is available from the British Library.

ISBN: HB 978-1-78552-227-7

**Library of Congress Cataloging-in-Publication Data**

ISBN: 978-1-78552-227-7 (cloth : alk. paper)
ISBN: 978-1-78552-299-4 (electronic)

ecpr.eu/shop

# Contents

List of Tables vii

List of Figures ix

Preface x

**1** Yes, They Can – Partisan Impact on Welfare State Change 1

1.1 Party Governments and Their Influence on Welfare States – Outline of the Argument 6

1.2 Key Findings and Contributions of the Book 10

1.3 Organisation of the Book 13

**2** The Politics of Welfare State Retrenchment – A Re-Assessment 15

2.1 Opposing Views on Retrenchment and Welfare State Reforms 15

2.2 Ideological or Strategic Policy-Making? An Assessment of Contradictory Theories 18

2.3 Chapter Appendix 31

**3** Party Politics and Political Constraints 36

3.1 Changing Demands for Social Policies and Social Protection 38

3.2 The Role of Social Policy in Political Competition 45

3.3 Party Governments, Political Constraints and Welfare State Reforms 46

**4** Austerity, Party Governments and Welfare State Output 58

4.1 Estimation Technique and Basic Empirical Model 58

4.2 Discussion of the Results 62
4.3 The Modifying Effect of Political Constraints 66
4.4 Changing Patterns of Partisan Effects over Time? 73
4.5 Conclusion 74

**5** The Mechanisms of Clientelistic Politics – Case Study Framework 78
5.1 Selection of Countries 79
5.2 Selection of Reforms 83

**6** Germany 90
6.1 Welfare System and Labour Market 90
6.2 Institutional Framework and Political Actors 92
6.3 Economic Context of Labour Market Policy-Making (from 1970s until the Mid-1990s) 95
6.4 Analysis of Recent Labour Market Reforms 98
6.5 Beschäftigungsförderungsgesetz (BeschfG1994) 102
6.6 Gesetz zur Reform der Arbeitsmarktpolitischen Instrumente 2001 (JobAQTIV) 113
6.7 Discussion and Outlook 124

**7** Ireland 135
7.1 Welfare System and Labour Market 135
7.2 Institutional Framework and Political Actors 138
7.3 Economic Context of Labour Market Policy-Making (from 1970s until the Mid-1990s) 142
7.4 Analysis of Recent Labour Market Reforms 146
7.5 Financial Act and Social Welfare Act 1996 150
7.6 Financial Act and Social Welfare Act 2001 162
7.7 Discussion and Outlook 170

**8** Discussion and Conclusion 180
8.1 Contextualisation of the Results 181
8.2 Main Findings and Implications 186
8.3 Concluding Remarks 196

Bibliography 202

Index 223

About the Author 233

# Tables


| | | |
|---|---|---|
| 2.1 | Political Determinants of Consolidation | 22 |
| 2.2 | Determinants of Retrenchment Size | 27 |
| 2.3 | Summary Statistics | 32 |
| 2.4 | Data Sources and Operationalisation of Variables | 32 |
| 3.1 | New Class Scheme Based on Work Logics and Skills | 41 |
| 3.2 | Labour Market Insiders and Outsiders in a Globalised Economy | 44 |
| 3.3 | Expected Effects of Partisanship and Political Constraints on Programme Generosity | 53 |
| 3.4 | Expected Effects of Partisanship and Political Constraints on Social Spending | 53 |
| 4.1 | Summary Statistics | 62 |
| 4.2 | Regression Estimates for Determinants of Δ Generosity and Δ Social Spending | 63 |
| 4.3 | Conditioning Effects of Political Constraints: Estimates for Determinants of Δ Generosity and Δ Social Spending | 68 |
| 4.4 | Marginal Effects of Programme Generosity and Social Spending for Two Time Periods and Different Levels of Political Constraints | 74 |
| 5.1 | Generosity | 86 |
| 5.2 | Spending | 86 |
| 6.1 | Reforms in Germany | 99 |
| 6.2 | Key Policy Proposals Included in the 'Beschäftigungsförderungsgesetz, 1994' | 104 |
| 6.3 | Policy Proposals Affecting the Generosity Dimension, BeschfG 1994 | 107 |

| | | |
|---|---|---|
| 6.4 | Policy Proposals Affecting the Spending Dimension, BeschfG 1994 | 108 |
| 6.5 | Reform Issues and Direction of Changes 'Beschäftigungsförderungsgesetz, 1994' | 112 |
| 6.6 | Key Policy Proposals Included in the 'JobAQTIV Law, 2001' | 114 |
| 6.7 | Policy Proposals Affecting the Generosity Dimension, JobAQTIV 2001 | 118 |
| 6.8 | Policy Proposals Affecting the Spending Dimension, JobAQTIV 2001 | 120 |
| 6.9 | Reform Issues and Direction of Changes 'JobAQTIV Law 2001' | 125 |
| 6.10 | Summary Hartz Reforms | 127 |
| 7.1 | Reforms in Ireland | 148 |
| 7.2 | Key Policy Proposals Included in the 'Financial and Social Welfare Bill, 1996' | 153 |
| 7.3 | Policy Proposals Affecting the Spending Dimension, 1996 | 157 |
| 7.4 | Reform Issues and Direction of Changes 'Financial and Social Welfare Bill, 1996' | 161 |
| 7.5 | Key Policy Proposals Included in the 'Social Welfare Act, 2001' | 164 |
| 7.6 | Policy Proposals Affecting the Spending Dimension | 168 |
| 7.7 | Reform Issues and Direction of Changes 'Social Welfare Act, 2001' | 171 |
| 8.1 | Active Labour Market Policies (Ideal Types) | 184 |
| 8.2 | Categorisation of Reform Issues Based on Bonoli's Ideal Types of ALMP | 185 |

# Figures


2.1 Probability of Retrenchment Events over Electoral Cycle 25
3.1 Preferences for Redistribution Based on Occupational Class 46
3.2 Development of Electoral Platforms for Four Party Families, over Forty Years 47
3.3 Preferences for Redistribution Based on Occupational Class (in Germany and Ireland) 49
4.1 The Modifying Effect of Political Constraints on the Redistributive Generosity of Welfare State Programmes 69
4.2 The Modifying Effect of Political Constraints on Social Spending 70
4.3 Predicted Changes for Left- and Right-Wing Governments (Programme Generosity) 72
4.4 Predicted Changes for Left- and Right-Wing Governments (Social Spending) 72
5.1 Political Spectrum Germany 81
5.2 Political Spectrum Ireland 83
6.1 Annual Economic Growth Rates in Germany: 1970–2012 96
6.2 Unemployment Rate in Germany (as Percentage of Total Labour Force) 97
6.3 Net Income Inequality in Germany (1990–2012) 130
7.1 Annual Economic Growth Rates in Ireland: 1970–2012 144
7.2 Unemployment Rate in Ireland (as Percentage of Total Labour Force) 145
7.3 Net Income Inequality in Ireland (1990–2012) 175

# Preface

The origin of this book is my PhD thesis written at the European University Institute in Florence under the supervision of Peter Mair, whose intellectual brilliance and kindness is still very much alive in my memory.

In between the original dissertation and the book, many things happened in my life. While the majority of the changes were of positive nature, they had the negative effect of slowing down the work on the manuscript. Starting a job as junior faculty at the Central European University in Budapest was bliss but also meant that the seemingly endless chores of teaching made it – at times – difficult to single out time for research and publishing. Still, I could not have wished for a better place to start my career. CEU, and in particular the School of Public Policy, provided me with a stimulating and challenging environment that allowed me to grow professionally. At SPP, I am particularly thankful to my colleagues Marie-Pierre Granger, Agnes Batory, Achim Kemmerling and Thilo Bodenstein for their friendship and support throughout the past years. Throughout all these years, I could always rely on the friendship and support of Kathrin Frey and Kaat Smets, both of whom I unfortunately don't see as often as I would like. Thank you for many great hours spent talking, laughing and discussing the various facets of our lives.

The birth of my two children alienated me from the manuscript and the plan to focus on finding a final home for it. However, their presence makes my life richer, and they prove to be an endless source of joy and laughter. Thus, the work on this manuscript and revisions was marked by a number of interruptions and was at times characterised by stagnation rather than progress. Finishing the manuscript has been facilitated by the patience of my publisher and the various people at ECPR Press whom I communicated with throughout the past years. I would also like to thank Louise Cooper for her extremely careful and considerate copyediting and Colin Walder for helping me putting together the final manuscript. All remaining errors are mine.

This book is dedicated to my family, in particular my husband Thomas. I cannot imagine a better partner to share my life with. It is through his love, patience and clarity of thought that this book sees the light of the world and that a long process finally comes to an end.

*Chapter 1*

# Yes, They Can – Partisan Impact on Welfare State Change

Welfare states and social policy play a key role in political competition in modern democracies. These institutions and policies are crucial in mitigating some of the most important risks, such as the loss of income, sickness and unemployment, that individuals in industrialised countries face in modern times. The position of parties and their propositions on how to address social risks, therefore, are crucial for social groups with diverging exposure to these risks. Accordingly, among the variety of approaches that explain the development of welfare states and their differences, a majority of them attribute an important, if not crucial, role to political parties (Esping-Andersen 1990; Korpi 1978; Manow 2015; van Kersbergen 1995). The ability of parties and party governments to offer and implement distinct social policies to meet these diverging policy preferences is an essential component of political competition and democratic politics. From this perspective, the development of differing welfare state regimes and social policy schemes across countries can be viewed as an exemplar of democratic political competition.

Although the influence of party politics and party governments has preoccupied political scientists since the emergence of the discipline and has been assessed in a number of policy fields, most prominently in economic policy-making (i.e. Hibbs 1977), the study of welfare states and party politics stands out as there is hardly any citizen who is unaffected by social policies, either as a contributor to social security schemes or as a recipient of benefits. The comparative welfare state literature has produced a great number of studies which examine the effects of party politics on welfare state development, structure and design. One of the reasons why comparative welfare state research is so rich in studies that focus on how party governments, in particular left-wing governments, shape welfare states is the fact that social and labour market policies affect such a large number of citizens in a country.

While historically welfare state policy has been a central component of political competition, citizens and researchers nowadays often have doubts about whether political competition in this policy area still works as well as it used to. With increasing international economic interdependence, the role of politics, and in particular the influence of party governments on social policies, has been questioned and critically scrutinised. Additional factors, such as a changing regulatory environment for global financial flows, and structural changes in the domestic economic environment have further nourished the emerging claim about the diminishing room to manoeuvre of party governments. Scholars concerned with questions having to do with welfare state retrenchment and the nature of party competition in Western democracies have also developed a more critical view about the ability of political parties to shape the development of public policies according to their electoral platform. A common conclusion is that economic globalisation imposes serious constraints on political parties and welfare state policy-making (Huber and Stephens 2001; Pierson 2001). Following their argumentation, the politics of retrenchment follow a different underlying logic, less susceptible to partisan politics and preferences than the politics of welfare state expansion and growth. As an example, Pierson (1996) proposes that the politics of welfare state reform and retrenchment are mainly characterised by strategies that help to avoid blame and obfuscate the implications and impact of reforms. Based on these key assumptions, parties in government try to delay unpopular reforms and obscure their impact (Hübscher and Sattler 2017; Vis 2010; Wenzelburger 2014).

In a separate literature focusing on other forms of party competition, researchers have come to similar conclusions. They assess the role of political parties in Western democracies from a broader perspective and propose that the policy positions and electoral platforms of political parties have converged (Katz and Mair 2009; Mair 2000; Nanou and Dorussen 2013). Furthermore, competition among parties around political issues has declined or is no longer taking place (Mair 1995, 2008). The reasons that party scholars put forward to explain this development are similar to the ones that are prominent in the comparative welfare state literature. Due to international interdependence and increasing budgetary pressures, political parties find themselves deprived of the possibility of shaping large areas of economic policy-making according to their ideological roots. In addition to the shrinking room to manoeuvre in terms of preferred policy choices, party scholars observe an increasing alienation of parties from their voter base and a convergence of policy positions among parties which have historically presented different policy solutions.

The inability of parties in government to pursue their ideological agenda or their electoral platforms has implications for representative democracy and the way in which voters perceive political parties. It negatively affects people's trust in government and the democratic processes and eventually leads to a decline in political participation (Armingeon and Guthmann 2014; Armingeon and Schädel 2015). It is widely agreed that the role of political parties and party governments is fundamental to democratic and representative politics (Gallagher, Laver and Mair 1992; Manin 1997; Przeworski, Stokes and Manin 1999). Political parties have a key role in shaping and reforming public policies in general, and social and welfare policies more specifically. Democratic rule and representative democracy is meaningful only if political actors have the ability to propose and implement diverging solutions to social, economic and political problems, and if citizens have a choice between different sets of policies. Without political competition over different policies and strategies to address issues that are salient to the electorate, the significance of core democratic institutions diminishes because the importance of elections and representative government becomes increasingly insignificant. Diminishing party competition therefore reduces both interest and trust in political institutions, a phenomenon that has been well documented in many industrialised democracies over the recent years (Katz and Mair 2009; Mair 2008).

Despite these pessimistic assessments of party governments and their room to manoeuvre, the welfare state literature has started to challenge the idea that social policy is 'locked in' and cannot be changed. While it is true that most policy change is associated with retrenchment, we still see significant variation in social policy developments. Contrary to popular predictions, continental welfare states such as France, the Netherlands, Switzerland and Germany did cut social rights in not only several policy fields, especially pensions (Germany, Switzerland and France) but also unemployment insurance schemes (the Netherlands) (Green-Pedersen 2002, Häusermann 2010a; Huber and Stephens 2001; Seeleib-Kaiser, van Dyk and Roggenkamp 2008). These findings clearly go against the notion of path dependence and stasis proposed by proponents of the 'New Politics' thesis. Furthermore, party politics, coalition building with extra-parliamentarian actors and the ideology of the incumbent government played an important role in these country-specific reform processes and significantly shaped their outcome. While some fields of welfare state policy-making underwent retrenchment, others, such as family and child-care policies, experienced significant expansion and increasing attention by policy-makers and citizens (Morgan 2013; Taylor-Gooby 2004). Many older studies also fail to explain why some governments have provided new policies directed at newly emerging social needs, such as child care, or why others fail to do so. These developments cannot be explained by the institutional theories which predominantly emphasise path dependency and ignore party politics.

More broadly, the empirical accounts of the functionalist view on policy-making in the post-golden era of the welfare state and the results found on the influence of partisanship on policy designs and reforms are contradictory. Although it is generally agreed that the pressure to reform social welfare institutions has been consistently high during recent decades, social policies continue to differ substantially across countries. The expected convergence of different types of welfare states did not take place, and the way countries take on welfare state reforms differs considerably. In light of these findings, the recent wave of welfare state research engages with alternative theoretical explanations, taking the role of politics and parties more seriously and reassessing the role of political parties as well as their vote- and policy-seeking motives in view of recent reforms and structural changes. Scholars have started to take a renewed interest in the key question concerning what parties in government really want, and whether their policy goals are representative of the party's public image and of their constituency's policy preferences. More recent contributions, therefore, show a more multi-faceted picture of welfare state development in the age of austerity (Green-Pedersen and Haverland 2002; Häusermann 2010a; Seeleib-Kaiser, van Dyk and Roggenkamp 2008).

This book stands in the tradition of these studies and aims at further developing and advancing our understanding of welfare state policy-making in times of budgetary and political constraints. It critically engages with traditional assumptions about the policy preferences of political parties, as well as their impact on public policies and on their traditional constituencies (Alexiadou 2013; Hübscher 2017; Jensen and Mortensen 2014). In particular, it deals with the question of which social groups benefit from which party constellation in government. Recent studies still maintain, at least implicitly, the idea that overall the salaried working class generally benefits from left-wing governments and that the working class also supplies the majority of votes for left-wing parties (Pontusson and Rueda 2010). This key assumption, however, has been seriously questioned by researchers assessing the changing class structure of societies and political parties (Oesch 2006b, 2008; Rehm 2009). Together with this well-documented knowledge about ongoing economic and structural changes, the long-held views on the party preferences of individuals also need to be assessed and revised. Newer contributions to the literature thus more critically assess the link between government partisanship and public policies with a particular focus on the reform of popular welfare state institutions and the development of new social policies (Häusermann, Picot and Geering 2013). The type of policy instruments and means that political parties choose from to reform policies in times of budgetary constraints may deviate from our expectations, which are still grounded in the traditional, one-dimensional approaches.

Recent work also proposes that the strategic aspects of policy-making have gained more importance in an environment of permanent austerity and budgetary constraints (Hübscher and Sattler 2017; Wenzelburger 2014). The increasing importance of strategic aspects of public policy-making substantiates and confirms the insight that the New Politics literature was accurate in its assessment that welfare state and social policy reforms are unpopular with the electorate. Governments are aware that, while necessary, the implementation of welfare state and labour market reforms can deploy negative electoral effects. Yet, the fact that such reforms are electorally risky does not mean that governments refrain from embarking on reforming welfare state institutions. Party governments are able to successfully address these challenges and also implement the necessary reforms, for example, by strategically timing the reform within the electoral cycle (Hübscher 2016). Alternatively, governments may make use of specific policy instruments which obfuscate the true nature of the changes (König and Wenzelburger 2014; Vis and van Kersbergen 2013). Current research, however, should carve out these strategies more carefully.

With regard to strategic behaviour, institutional setups play a crucial role. However, our knowledge of the interplay between political strategy and institutional context is still sparse. On the one hand, it is commonly acknowledged that institutional factors matter for policy-making. On the other hand, the dominant theories explaining welfare state development and change are surprisingly agnostic when it comes to the effect of institutional contexts on the reform strategies of parties in government. The institutionalist literature mostly conceptualises institutions as preservers of existing policies and says little on how institutions condition policy change. However, institutions not only influence the paths reforms of the social insurance schemes can take but also constitute a framework to mobilise and unite beneficiaries of the schemes. The way political institutions, existing social policy schemes and political actors mutually influence each other and affect the reforms that political parties propose has not been systematically assessed. An exemption is an emerging literature that engages with the question of how institutional contexts and constraints may enable some parties but restrict others in pursuing their preferred reform paths (Abou-Chadi and Immergut 2014; Jensen and Mortensen 2014). Overall, however, there is a clear need to examine how reform strategies and their impact on specific societal groups differ across institutional context and party government.

The argument presented in chapter 3 addresses these shortcomings. In short, it proposes an explanatory framework that highlights the following building blocks: the first building block of the argument suggests that social policies are multi-dimensional. More specifically, this means that the room to manoeuvre that is available to party governments is not only limited by their ability to influence the spending dimension. In times of fiscal austerity, governments can also alter the redistributive characteristics of a given social security scheme and therefore privilege or discriminate against specific societal groups. The second building block of the argument is the explicit modelling of the interactions between institutional constraints and the reform strategies of political parties in this multi-dimensional policy space. The political constraints configure the room to manoeuvre available to party governments. Depending on the given configurations, governments are able to propose and implement social policy reforms which address the preferences of the electorate on both dimensions. However, this scenario is plausible only if political constraints are low. If political constraints are high, the policy-making opportunities of party governments are significantly limited and they have to compromise with the demands of the opposition party with regard to one dimension, usually the spending dimension. In such cases, policy proposals will be designed in such a way that they preserve the privileges of the core workforce, the traditional working class, in order to maintain their electoral support.

The last building block of the argument is the emphasis on the strategies of left-wing governments to compensate the well-organised part of the labour force ('insiders') at the expense of the poorly organised and politically inactive labour force ('outsiders'). In a political environment characterised by high levels of constraint, left-wing party governments have to come to an agreement with the parties in the opposition, which is often reached by limiting expenditures on social security, all the while attempting to ensure that they don't lose the support of their core constituency. This balancing act can be achieved through the compensation of the core labour force, specifically by increasing the redistributive generosity of core social security schemes.

## 1.1 PARTY GOVERNMENTS AND THEIR INFLUENCE ON WELFARE STATES – OUTLINE OF THE ARGUMENT

A defining feature of many contributions assessing the impact of party politics on changes to the welfare state is their focus on a uni-dimensional conceptualisation of welfare state and labour market policies. In other words, they mostly examine the extent to which spending on specific programmes has increased or decreased. The dominant focus on a single dimension of policies does not allow for the observation of the more finely grained and nuanced choices that political parties have for the further development of public policies. Having a more nuanced way of assessing the impact of politics is particularly relevant in these times when (mostly left-wing) political parties are increasingly deprived of any possibility to expand traditional social security schemes due to budgetary pressures. The newly emerging policy-making landscape, however, requires that political parties consider additional policy options and strategies to compensate their constituency and distinguish themselves from their political opponents. This means that social policy-making should be perceived as a multi-dimensional exercise rather than as a battle to implement the least cost-saving policies.

The argument of this book proposes that the way in which a government reforms social policies under these circumstances depends on two key factors: first, its partisanship and policy preferences influenced by its underlying ideology; and second, the institutional constraints that the government faces. The existing institutional constraints alter the reform strategy of party governments and influence the set of policies available to a government. Institutional constraints determine whether a party government has to gain support from opposition parties (e.g. in a bicameral system) to implement a reform, and the extent to which interest groups can access the policy-making process and block a reform proposal. The theoretical framework highlights the logic in which the ideology of party governments *jointly* with institutional constraints determines the outcome of welfare state reforms.

An important aspect of this process is the ability of party governments to build broader reform coalitions or to obtain the support of interest groups, mainly that of trade unions, in order to overcome institutional barriers. This argument is centred on the idea that social policy-making encompasses two main dimensions, specifically, an expenditure dimension and a dimension capturing the redistributive generosity of social policy programmes. By taking into account more than just the spending dimension, we are able to understand how governments exploit leverage on one dimension in order to be able to compromise on the other. While party governments are likely to face constraints on one dimension, particularly the spending dimension, they have greater room to implement their preferred policy choices on the other dimension. This setting also allows them to overcome and bridge diverging preferences on one of the two policy dimensions. Thus, party governments can gain the support of pivotal, well-organised societal groups and overcome institutional constraints by partly compensating them for social cuts through greater concessions on other policy dimensions.

The institutional setting of a country decisively influences how governments strategically use the trade-off between these two dimensions. In particular, institutions define which societal groups are pivotal and need to be considered in policy reforms. Governments therefore adjust policy depending on the importance of different societal groups. For instance, governments which face opposition in a second parliamentary chamber are likely to compromise on aspects that are of particular importance to their political opponents. Giving in on aspects that are important to the opposition, however, can provoke outrage and anger among the core supporters of the party in government. In order to prevent such outrage, the party in government can shield its supporting base from significant losses at the expense of other groups that are less relevant for the political success and survival of the party in government. Examining the joint impact of party government and constraints on welfare states is therefore important in understanding the mechanisms of reforms politics and how their outcomes differ across institutional and political settings, often at the expense of less organised social groups.

To sum up, the argument suggests that a right-wing government that does not face high institutional constraints will mainly cut social spending, but will not offer any compensation for the losers of the reform through redistribution. The situation is different for a right-wing government in a country where institutional constraints are high. These governments will often end up with small-scale social policy reforms that bring little change in terms of both redistributive generosity and retrenchment. The implementation of more substantial spending cuts can be prevented by interest groups – mainly trade unions and employers' organisations – through their influence on opposition parties or the government. Traditionally, trade unions demand compensation for their constituencies while employers, with close connections to conservative and liberal parties in power, oppose such compensatory measures. The result will be a failed reform or one that is incomplete and has little impact on social policies.

The reform outcomes will differ when a left-wing government is in power. Left-wing governments in countries with few institutional constraints will tend to implement welfare state reforms that reduce spending and at the same time compensate the broader workforce through greater redistribution. A broad range of working-class citizens exposed to social risk will benefit in a roughly similar manner from the compensation measures. When a left-wing government faces high institutional constraints, however, it will have to accommodate conservative political forces and thus offer greater retrenchment to reach an agreement with the opposition party. The left-wing government will also have to make sure that well-organised constituencies, so-called insiders, which are represented by trade unions, are not too greatly affected by the reform. At the same time, compensation cannot come from the wealthy because this would provoke resistance from right-wing parties. The solution will be a disproportionate retrenchment on the side of the poorly organised, precariously employed workforce ('outsiders') to satisfy the needs of the well-organised 'insiders' and simultaneously achieve a sufficient reduction in social expenditures to accommodate the opposition.

Using the analytical framework described earlier, the study generates the following substantive implications. It suggests that more encompassing reforms are often proposed and implemented by left-wing governments. This is in line with existing research by Armingeon et al. (2016) and earlier contributions by Green-Pedersen (2001b). My argument resembles a so-called Nixon-goes-to-China logic (Baggesen Klitgaard 2007; Ross 2000a) although the mechanism is different. In the standard argument, the electorate of a government consisting of pro-welfare parties does not expect this government to dismantle popular social policy institutions. Due to the fact that leftist parties 'own' the welfare state issue (Petrocik 1996), they enjoy a high level of credibility among their voters when it comes to the design and implementation of social policy reforms. According to the literature, this high level of credibility gives left-wing governments some more leeway to negotiate reforms together with their social partners. In contrast, my argument suggests that the left-wing party is able to get away with the reform because it compensates key constituencies but is able to do so only by disadvantaging other social groups that are electorally less relevant.

The second key implication of this book is that left-wing parties can adversely affect the societal rights and standing of labour market 'outsiders' in situations where the opposition has the ability to veto the government's legislative proposal (see also Rueda 2007, 2008). This negative impact of left-wing governments on labour market 'outsiders' results from the fact that these parties when governing in a context of high levels of institutional constraints are pressured to seek a compromise with the opposition on policy issues that are of crucial importance to them. Achieving a compromise with the opposition comes at some cost and entails cutting back on some of the initially proposed policies. The resulting compromise is likely to come at the expense of weaker labour market participants who are not well organised and are less influential in the policy-making debate with the government. The conscious preferential treatment of the core workforce adds a clientelistic touch to the policy-making qualities of a left-wing government that is subject to political constraints. This finding is counterintuitive and goes against the common wisdom that the Left represents the interests of the overall workforce, including the least privileged people in society.

Third, these arguments have important implications for political competition and partisan support. Mainstream left-wing political parties whose policies are directed at a specific segment of the labour force, mainly labour market 'insiders', are likely to lose the support of less privileged segments of the labour market. Depending on the overall structure of the party landscape, these voters then have reason to support parties which take a more pronounced leftist potentially populist position and more forcefully advocate redistributive justice. Or they turn towards political parties that campaign on platforms that promote less immigration and more cultural homogeneity in order to appeal to voters who are disappointed with the offerings of the traditional parties. Overall, this development further contributes to the polarisation of the political landscape as we have seen in many countries.

## 1.2 KEY FINDINGS AND CONTRIBUTIONS OF THE BOOK

The book shows that party governments resort to different strategies in different institutional contexts to pass social policy reforms. As a result, the political ideology of the party in government does make a difference to the type of policy reform outcome. This is shown by the quantitative and qualitative analyses. In short and contrary to earlier research, this study finds clear partisan effects. This implies that the importance of political parties in shaping public policies in times of fiscal austerity and open economies should not be underestimated. Rather than convergence of partisan positions, we observe the mushrooming of new political contestants which increases the need for strategic policy-making and well-designed reforms which appeal to a majority of the stakeholders. This study also empirically traces the emergence of new, clientelistic patterns of policy-making by left-wing party governments which contradicts long-held views that one of the top priorities of left-wing governments is to work towards a more egalitarian society. The development towards clientelistic policy-making that benefits specific segments of the electorate has the potential to affect societal structures in the long-run and to limit social rights, particularly for people in low-skill and low-wage sectors.

More specifically, the quantitative analyses reveal a clear partisan effect on the redistributive generosity dimension of social policy-making. The influence of party governments on the redistributive generosity of core welfare state programmes that benefit the well-organised labour force ('insiders'), such as unemployment insurance and pension schemes, remained intact during the period of increasing fiscal austerity, with left-wing party governments having a tendency towards a positive impact on redistributive generosity which primarily benefits labour market insiders. The positive impact of left-wing governments on redistributive generosity tends to increase the more political constraints the government faces. The influence of party governments on the spending dimension, however, has vanished, with economic determinants, such as unemployment and low economic growth, having a statistically significant positive, respectively negative effect on social expenditure. This finding can be explained by the increasing financial constraints and liabilities that governments are facing in post-industrial economies.

The results from the in-depth case studies of labour market reforms in Germany and Ireland assess the underlying policy-making processes which lead to these outcomes. The analysis of the reform processes shows how different party governments draft reform proposals to find a majority and overcome potential veto points, depending on the institutional constraints they face. The analyses show that institutional constraints, jointly with government partisanship, affect the design and content of reform proposals. As an example, the Conservative German government in 1994, facing a Social Democratic majority in the second chamber (the 'Bundesrat'), ended up with a de facto small-scale reform of the labour market and limited retrenchment. This occurred because it did not want to offer more compensation for further retrenchment. In contrast, the subsequent left-wing government imposed greater retrenchment measures but, at the same time, accommodated trade unions more than was originally planned. The main losers were low-skilled labour and the poor who were less able to organise efficiently and were only marginally represented by the large and powerful unions. In Ireland, the situation for the left-wing 'rainbow' coalition government in 1996 was different. The lack of powerful veto points enabled the government to implement labour market policy reforms that were mainly directed towards 'outsiders'. The emphasis on the re-integration of the long-term unemployed and the improvement of the social insurance coverage for part-time employees are two examples that show how party governments are able to direct and link policy changes with their ideological preferences.

Taken together, this study's main theoretical contributions are threefold. First, it conceptualises (social) policies as multi-dimensional and therefore moves beyond the uni-dimensional characterisation of policies that highlights only the expansion or retrenchment of spending on a given policy. Assessing social and labour market policies on more than just the spending dimension allows us to assess how party governments go about reforming popular social policies in times of fiscal austerity in a more nuanced way. The theoretical interest in the multi-dimensionality of social and labour market policies is additionally inspired by empirical evidence that while both Social Democratic and Conservative governments are implementing cost-cutting reforms, left-wing governments manage to maintain welfare state programmes which protect the core workforce. The analysis of multiple dimensions of policy-making yields different results from those produced by a one-dimensional approach that exclusively focuses on social spending (Huber and Stephens 2001). It particularly implies that party politics continues to matter but in a way that the many macro studies that solely examine social spending size are unable to capture.

This leads to the second theoretical contribution: taking into account that social policy-making goes beyond expanding or retrenching specific schemes allowed me to focus on how party governments strategically exploit the multi-dimensionality of social policies when reforming and adjusting social policies, in particular labour market policies. A focus on strategic policy-making sharpens our understanding of how party governments are able to design policies which can overcome political hurdles and find sufficient support among the decisive actors. If compromises on the spending dimension are not possible due to budgetary constraints, the party government will try to design the reform in a way that offers compensation to potentially opposed actors on dimensions other than spending, particularly redistributive generosity.

Third, the theoretical argument systematically connects the multi-dimensionality of policy-making to the interdependence between government partisanship and institutional constraints. The framework explicitly proposes that the political constraints differ for left-wing and right-wing party governments. This allows for a more sensitive examination of how institutional constraints, access opportunities for organised interests to decision-making arenas and changing relationships between political parties and societal groups all influence government policy-making. The framework thus extends our knowledge of how political parties are dealing with new economic realities, emerging political conflict lines and more volatile voter bases under diverging political settings.

Empirically, the study provides a comprehensive picture of social policy reforms by combining an encompassing quantitative analysis with multiple case studies. It covers core welfare state policies, specifically sick pay, unemployment insurance and pension programmes (in the quantitative macro section), and specifically focuses on the reform of unemployment insurance and active labour market policies in the country case study section. The choice of these policy fields is justified because the aforementioned social security schemes are seriously affected by internationalisation and structural change. The qualitative case studies systematically link party politics with the institutional context which configures political relations and power structures. This aims at assessing the important question of how the political preferences of the core workforce are translated into specific policies, and under which circumstances, and what the role of special interest groups are.

The empirical part of the study is modelled on a mixed-methods design which combines quantitative research with detailed qualitative case studies of labour market reforms in Germany and Ireland. While the quantitative section allows me to assess the proposed relationship between party governments, economic factors and policy reforms on the macro level, the case study chapters assess the underlying political mechanisms and policy deals among key actors. Also, while the quantitative section examines the relationship over a period of roughly thirty years, the case study chapters offer a more precise snapshot of reforms designed by party governments with different ideological agendas, taking place in specific institutional settings characterised by varying levels of political constraints. This shift away from a purely quantitative framework based on the analysis of aggregate (spending) data in comparative welfare state research is a fruitful way of assessing the underlying mechanisms proposed in the theoretical framework and allows us to evaluate party competition in a new light.

The case studies highlight reform processes in Ireland and Germany during the 1990s and early 2000s. While Germany receives a lot of attention in welfare state research, the Irish case is often excluded from comparative studies and not well linked and compared to general developments in the study of welfare state reforms in advanced industrial societies. The Irish case, however, adds interesting insights in policy-making processes by coalition governments which are not subject to high levels of institutional constraints and which include political parties with very distinct welfare and labour market agendas.

## 1.3 ORGANISATION OF THE BOOK

The remainder of this book is divided into two parts. The first part, consisting of chapters 2 and 3, first provides an overview of the recent developments in literature and then provides a first empirical assessment of the contradictory theories on the impact of government partisanship on policy outcomes in times of budgetary constraints. Using a novel data set capturing episodes of fiscal consolidation in post-industrial democracies, chapter 2 examines the capacity of party governments to influence both the timing and the extent of retrenchment measures. It confirms that although governments find it difficult to avoid retrenchment measures, left-wing governments seem to implement smaller packages than right-wing, conservative governments. This lends support to the key theoretical contribution of this book that party governments still enjoy a certain room to manoeuvre which allows them to tailor reforms.

Chapter 2 then proposes the theoretical framework guiding the subsequent chapters, including the quantitative and qualitative analyses. The chapter first describes the tension that governments face because globalisation leads to new demands and at the same time constrains the supply of social policies. The second part presents the logic of partisan social policy-making in which actors can choose both the size of spending and the amount of redistribution. The theoretical argument also presents the mechanism by which institutions interfere with party politics in the two-dimensional social policy space and shape the policy outcomes accordingly.

The second part, which includes chapters 4, 5, 6 and 7, consists of the empirical analyses assessing the proposed theoretical framework. Chapter 4 quantitatively assesses the impact of party governments on the redistributive generosity of core social policy programmes and social expenditure. In line with the findings of existing work, the results show that party governments have no statistically significant impact on the spending dimension anymore. The analysis, however, reveals that left-wing party governments have a significant and positive impact on redistributive generosity, which primarily benefits labour market insiders. The positive impact of left-wing governments on redistributive generosity tends to be even greater the more political constraints the government is facing.

Chapters 6 and 7 are dedicated to the in-depth case studies. The first of the case study chapters discusses the rationale for the selection of the countries and the reform processes which are assessed in each of the two countries. Chapters 6 and 7 analyse labour market reforms in Germany and Ireland. The analysis of the underlying reform processes shows how different party governments draft reform proposals to find a majority and overcome potential veto points, depending on the institutional constraints they face. The book ends with chapter 8, which includes a summary of the combined evidence and a discussion of the potential implications of the study and finishes by offering some conclusions.

*Chapter 2*

# The Politics of Welfare State Retrenchment – A Re-Assessment

This chapter engages with a large body of literature that deals with a fundamental question in political science and welfare state research, namely, whether and how the partisanship of a government influences policies and the macroeconomic environment. This question attracted a lot of attention in the early days of welfare state research (i.e. Alt 1985; Blais, Blake Dion 1993; Castles 1982) but gained more prominence again with the increasing interdependence of domestic economies and the fiscal pressure many governments started to experience over the past decades (i.e. Garrett 1993, 1998; Huber and Stephens 1998, 2001; Pierson 1994). This chapter reviews opposing views on retrenchment and welfare state reforms from the 'politics matter' perspective and empirically reassesses its key claims.

## 2.1 OPPOSING VIEWS ON RETRENCHMENT AND WELFARE STATE REFORMS

During the 1990s, the focus of the research on the political economy of welfare states shifted from explaining the rise and different shapes of welfare states to the analysis of welfare state stasis, reform and retrenchment. Broadly speaking, we can distinguish between two different views taken in political economy research concerning the role of politics for economic and social policy reforms in post-industrial welfare states which have to cope with diminishing revenues and increasing public debt. On the one hand, a significant literature suggests that governments have lost their ability to design and implement policies according to their party preferences (Kitschelt 2001; Mair 2006; Pierson 2001). On the other hand, and in contrast to the aforementioned apolitical and functionalist perspective of policy change and reform, there is a second strand of research that ascribes to political parties, in particular the Left, an important role in reforming mature welfare states (Green-Pedersen 2001a, 2002; Levy 1999).

These literatures yield a great variety of findings about the ability of governments to reform, cut back and shape social policies, which are at times contradictory and inconclusive. In the meantime, independent from the theoretical perspective, welfare states have by no means remained frozen landscapes over the past years, as both incremental and significant reforms have been implemented in a large number of countries. These reforms took place despite the overwhelming public support welfare state institutions enjoy across Western democracies. What is up for debate, however, are the determinants and underlying mechanisms of recent and current reforms in post-industrial welfare states. The pages that follow will briefly summarise the key elements of the opposing views and present original empirical evidence that constitutes an empirical puzzle and lends initial support to one of the aforementioned theories. The chapter thus serves as an empirically driven literature review which assesses the key theoretical strands that underpin scholarship on welfare state development and retrenchment over the past years, namely the 'partisan' approach and the 'New Politics' approach.

In order to assess these two contradictory views on partisan impact, the empirical contributions in this chapter rely on a novel data set consisting of information about retrenchment *events* and their *size*. The nature of the data allows retrenchment processes to be split into the actual event (i.e. whether or not retrenchment takes place), and the size of any eventual retrenchment. The separation of the two gives us a clearer picture about the nature of partisan impact and its constraints in times of permanent austerity.[1] The data cover discrete consolidation events in sixteen Western democracies and includes a total of 159 instances of fiscal adjustments between 1978 and 2009 (Devries et al. 2011).[2] The selection of the consolidation events included in the data set is based on official announcements by public authorities of fiscal deficit cuts in nominal terms measured as the percentage of gross domestic product (GDP). Consolidation events are thus identified qualitatively based on the most important policy documents in each country, including Budget Reports, Budget Speeches, OECD Economic Surveys and IMF Staff Reports. These documents 'explicitly provide evidence of what policymakers believed at the time that the decisions were taken' (Devries et al. 2011, p. 4). Assessing the predictive power of key welfare state theories using data on fiscal consolidation events is helpful as such reforms hardly go unnoticed. It is therefore more likely that an association will be found between strategic, political or economic factors and across-the-board retrenchment in quantitative macro studies than in an assessment of these impacts on specific social security schemes or changes in public spending. Indeed, the implementation of small-scale programme reforms can be hidden more easily by governments and often raises less public outcry. In addition, assessing the impact of political and socio-economic factors on retrenchment events and size rather than incremental changes in general public or social spending has the advantage that the former represent pure political acts, that is, government decisions, which need to be legislated by parliament. The retrenchment events included in the data set are therefore based on conscious decisions of the cabinet and represent the political and strategic considerations of policy-makers more properly than gradual outcome variables like spending.[3]

For the retrenchment events that are identified, the size of the respective measures is then specified by assessing the impact these cuts had on the overall fiscal balance of a given country expressed as a percentage of the overall GDP. The data set therefore captures the governmental decisions, which can be publicly identified and were debated, as consolidation events. The raw data indicate the size of fiscal consolidation in the year it took place. Using this information, a time-series cross-section data set is first constructed, with a discrete dependent variable that takes the value 1 for the year in which the data set reports that a consolidation event occurred, and the value 0 for years in which no event is reported. This yields a balanced data set from 1978 to 2009 which can be used to estimate the *probability* of a consolidation event given a specific political and economic context. To examine the *size* of consolidation, another variable is constructed which takes the value 0 when no fiscal cut took place, or a value corresponding to the amount of consolidation as listed in the original data for the year when the government implemented the reform.

The explanatory variables included in the analysis represent the various factors that prominent welfare state theories hold accountable for having an influence on decision-making capacity of governing parties and their room to manoeuvre in times of austerity. Hence, the key political independent variables are government ideology, political constraints (Henisz 2006) and different electoral variables. Government ideology is measured using an index suggested by Kim and Fording (1998, 2002). The measure is based on the left-right index from the Comparative Manifesto Project and takes into account the weighted seat share in parliament of each party in the cabinet. The original index varies from −100 (most left-wing position) to 100 (most right-wing position). This index has been rescaled for this analysis to range between 0 and 1. Lower values still indicate more left-wing party governments. Political constraints are measured using the general constraints index by Henisz (2006). To assess the strategic dimensions of retrenchment politics, two electoral variables are used which capture the effect the electoral cycle has on government reform activity. The first is an electoral counter counting the years between two elections. The second comprises different electoral dummies for each year after the election. Last, the main macro- and socio-economic measures representing the economic constraints governments face are unemployment, economic growth, demographic change and financial openness, which come from Armingeon et al. (2012).[4] In all the empirical models, the socio-economic variables are lagged by one year, as I expect the impact of these variables to take effect only during the next budgetary year.

## 2.2 IDEOLOGICAL OR STRATEGIC POLICY-MAKING? AN ASSESSMENT OF CONTRADICTORY THEORIES

Whereas party politics was considered to be important and decisive in influencing the design and output of social security schemes during the 'golden age' of the welfare state (Bradley et al. 2003; Esping-Andersen 1985, 1990; Hicks and Swank 1992; Huber, Ragin and Stephens 1993; Korpi 1989), more recent research yields unstable or even contradictory results regarding the impact of partisan preferences and party governments on public policies in times of austerity and declining fiscal revenues (Huber and Stephens 2001; Kittel and Obinger 2003). Scholars mainly attribute this to the fact that the room to manoeuvre in politics has significantly decreased over the past decades, particularly for cost-intensive social and welfare policies. The main reasons for this have to do with the increasing international interdependence of domestic economies (Castles and Obinger 2007; Cusack 1999; Kittel and Obinger 2003; Swank 2001). With the liberalisation of financial and labour markets, the increasingly mobile means of production, and the search by companies for ever lower production costs, nation states are in competition to offer the most attractive conditions for corporations. The outsourcing of industrial production sites to cheaper locations triggered fundamental structural changes of the economy in advanced industrial democracies. In addition to these structural economic changes, Western democracies are undergoing significant socio-demographic transformations, such as demographic ageing and decreasing fertility, placing additional pressure on welfare state institutions, particularly on pension schemes (Iversen and Cusack 2000; Iversen and Wren 1998; Schwartz 2001). The increasing interdependence of macroeconomics and the socio-demographic developments in the domestic arena led to the development of a 'functionalist' view of the politics of reform, policy change and party competition (Cameron 1978; Castles 2005; Huber and Stephens 2001; Rodrik 1998).

When it comes to research on the welfare state and the underlying politics of social policy reforms, this 'functionalist' view is mostly represented by the 'New Politics' literature (Pierson 1994, 1996, 2001), which sees countervailing pressures on the welfare state as the main source of declining political competition over policy change and reforms. The declining room to manoeuvre for politicians aiming at reforming welfare state institutions is further exacerbated by the large popular support that these institutions enjoy in post-industrial democracies (Boeri et al. 2001; Brooks and Manza 2007; Larsen 2006, 2008; Matthews and Erickson 2008; Rehm 2005; Svallfors 1997). According to the 'New Politics' literature, the combination of public support and a strong path-dependency created by social security schemes makes welfare states largely resilient to radical change and cutbacks (Pierson 1996; Vis 2009a). The widespread popular support social policies enjoy among the electorate led to a key claim of the 'New Politics' literature, which contends that 'frontal assaults on the welfare states carry tremendous electoral risks' (Pierson 1996, p. 179). The riskiness of such reforms stems from the characteristics of welfare state institutions which generate their own constituencies and powerful interest groups who oppose major changes to social policies from which they currently benefit or expect to benefit in the future (Pierson 1996, p. 147). The recipients of welfare state benefits, in particular old-age pensioners, are well-defined groups which can easily be mobilised. In addition, some groups, such as unionised workers, have a strong and powerful lobby with close links to the political establishment. This adds an additional layer of complexity to welfare state policy-making, namely the fact that politicians perceive the reform of social security schemes as an exercise in blame avoidance rather than credit claiming. Hence, party governments of all colours shy away from openly undertaking potentially, electorally costly reforms and resort to a variety of strategies to cope with the mounting pressure to cut welfare state spending and to deal with the increasing structural problems. Due to the fact that established welfare state institutions represent a status quo which provides many advantages for various political actors, and also led to the emergence of new actors, changes to these institutions are extremely path-dependent. The characteristics and nature of the existing programmes determine to a great extent the reform opportunities which are available to political actors.

Large parts of the theoretical literature on the 'New Politics' of the welfare state emphasise the importance for governments of avoiding blame and obfuscating the real impact of potentially costly reforms (Pierson 1996; Vis and van Kersbergen 2013; Wenzelburger 2011). The reason why the avoidance of blame has become such a defining issue in reform politics has to do with the shrinking financial resources available to politicians, which impede the implementation of expansionary policy changes which could be used to claim credit. According to the 'New Politics' literature, 'retrenchment is generally an exercise in blame avoidance . . . because the costs of retrenchment are concentrated (and often immediate)' (Pierson 1996, p. 145). The literature distinguishes several strategies to avoid blame. The easiest and most radical method of blame avoidance – at least in the short run – is not to change existing social policy programmes at all. Both left-wing and right-wing governments do their utmost to stay away from cutting welfare state policies in times when economic growth is sluggish and the popular demand for social policies is high. Cutting back welfare state institutions in such times is extremely unpopular and decreases the chances of getting re-elected (Hübscher and Sattler 2017). However, inaction and stasis are not always possible, and most mature welfare states have experienced retrenching reforms affecting pension schemes or unemployment insurance schemes, for instance (Häusermann 2010b; Vis 2010).

Research following the 'New Politics' tradition therefore illuminates various strategies which help party governments to reform social security schemes without necessarily alienating the electorate, or at least to cushion the expected negative electoral effects. Complex reforms of social security schemes offer many possibilities to mask cutbacks, such as obfuscation or automatic retrenchment, the intentional division of certain societal groups opposing the legislation and conversely the direct compensation of such groups (König and Wenzelburger 2014; Vis 2009a; Wenzelburger 2014). Making use of specific framing strategies can also help the government to successfully reform popular social security institutions such as unemployment insurance and pension schemes. However, social policy-making in times of austerity is not only an exercise in blame avoidance and careful strategic planning. Due to the societal and labour-market changes, demand for new types of social policies, such as family and childcare policies, has been created (Häusermann 2006; Morgan 2013; Taylor-Gooby 2004). Hence, governments in mature welfare states, particularly continental welfare states, in which such policies are lagging behind, still have the opportunity to claim credit for social policy-making. The context of cutting on the one hand and creating new policies on the other sometimes also gives rise to new actor-coalitions which can have a decisive influence on the further development and reform of welfare state institutions (Häusermann 2010a). The expectations based on theories that belong to the 'New Politics' paradigm thus give rise to the following propositions:

**Proposition 1:** *Political considerations have no influence on the probability of fiscal consolidation.*

**Proposition 1a:** *The probability of a consolidation event is smaller when the incumbent is a left-wing party government and bigger with a conservative incumbent.*

**Proposition 2:** *An increase in economic pressure on the government has a positive effect on the probability that the government will implement measures to consolidate the budget.*

Finally, there are important strategic considerations influencing governments' reform plans. In principle, major consolidation events are considered a risky enterprise for governments. Given the political risk associated with fiscal reforms and in line with the scholarship outlining how governments strategise policy-making, it is reasonable to expect that governments would strategically time these events to maximise political gains or minimise potential losses. According to the substantial literature on electoral effects on economic policy (Alesina 1987; Downs 1957; Erikson, MacKuen and Stimson 2002; Nordhaus 1975; Stimson 1999), it is plausible that fiscal consolidation tends to occur early in the electoral cycle for a number of reasons. First, the electoral cycle structures governments' legislative activity, with government activity being highest at the beginning of the term and declining in the second half of a legislative term (Becker and Saalfeld 2004; Heller 2001; Martin and Vanberg 2004). A second reason is the time-horizon of voters, which previous research has found to be relatively short (Bartels 2005). If this is right, governments can hope that the negative effects of fiscal consolidation packages will be remembered less well by the time of the next election. In addition, if governments cut spending at the beginning of the legislative term, the positive impact of these measures may become noticeable right before the next election, which can be used as a political asset by the incumbent and may convince voters to support the present government in the next election. According to this logic, the probability of governments implementing a substantial reform decreases as the next election approaches. It would therefore be expected that elections would mostly affect the timing of the reform event. If, however, an incumbent decided that it was strategically wise to cut spending before an election, it is unlikely that its size and content would be affected by the fact that an election was to occur in the near future.

**Proposition 3:** *The probability of a consolidation event is highest right after the election and decreases over the legislative term.*

In order to empirically examine the aforementioned propositions representing a view of public policy-making that is guided more by strategic decisions and reactions towards constraints rather than partisan ideology, the *probability* of a consolidation event occurring given specific economic and political factors needs to be assessed. Because of the binary nature of the dependent variable (1 if a consolidation event happened, and 0 if no event took place), a probit model is used to estimate the likelihood of a consolidation event occurring in a particular year. To account for time in a time-series cross-section setting with a binary dependent variable, the procedure used is that is proposed by Carter and Signorino (2010), which has become a standard approach to dealing with this problem in political economy research. The variable $t$ captures the time that has passed since the last consolidation event; that is, it takes the value 0 after a fiscal consolidation episode and increases linearly until the next consolidation event in that country occurs.

I have also added $t^2$ and $t^3$ to the model to capture the potentially nonlinear effects of time on the probability of an event. These variables together capture the probability of a reform, given the number of years that have passed since the last reform.[5]

Table 2.1 presents the results assessing how the probability of fiscal retrenchment depends on political and macroeconomic circumstances. The

**Table 2.1. Political Determinants of Consolidation**

| | *Economic Baseline* | *Ideology* | *Electoral Counter* | *Election Dummies* | *All Relevant* |
|---|---|---|---|---|---|
| Ideology | | 1.400 | | | 1.215 |
| | | (0.900) | | | (0.919) |
| Constraints | | | | | −0.926 |
| | | | | | (1.227) |
| Election counter | | | −0.165*** | | −0.158*** |
| | | | (0.059) | | (0.059) |
| Postelection year 2 | | | | −0.248 | |
| | | | | (0.188) | |
| Postelection year 3 | | | | −0.511** | |
| | | | | (0.206) | |
| Postelection year 4 | | | | −0.421** | |
| | | | | (0.198) | |
| Postelection year 5 | | | | −0.633 | |
| | | | | (0.396) | |
| $Growth_{t-1}$ | −0.078** | −0.077** | -0.087*** | −0.087*** | −0.086*** |
| | (0.034) | (0.033) | (0.034) | (0.034) | (0.033) |
| $Unemployment_{t-1}$ | 0.159*** | 0.152*** | 0.162*** | 0.163*** | 0.157*** |
| | (0.031) | (0.031) | (0.031) | (0.031) | (0.032) |
| $Elderly_{t-1}$ | 0.208** | 0.215** | 0.207** | 0.212** | 0.195** |
| | (0.093) | (0.093) | (0.095) | (0.096) | (0.096) |
| $Openness_{t-1}$ | −0.646*** | -0.673*** | −0.636*** | −0.643*** | −0.609*** |
| | (0.207) | (0.207) | (0.209) | (0.211) | (0.216) |
| t | −0.811*** | -0.793*** | −0.829*** | −0.838*** | −0.806*** |
| | (0.164) | (0.162) | (0.165) | (0.167) | (0.161) |
| $t^2$ | 0.088*** | 0.085*** | 0.089*** | 0.091*** | 0.086*** |
| | (0.027) | (0.027) | (0.027) | (0.028) | (0.026) |
| $t^3$ | −0.002** | −0.002** | −0.003** | −0.003** | −0.002** |
| | (0.001) | (0.001) | (0.001) | (0.001) | (0.001) |
| Constant | 0.703 | −0.003 | 0.969 | 0.989 | 0.698 |
| | (0.813) | (0.941) | (0.836) | (0.842) | (1.098) |
| $\chi^2$ | 162.12 | 162.39 | 171.99 | 170.87 | 175.18 |
| p-Value | 0.000 | 0.000 | 0.000 | 0.000 | 0.000 |
| Pseudo $R^2$ | 0.32 | 0.32 | 0.33 | 0.33 | 0.33 |
| N | 480 | 480 | 480 | 480 | 480 |

All models include fixed effects. Robust errors in parentheses. * = p<0.1, ** = p<0.05, *** = p<0.01.

first column presents the baseline model including only the socio and macroeconomic determinants of fiscal retrenchment, and the three variables controlling for time since the last retrenchment events. The economic variables assessing the impact of growth, unemployment and financial openness on the likelihood of a fiscal retrenchment event are statistically significant. Greater economic growth during the previous year significantly decreases the probability that the government will consolidate. Higher levels of unemployment unambiguously increase the probability of fiscal retrenchment, which is in line with proposition 2. The same applies to demographic change, although this effect is less pronounced. The coefficient on government ideology is not statistically significant at conventional levels but points in the expected direction, which implies that right-wing governments are more likely to implement retrenchment measures. This finding is consistent with the apolitical 'New Politics' literature, which attributes to party politics little influence on policy reforms in an economic environment that is characterised by scarce resources. This result is further corroborated by recent findings by Vis (2009a, b) and Green-Pedersen (2002) who find that both left-wing and right-wing governments implement reforms, lending support for proposition 1 and defeating proposition 1a. Overall, economic pressure dominates party ideology and institutional constraints when it comes to the implementation of significant retrenchment packages.

The models presented in columns 2 to 4 capture the strategic dimension of government policy-making represented in proposition 3. All models show a strong and statistically significant effect of the different variables which capture electoral politics. The finding that elections have the strongest effect on retrenchment decisions is in line with the 'New Politics' literature and research that stresses the importance of strategic planning of government reform activities. If we include dummies for each year except the post-election year, we see that the probability of fiscal retrenchment decreases over the term (see column 3). The effect is even more pronounced for the electoral counter which linearly increases during the electoral cycle (column 4). This also confirms qualitative and quantitative findings about the strategic manoeuvres of governments (Wagschal and Wenzelburger 2012). If governments take the decision to consolidate the budget, they are likely to implement the cuts at the beginning of the electoral cycle. In principle, major retrenchment events are considered a risky enterprise for governments. Despite the electoral riskiness of reforms, research shows that governments regularly implement unpopular reforms taking into account any potential punishment from the electorate (Vis and van Kersbergen 2007). This strategy can be considered as a way to avoid blame or a drop in popularity during the most significant time of the legislative cycle, namely during the run-up to the next elections.[6] These results strongly support proposition 3.

Given the strong and important effect of elections, figure 2.1 explores the role of the electoral cycle in greater detail. The top graph is based on the fourth model in table 2.1 with the electoral counter, while the bottom graph is based on the third model in table 2.1 with several dummies for each post-election year. Both graphs show that governments are significantly more likely to implement reforms at the beginning of their term in office than towards the end. The probability for a retrenchment event decreases from around 39 per cent at the beginning of the electoral cycle to approximately 24 per cent at the end. Overall, the results presented in table 2.1 support the rather apolitical view of the 'New Politics' literature and seemingly speak in favour of theories that emphasise the desire of politicians to avoid blame in order to stay in office. Based on the results discussed earlier, it would seem that strategic political considerations play a major role in the timing of fiscal retrenchment. This result is in line with and extends previous qualitative contributions to the literature, which show how governments resort to strategic manoeuvres to implement reforms and also make use of strategic communication and framing of reforms (Wenzelburger 2011). It also yields interesting implications in combination with recent findings that governments are not necessarily punished when implementing unpopular reforms (Armingeon and Giger 2008; Giger and Nelson 2011). Possibly, electoral punishment is small because governments implement unpopular reforms at the beginning of the electoral cycle precisely to minimise this punishment. In fact, thirteen out of eighteen retrenchment events which improved the cyclically adjusted fiscal balance by two percentage points or more took place in the first or second year after the inauguration of the new government.[7]

Research assessing the likelihood of governments to engage in consolidation and risky reforms reveals that partisanship is indeed not the most important determinant of reform activities. However, the evidence speaking in favour of the 'parties matter' literature was mostly based on data measuring changes in the size of specific social programmes or public expenditure. This is why the present work exploits the nature of this novel data to assess whether government ideology affects the size of consolidation events. Based on the standard logic of the long-established 'parties matter' literature, left-wing governments should be less supportive of fiscal retrenchment than those on the right, but this can manifest itself in different forms. Public support for redistributive policies and the welfare state is particularly significant during economic downturns and in times of fiscal constraints (Blekesaune 2007; Jensen 2007). Since left-wing governments generally represent constituencies that rely more heavily on redistributive policies, these governments are particularly vulnerable to losing political support in response to fiscal retrenchment. Left-wing governments may not therefore want to be associated with

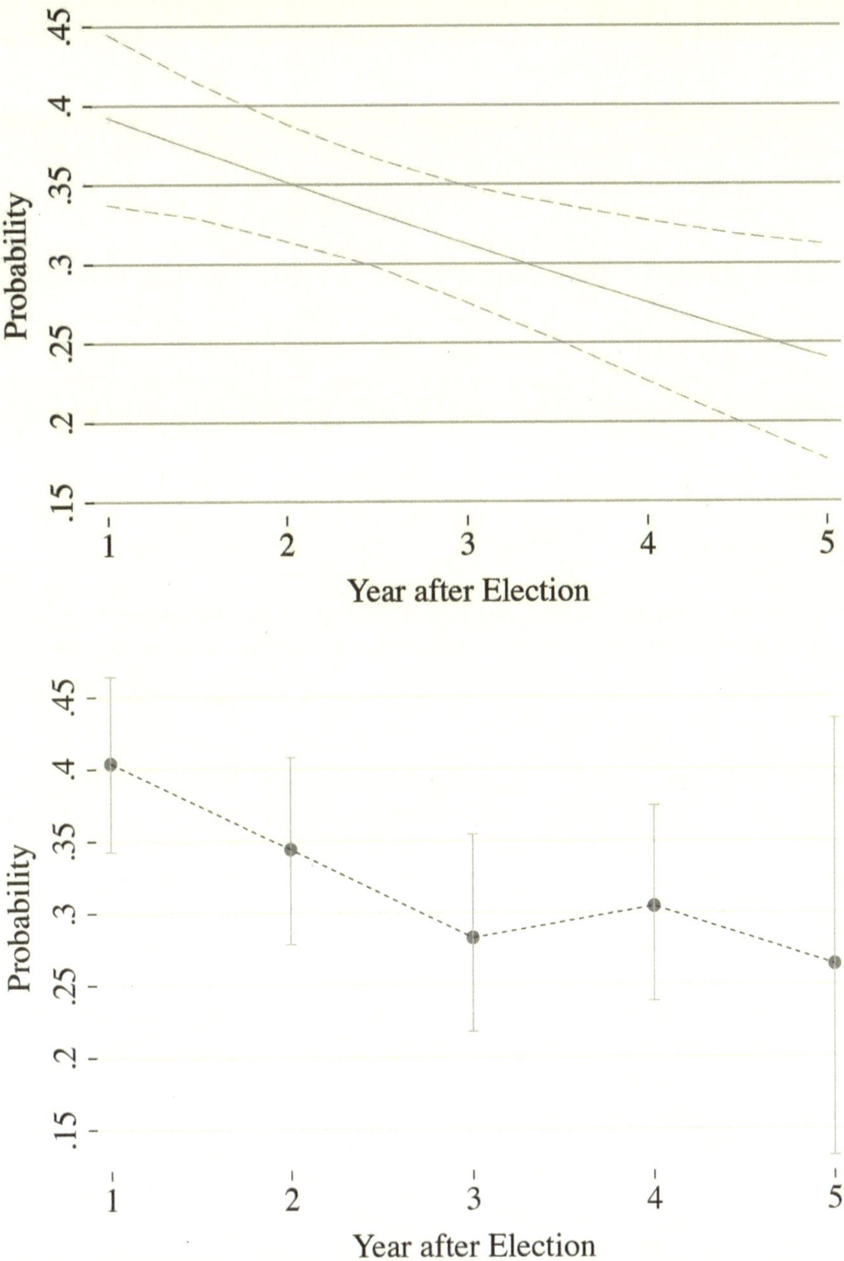


**Figure 2.1. Probability of Retrenchment Events over Electoral Cycle**

retrenchment measures and may hence try to avoid them. This argumentation implies that left-wing governments are less likely to initiate retrenchment measures in the first place. If such a government were to be pressured into implementing retrenchment measures, the impact of party ideology should have a straightforward effect on the size and extent of the reform. In times, when the economic pressure on governments is too high to refrain from implementing unpopular reforms, a left-wing government should implement smaller reform packages than those legislated by right-wing governments (Allan and Scruggs 2004). Smaller cuts are in line with the core preferences of left-wing parties who traditionally prefer higher taxes and more generous public expenditure over budget cuts. To build a reform coalition, the Left would also need to guarantee that it keeps spending cuts to the absolute minimum. The 'parties matter' theory thus leads to the following proposition:

**Proposition 4:** *Given that a consolidation event occurs, the size of retrenchment is lower under left-wing governments than under conservative governments.*

In order to assess whether government ideology influences the design, in particular the size, of retrenchment events, the factors determining the size of retrenchment events will be assessed. However, empirically examining the size of consolidation raises some tricky econometric issues. First, if we examine consolidation size by looking at consolidation episodes only, we get biased estimates because of selection problems. Specifically, the set of governments that consolidates is systematically different from those that do not because they face different macroeconomic and political situations. Second, if we examine all country-years (including those when consolidation is 0), we still have the problem that governments that do not consolidate (those for which the dependent variable is 0) are all treated in the same way in a standard regression model. This is problematic, because some of those governments only marginally decided against reform, while others were far from implementing a reform (Bortolotti and Siniscalco 2004; Hicks 2016). Theoretically, the problem arises because, as the previous literature has argued, the political processes that lead to consolidation differ from the political processes that lead to expansions (Pierson 1996, 1998). We therefore cannot simply expand the distribution to include both consolidations and expansions because the variables and their expected impacts differ for the two processes. These problems are addressed using Heckman models.

These selection models first assess the likelihood of retrenchment events and, in a second step, estimate the determinants of the size of the respective fiscal cuts. The dependent variable of the Heckman models therefore is the *size* of the retrenchment package. Table 2.2 shows the results of this

**Table 2.2. Determinants of Retrenchment Size**

| | Tobit | Tobit | Tobit | Heckman | | Heckman | | Heckman | |
|---|---|---|---|---|---|---|---|---|---|
| | | | | Outcome | Selection | Outcome | Selection | Outcome | Selection |
| Ideology | 2.636*** | | | 1.452** | | | | | |
| | (0.979) | | | (0.671) | | | | | |
| Election counter | | −0.181** | | | −0.133*** | −0.102 | −0.179*** | | −0.128*** |
| | | (0.074) | | | (0.048) | (0.068) | (0.058) | | (0.049) |
| Constraints | | | −3.155** | | | | | 0.422 | |
| | | | (1.402) | | | | | (0.758) | |
| $Growth_{t-1}$ | −0.139*** | −0.148*** | −0.140*** | −0.140*** | −0.100*** | −0.145*** | −0.099*** | −0.136*** | −0.096*** |
| | (0.037) | (0.036) | (0.037) | (0.034) | (0.031) | (0.035) | (0.031) | (0.034) | (0.031) |
| $Unemployment_{t-1}$ | 0.277*** | 0.298*** | 0.295*** | 0.083*** | 0.149*** | 0.076*** | 0.144*** | 0.074*** | 0.144*** |
| | (0.036) | (0.037) | (0.037) | (0.019) | (0.027) | (0.019) | (0.027) | (0.019) | (0.027) |
| $Elderly_{t-1}$ | 0.385*** | 0.363*** | 0.318*** | 0.032 | 0.197*** | 0.026 | 0.205*** | 0.033 | 0.200*** |
| | (0.112) | (0.111) | (0.108) | (0.038) | (0.074) | (0.037) | (0.076) | (0.039) | (0.075) |
| $Openness_{t-1}$ | −1.137*** | −1.069*** | −0.931*** | −0.117 | −0.542*** | −0.112 | −0.565*** | −0.147 | −0.562*** |
| | (0.256) | (0.256) | (0.261) | (0.130) | (0.166) | (0.128) | (0.170) | (0.141) | (0.169) |
| t | | | | | −0.677*** | | −0.663*** | | −0.649*** |
| | | | | | (0.162) | | (0.168) | | (0.171) |
| $t^2$ | | | | | 0.074*** | | 0.072*** | | 0.069*** |
| | | | | | (0.022) | | (0.022) | | (0.023) |
| $t^3$ | | | | | −0.002** | | −0.002** | | −0.002** |
| | | | | | (0.001) | | (0.001) | | (0.001) |
| Constant | −2.916*** | −1.338 | −0.407 | −0.727 | 0.520 | 0.268 | 0.555 | −0.010 | 0.515 |
| | | | | (0.693) | (0.725) | (0.576) | (0.734) | (0.637) | (0.727) |
| P | – | – | – | 0.88 | | 0.86 | | 0.87 | |
| F- /$\chi^2$ – statistic | 7.21 | 7.55 | 7.73 | 34.85 | | 31.48 | | 29.67 | |
| p-Value | 0.000 | 0.000 | 0.000 | 0.000 | | 0.000 | | 0.000 | |
| N (N censored) | 480 | 480 | 480 | 480 (321) | | 480 (321) | | 480 (321) | |

All models include fixed effects. Robust standard errors in parentheses. * $p < 0.1$, ** $p < 0.05$, *** $p < 0.01$.

assessment. The influence of the socio-economic variables is as expected: economic growth negatively affects the size of budget retrenchment, which means that retrenchment will be smaller when the economy performs well. In contrast, high levels of unemployment have a positive effect on the size of fiscal retrenchment measures. The percentage of elderly people in the population and financial openness are statistically significant in the selection equation of the Heckman model, but show no statistically significant effect in the outcome equation of the Heckman model examining the *size* of fiscal retrenchment events. Overall, this implies that they mostly influence the probability that governments consolidate and less the extent to which governments consolidate.

Among the political variables, ideology has the strongest and most robust effect on retrenchment size. The variable in the Heckman models is statistically significant and has the sign in the expected direction. This implies that, although government partisanship does not significantly affect the likelihood of a reform, as previously shown, the political hue of the government still has a significant impact on the size of government cuts. The results show that right-wing incumbents cut spending much more than left-wing governments. The first finding for the probability of reforms means that sceptics are right to think that economic pressures push both left- and right-wing governments towards reforms. However, the result for retrenchment size suggests that governments still have room to implement different retrenchment measures according to their political preferences. Right-wing governments grab the opportunity to cut spending as much as possible, while those on the Left will do only as much as absolutely required. As expected, constraints and elections do not have a robust effect on retrenchment size. In fact, for constraints, the coefficient in the Heckman outcome equation is not in the expected direction.

The initial analyses presented earlier suggest that the overall picture is more complex than existing research and traditional theories suggest. There are some stages of the reform processes – in particular whether retrenchment events take place – where politics and party ideology is unimportant. Overall, when controlling for the same strategic, structural and socio-economic factors, retrenchment events seem to be equally likely under left- as under right-wing governments. This finding contradicts the general expectations that there is a linear link between government partisanship and policy output. If the propositions of the traditional 'parties matter' theory still held, one would expect to find a significant difference in the retrenchment activities between left and right-wing governments. The fact that there is no such difference implies that governments have lost some room to manoeuvre, mainly the liberty not to engage in spending cuts.

While there is no difference in whether governments engage in efforts to cut spending, however, one can observe significant discrepancies in how big the cost-cutting reforms are. At this level, there appear to be clear-cut partisan differences between left and right-wing governments. The results on how ideological differences of governments affect the size of retrenchment are in line with the traditional partisan theory. However, despite the fact that the retrenchment measure used in the aforementioned analyses reflects the decisions made by governments to cut spending and also indicates the extent of the cuts, the analyses do not reveal whether the cuts are targeted at specific programmes or spare strategically selected policy areas. In the light of theories on representative government and mandates, it is important to see that governments still make a difference. It is, however, even more important to focus on how these seemingly intuitive findings are translated into specific policies and whom these policy changes are beneficial for or what kind of societal groups are most affected by spending cuts and reforms. This endeavour includes a more in-depth assessment of the underlying political mechanisms which also takes into account a number of developments which were not fully taken into account in existing studies about politics and welfare state development.

The insights from the aforementioned analyses suggest that governments are likely to act very strategically when planning costly and unpopular reforms; this observation is true for governments across all party families. Still, there are significant differences across party lines when it comes to the size of the reforms. The combined insight of these analyses shows that while no party government is able to postpone or sit out important reforms for too long, there is still room for party governments to implement distinct types of reforms which reflect the ideological preferences of the respective government. Overall, the picture painted earlier is less disenchanting for the way representative democracy and party governments work in times of austerity.[8] The findings also contradict the predictions by globalisation sceptics who have proposed that political motivations have become irrelevant for policymaking in times of austerity and global economic interdependence. Thus, some of the most important and fundamental assumptions about political parties, namely that political parties matter, still hold. However, the aforementioned analyses do not show whether our traditional views about how exactly political parties in government make a difference are still accurate. In particular, which social groups benefit from which party constellation in government? At least implicitly, the majority of recent studies maintain the idea that, overall, the salaried working class generally benefits from left-wing governments and that the working class also supplies the majority of votes for left-wing parties (Pontusson and Rueda 2010).[9]

This key assumption, however, has been seriously questioned in the literature assessing the changing class structure of societies and political parties (Oesch 2006b, 2008; Rehm 2009). They also propose that changes among the electorate of mainstream parties result in strategic adjustments of the policy preferences and positions of political parties, with the aim of retaining the core electorate or attracting new supporters. Together with our well-documented knowledge about ongoing economic and structural changes, the long-held views about the party preferences of individuals also need to be assessed and revised. Recent contributions to the literature thus more critically assess the link between government partisanship and public policies with a particular focus on the reform of popular welfare state institutions and the development of new social policies (Häusermann, Picot and Geering 2013). The studies reintegrate politics into the study of welfare state development and aim at reconciling the two key theoretical strands which dominate research on welfare state change and reform. In particular, they share the view of the 'New Politics' literature that the underlying mechanisms of welfare state cuts and reforms in times of austerity differ from the mechanisms observed during the golden age of the welfare state, when social policy-making was mostly about creating new social security schemes and expanding existing schemes. In line with 'parties matter' literature, such relatively recent research again assigns to political parties a significant role in crafting and designing reform programmes. The type of policy instruments and means chosen by political parties within the framework of the reforms may deviate from our expectations and scholars may find that – together with the changing mechanisms – political parties serve their own interests with an updated toolbox of policy solutions and an updated strategy of whom their policies should benefit.

In addition to the effort to update our knowledge on the linkages between political parties and their preferred policy choices, researchers have again started to take more seriously institutions and the way they intervene in politics. While it was commonly acknowledged that institutional factors matter for policy-making, the two dominant theories which aim at explaining welfare state development and change are surprisingly agnostic when it comes to theorising on how institutional contexts condition the policy preferences and reform strategies of parties in government. Recently, however, there has been an emerging literature which engages more seriously with how institutions and context may enable some parties but restrict others (Abou-Chadi and Immergut 2014; Jensen and Mortensen 2014; Iversen and

Soskice 2006a). Overall, there is a need to engage in more finely grained analyses of reform processes and their impact on specific societal groups given a particular institutional context and party government. In the following chapter, I will outline how governments in times of fiscal constraints and austerity are able to influence policies in ways that is in line with their party preferences while coping with existing institutional and economic constraints.

## 2.3 CHAPTER APPENDIX

*Fiscal retrenchment*: The data cover discrete retrenchment events in sixteen Western democracies and include a total of 159 instances of fiscal adjustments between 1978 and 2009 (Devries et al. 2011).[10] The selection of the retrenchment events included in the data set is based on official announcements by public authorities to cut fiscal deficits in nominal terms measured as a percentage of GDP. It represents how these actions reflect on the budgetary balance of the national government and therefore avoids a situation where deficits, which can be shifted to lower levels of government, are missed. Retrenchment events are identified qualitatively, based on the most important policy documents in each country, including Budget Reports, Budget Speeches, OECD Economic Surveys and IMF Staff Reports. These documents 'explicitly provide evidence of what policymakers believed at the time that the decisions were taken' (Devries et al. 2011, p. 4). For the events that are identified, the size of the respective measures is then specified by assessing the impact that the cuts had on the overall fiscal balance. The data set therefore captures the governmental decisions that can be publicly identified and were debated as retrenchment events.[11] The retrenchment events cover both retrenchment through spending cuts and retrenchment through changes in taxation.[12]

The raw data indicate the size of fiscal retrenchment in the year it happened. Using this information, a time-series cross-section data set was constructed with a discrete dependent variable that takes the value 1 for the year in which the data set reports that a retrenchment event occurred, and the value 0 for years in which no event was reported.[13] This yields a balanced data set from 1978 to 2009, which can be used to estimate the *probability* of a retrenchment event. To examine the *size* of retrenchment, another variable was constructed, which takes the value 0 when no fiscal cut took place and the amount of retrenchment as listed in the original data for the year when the government implemented the reform.

The following tables, 2.3 and 2.4 include the summary statistics (2.3) and the information on the sources of the data used in the analysis presented in chapter 2.

**Table 2.3. Summary Statistics**

| *Variable* | *Mean* | *Std. Dev.* | *Min.* | *Max.* | *N* |
|---|---|---|---|---|---|
| Retrenchment event | 0.331 | 0.471 | 0 | 1 | 480 |
| Retrenchment size (including 0s) | 0.333 | 0.707 | −0.75 | 4.49 | 480 |
| Retrenchment size (events only) | 1.005 | 0.915 | −0.75 | 4.49 | 159 |
| Ideology | 0.45 | 0.096 | 0.207 | 0.686 | 480 |
| Political constraints | 0.452 | 0.123 | 0.12 | 0.72 | 480 |
| Popular unrest | 0.288 | 0.453 | 0 | 1 | 480 |
| Postelection year 2 | 0.273 | 0.446 | 0 | 1 | 480 |
| Postelection year 3 | 0.237 | 0.426 | 0 | 1 | 480 |
| Postelection year 4 | 0.175 | 0.38 | 0 | 1 | 480 |
| Postelection year 5 | 0.033 | 0.18 | 0 | 1 | 480 |
| Election counter | 1.406 | 1.165 | 0 | 4 | 480 |
| Growth | 2.749 | 2.282 | −7.565 | 11.877 | 480 |
| Unemployment | 8.104 | 3.768 | 1.62 | 24.17 | 480 |
| Elderly | 14.16 | 2.247 | 9 | 20.2 | 480 |
| Openness | 5.17 | 0.809 | 3.436 | 7.853 | 480 |
| t (times since last event) | 4.277 | 3.783 | 1 | 20 | 480 |

*Source:* Author's elaborations.

**Table 2.4. Data Sources and Operationalisation of Variables**

| *Variable* | *Operationalisation* | *Source* |
|---|---|---|
| Consolidation event | Consolidation events are identified qualitatively based on the most important policy documents in each country, including Budget Reports, Budget Speeches, OECD Economic Surveys and IMF Staff Reports. These documents 'explicitly provide evidence of what policymakers believed at the time that the decisions were taken' (Devries et al. 2011, p. 4). | IMF, Devries et al. (2011) |
| Consolidation size | The size of fiscal consolidation consists of the combined effect of tax-based and spending-based measures implemented to reduce the deficit. The size of consolidation is then expressed as the impact the cuts have on the overall fiscal balance (in percentage of GDP). | IMF, Devries et al. (2011) |

| *Variable* | *Operationalisation* | *Source* |
|---|---|---|
| Government ideology | Government ideology is based on the CMP RILE index. In order to capture overall cabinet ideology, I use the weighted (based on each government party's seat share in parliament) average of the left-right score of all parties constituting the cabinet. The score is rescaled to range between 0 and 1, where 0 marks the extreme Left and 1 indicates the extreme Right of the political spectrum. The information about government composition comes from the European Representative Democracy data set (Andersson et al., 2012). | Comparative Manifesto Project (https://manifesto-project.wzb.eu/); European Representative Democracy data set (http://erdda.se/index.php/projects/erd) |
| Political constraints | Henisz measure of political constraints measures the number of actors involved in the policy-making process. It takes into various institutional features that determine the level of political constraints. | Henisz (2006), http://www-management.wharton.upenn.edu/henisz/. |
| Economic growth | Economic growth is measured as real growth of GDP (in per cent). | Comparative Political Data Set (CPDS), Armingeon et al. (2012). CPDS. |
| Unemployment | Unemployment refers to the rate of unemployed people as percentage of the overall civilian labour force. | Comparative Political Data Set (CPDS), Armingeon et al. (2012). CPDS. |
| Elderly | Elderly refers to the percentage of people over the age of sixty-five as percentage of the population total. | Comparative Political Data Set (CPDS), Armingeon et al. (2012). CPDS. |
| Capital openness | Financial openness is the log of the sum of foreign assets and foreign liabilities of a country over GDP. | Lane and Milesi-Ferretti (2007) http://www.philiplane.org/EWN.html. |

## NOTES

1 The focus on event data rather than looking at different types of spending data also addresses the long-discussed 'dependent variable' problem in welfare state research (Clasen and Siegel 2007; Green-Pedersen 2004).

2 The following countries are included in the analysis: Australia, Austria, Belgium, Canada, Denmark, Finland, France, Germany, Ireland, Italy, the Netherlands,

Portugal, Spain, Sweden, the United Kingdom and the United States. An extensive discussion of the data and the econometric models presented in this section can be found in the appendix of the chapter.

3 Also, the effect of the key explanatory factors on reform data is straightforward and less ambiguous than for macroeconomic aggregates like spending. For instance, high levels of unemployment may be associated both positively and negatively with public spending. On the one hand, high levels of unemployment boost public expenditure because more benefits need to be paid. On the other hand, high levels of unemployment, in the long run, may lead to increasing pressure on governments to consolidate and cut public spending. By focusing on retrenchment events, we can avoid having the ambiguous relationship between incremental changes in public spending and macroeconomic factors cloud the empirical results (see also Hicks and Zorn 2005).

4 A full description of the operationalisation and sources of all variables can be found in the methodological appendix of the chapter.

5 The procedure used here is a variant of a classic duration model accounting for the hazard that an event takes place over time (Box-Steffensmeier and Jones 2004).

6 These results complement the findings by Mierau Jong-A-Pin and de Haan (2007) who show that the probability of fiscal adjustments is significantly lower in the year before a general election.

7 In 1993, Italy implemented one of the biggest reform packages (4.5 percentage points) in the year right after the general election; a similarly encompassing package was implemented in Sweden (3.5 percentage points) also in the wake of a general election.

8 In the literature, the 'de-politicisation' of social policy-making was significantly questioned by observations that many countries, while not dismantling the welfare state completely, still implemented social security reforms that did not go unnoticed by the public. The claim by adherents of the 'New Politics' approach that retrenchment is hard or impossible to achieve has therefore to be refuted. In-depth case studies on core welfare state policies, such as pensions, healthcare and unemployment, have shown that a number of European countries have implemented significant cuts.

9 In early contributions to research assessing the link between the ability of different governments to implement reforms and their political ideology (and quite similar to the 'resource mobilisation' literature, which ascribes to left-wing parties a particular role in the founding years of welfare state development), there are a range of studies which again see left-wing parties as crucial actors for successful retrenchment. As the literature has shown, left-wing governments often successfully implement retrenchment measures and reforms mostly because they sometimes have more room to consolidate because of their historic record in building the welfare state. Citizens therefore trust left-wing parties more when it comes to welfare state reforms and do not expect them to fully dismantle social policies (Green-Pedersen 2001b, 2002; Levy 1999; Ross 2000a).

10 The IMF database on fiscal retrenchment does not cover Japan and New Zealand; these two countries are therefore excluded from the analysis.

11 Under the assumption that the government cannot implement serious fiscal cuts 'secretly', that is, in a way that they are not identifiable from budgetary reports and are therefore hidden from the public, the data set includes the full sample of fiscal retrenchment event in these countries.

12 The overall proportion of spending-based retrenchment versus tax-based retrenchment over time and across countries is 63 per cent spending as opposed to 37 per cent tax-based measures. Of the 159 fiscal retrenchment events included in the data set, 21 (13.2 per cent) were purely spending-based and 24 (15.1 per cent) purely tax-based. 114 (71.7 per cent) retrenchment measures consisted of a mix of spending-based and tax-based measures. A qualitative assessment of the data also shows that during the most recent decade, most retrenchment events were based on a mix of spending and tax measures.

13 For instance, no retrenchment event is listed for Germany in 2001, but the German government implemented a fiscal retrenchment programme that reduced the deficit by 0.7 per cent of GDP in 2000. The retrenchment event variable then takes the value 0 for Germany in 2001 and the value 1 for Germany in 2000.

# *Chapter 3*

# Party Politics and Political Constraints

The economic and social environment that party governments and policy-makers face has changed considerably since the golden age of post-war prosperity. New challenges such as the continuing internationalisation of the economy and financial markets as well as domestic structural and demographic changes therefore call for policy adjustments and reforms, particularly as the social security schemes that are most affected by these changes are the core welfare state institutions such as pension and unemployment insurance schemes (e.g. Bonoli 2003; Häusermann 2010a; Immergut, Anderson and Schulze 2007; Mares 2000; Seeleib-Kaiser, van Dyk and Roggenkamp 2008). Structural changes of the economy have led to more persistent and higher levels of unemployment in a number of countries, which, on the one hand, affects unemployment insurance schemes but also has an effect on pension schemes which receive fewer contributions. Public pension schemes are additionally challenged by demographic ageing and longer life expectancy that result in an increasing imbalance between contributions and benefits paid to eligible individuals. Economic globalisation and de-industrialisation have also resulted in a more heterogeneous workforce consisting on the one hand of a core workforce (mostly skilled workers with regular employment contracts and full time jobs) and on the other hand of people in more precarious work arrangements, such as temporary contracts and part-time work, with the majority in the latter group having few professional skills and working in the low-wage sector. The main beneficiaries of the core social security programmes today are those in the core workforce, as it is mostly people in permanent full-time jobs who usually earn the relevant rights for social insurance through regular contributions to the schemes. In contrast, people with temporary contracts or part-time jobs (labour market outsiders) have a less privileged situation in the labour market and often enjoy less coverage by core social insurance schemes.

Increasing reform pressure, high demand for and support of social policies and a more heterogeneous workforce all complicate the reforms of crucial welfare state institutions for party governments. This view is supported by a significant part of the literature that has been published during recent years suggesting that party governments have lost their ability to design policies according to their ideological preferences (Pierson 1994, 2001). This strand of the literature also implicitly indicates that competition over substantive policies has been declining and reform outcomes are converging. Empirical evidence, however, shows that policies across different welfare states have not converged as predicted by many researchers. This implies that despite the common pressures, reform paths across countries, as well as social policies in general, continue to differ significantly across countries. The more recent literature on welfare state reforms has as a consequence reintroduced politics into the analysis. In addition to the renewed interest in the influence of party politics in the welfare state literature, the field has started to more critically engage with the role of political parties in the reform processes and started to question established presumptions about the nature of the impact of political parties on welfare state reforms. The reintroduction of politics in the recent literature on welfare state reforms includes work that focuses on various reform coalitions across party lines, or that examines the particular impact of the Left on reforms of social policies (Green-Pedersen 2001b; Häusermann 2010a). Other contributions show that left-wing parties in government are sometimes better able to reform and retrench welfare state programmes as they generally enjoy more credibility among the beneficiaries of social security schemes and are better able to engineer reform coalitions (Green-Pedersen 2002; Ross 1997, 2000a). In addition to new insights about the reform capability of party governments, there is mounting evidence that the impact political parties have on reform outcomes may go against long established theories. Rueda's (2007) quantitative and qualitative evidence on the impact of left-wing party governments on social policy reforms, for instance, shows that left-wing governments tend to mostly cater towards their own clientele, that is, trade unions and the core workforce and shape policies accordingly in times of austerity.

This chapter proposes one possible explanation for the distinct reform paths and outcomes that we observe. It develops a framework which establishes the logic concerning the manner in which party governments, conditioned by institutional constraints, determine the outcome of welfare state reforms, particularly the reforms of core social security programmes such as pension and unemployment insurance. The theoretical argument covers three levels of analysis: the interests of the constituents; the policy preferences of political parties and how they differ across political systems; and the resulting outcomes on the macro level. I propose that party governments experience constraints in shaping and influencing the spending dimension of social policies according to their policy preferences but nevertheless still enjoy room to manoeuvre on the generosity dimension. The core of the argument centres around the idea that the impact of party governments on social policy-making and reform differs across institutional settings and that overtly left-wing party governments pursue clientelistic policies when facing high institutional constraints and austerity. This leads to a situation in which left-wing governments essentially cater towards the core workforce rather than designing policies for the full range of labour market participants, including those in precarious employment relations.

## 3.1 CHANGING DEMANDS FOR SOCIAL POLICIES AND SOCIAL PROTECTION

One reason why welfare states in industrialised countries have come under pressure to reform is the changing demand for social policies which results from increasing international trade in goods and a global reorganisation of industrial production. This change in demand was triggered by radical changes in the macroeconomic context of domestic economies. During the period of embedded liberalism (after the Second World War until the breakdown of the Bretton Woods system in 1973), international trade was limited through trade barriers, particularly high taxes and tariffs. Polanyi (1954, p. 132) described this period as a 'double movement' consisting of two components, with one component being the principle of economic liberalism, aimed at establishing a self-regulating market that allows for free trade and relies on the support of the trading classes. The second component was the principle of social protection, which should be upheld through state intervention and is aimed at supporting those who are most immediately and negatively affected by the deleterious actions of the market. This system worked well as long as the international monetary order was characterised by fixed exchange rates and very limited possibilities of cross-border financial flows. The economies of Western countries during this period were characterised by a broadly diversified and labour-intensive industrial sector, a still relatively substantive agrarian sector and a rather marginal service sector which mainly provided services for the domestic market. Domestic labour faced homogenous risks in the sense that the danger of losing employment was mainly related to domestic macroeconomic trends which could be influenced by domestic politics. Social policies mostly covered the core workforce against temporary loss of employment, old age, poverty and sickness.[1] The specific interests of employees, which were similar across groups within the workforce, mostly related to unemployment insurance for temporary job loss, safety at work, old age benefits and sector-specific issues. All these have traditionally been represented by trade unions, which aimed at influencing social policy-making processes at the national level.

However, increasing international trade in combination with the breakdown of the Bretton Woods system in the 1970s and a gradual liberalisation of capital flows led to a worldwide reorganisation of production. Labour-intensive industries, which employed a large number of low-skilled workers, took the opportunity to relocate production to countries where labour is cheaper and taxes are lower. The relocation of industrial production sites led to shrinking industrial sectors in Western countries and a declining demand for labour, especially for unskilled labour and for workers with a low degree of education. Substantial productive parts of the industrial sector in post-industrialised countries nowadays rely on highly specialised and skilled workers. Even though the service sector in post-industrial countries has been growing – albeit at a slow pace – it has not been able to absorb all the workers formerly employed in the industrial sector. The decreasing demand for labour thus led to an increase in unemployment and also decreased employment security among those still employed. This development undermined collective agreements between unions and employers and generally augmented the downward pressure on wages.

As a result, global competition and international trade have led to employment relations that are less stable and less predictable than before. For instance, the growing service industry increasingly offers temporary and part-time jobs for poorly qualified personnel (e.g. employees in shops and restaurants, call-centres and automated production). Similarly, the relocation of technologically simple, but labour-intensive, production sites to developing and emerging market economies has forced low-skilled labour in Western countries to find new employment opportunities or change their career paths. In addition, growing competition from developing and emerging market economies has put the relatively high wages paid in industrialised countries under downward pressure. These patterns generally apply to both skilled and unskilled employees across all economic sectors and in all industrialised Western countries.

Most important, the changes at the macro level have an effect on individual-level employment security and career prospects. However, greater international competition does not affect all individuals equally, and not all occupational groups are affected negatively by these developments. Even though highly educated people also tend to change their jobs more often and experience greater competition in the labour market, the labour market for these people offers more flexibility, and they tend to be more mobile and better able to change their careers. Generally, highly skilled and well-educated people do not face significantly higher risk exposure in open economies because they often have the possibility to take their skills to different economic sectors. Moreover, in many industrialised countries, there is a shortage of highly trained and specialised labour.[2] In contrast, workers with fewer skills are left with significantly limited options because their education and professional training does not meet the changing employment requirements.

Overall, the reorganisation of production and the following domestic changes has resulted in an increased diversification of the labour force. Whereas the interests regarding the provision of social policies and social protection of the workforce were fairly homogeneous in closed industrialised economies during the golden age, international trade and the integration of domestic companies in the international market have affected the degree to which particular workers are exposed to various risks, especially that of unemployment (Walter 2017; Walter and Maduz 2009). These differences in risk exposure have led to the development of social and labour market policies being required to cater to different needs of workers, depending on an individual's work relationship (e.g. part-time versus full-time, permanent employment contract versus freelance work) and economic outlook (the degree of vulnerability of their sector to increasing internationalisation or the general business cycle). The traditional class scheme used by political economy scholars, which treated the working class as a homogeneous group with shared interests that are represented by labour unions, has been questioned in the light of these developments and consequently adjusted, with the understanding of social classes and especially of the working class changing substantially over the past few years. Newly proposed class schemes are based on working relationships ('economic' classes) rather than shared social identities. In a recent attempt to categorise the 'working class', Oesch (2006a) addresses the earlier discussed changes within the workforce and proposes a refined class scheme that distinguishes between seventeen occupational groups which differ according to the work logic the occupation is based on and the level of skill an individual has. Table 3.1 shows Oesch's class scheme with a slightly reduced number of categories.

Generally speaking, the typical blue-collar worker in this class scheme has an occupation that is based on a technical work logic and has vocational skills that are – ideally – transferable from one company to another. Many jobs in this category, however, have been transferred to countries which allow for cheaper production processes and lower wages. In addition, many employment opportunities in the industrial sector have disappeared due to the increasing automatisation of production processes. This new heterogeneity of the workforce is particularly visible in the industrial sector where a gap has opened up between workers with vocational training and workers who have not enjoyed specific professional training and generally have few marketable skills due to low educational achievements. Nowadays, their employment

**Table 3.1. New Class Scheme Based on Work Logics and Skills**

| *Self-Employed* | *Employees* | | | |
|---|---|---|---|---|
| *Independent Work Logic* | *Technical Work Logic* | *Organisational Work Logic* | *Interpersonal Work Logic* | *Marketable Skills* |
| **Large Employers and Self-Employed Professionals** (e.g. firm owners, lawyers and medical doctors) | **Technical Experts and Technicians** (e.g. mechanical engineers and computer equipment operators) | **Higher and Associate Managers** (e.g. business administrators and tax officials) | **Socio-Cultural (Semi) Professionals** (e.g. university teachers, school teachers and social workers) | *Managerial* |
| **Small Proprietors with and without Employees** (e.g. restaurant owners, farmers and shopkeepers) | **Blue Collar** (e.g. carpenters and mechanics) | **White Collar** (e.g. secretaries and bank tellers) | **Skilled Service** (e.g. nurses and cooks) | *Vocational* |
| | **Routine Operatives and Agriculture** (e.g. agriculture, farm hands and gardeners) | **Routine Office** (e.g. call centre employees and messengers) | **Routine Service** (e.g. waiters and shop assistants) | *Low Skilled* |

Source: Based on Oesch (2006b, p. 68).

history is often marked by extended spells of unemployment, fixed-term contracts with temporary employment agencies and involuntary part-time employment. All these factors contribute to their overall disadvantaged position in the labour market and social security schemes.

A large number of jobs which have been established over recent decades are part of the service sector and follow an organisational or interpersonal work logic. However, unskilled employees in the service sector are facing the same problems of precarious work relations as people in the industrial sector. In addition, jobs in the service sector, as well as jobs based on an interpersonal work logic, are often particularly well suited to part-time employment and are therefore attractive for women who want to work in addition to being the main care giver to children in the household. This leads to the situation in which women – particularly in conservative welfare states – often have an extremely fragmented and short employment history. Their scattered work experience increases their economic vulnerability, particularly during economic downturns when they are often among the first to be laid off. Such fragmented employment histories also carry the risk that individuals (partially) lose their social rights, such as the right to unemployment benefits, if their contribution periods are too short and intersected by spells of unemployment. Young workers often face similar risks.

This implies that the structural changes that Western democracies were and are experiencing increase the existing divisions and also introduce new rifts into the workforce. The division between skilled and unskilled labour market participants is particularly marked, as is – depending on the country context – that between men and women. Based on the predominant work logic, unskilled people are more prone to finding themselves working part-time (i.e. as socio-cultural professionals), having fixed term contracts or being hired through job agencies which place them in the service and industrial sector. These developments exacerbate the division between workers with standard employment relations and people with precarious fixed-term or part-time jobs. The increasing heterogeneity of the labour force also has implications for politics as the social policy preferences of individuals are significantly influenced by their personal circumstances and their position in the labour market. These developments in turn have implications on how political economists model the policy preferences of individuals and political actors.

Labour economists have developed an interest in the micro- and company-level implications of the profound structural changes domestic economies were and are still experiencing (Blanchard 2006; Lindbeck and Snower 1988, 2001). They have proposed that these changes have a different impact on companies that are exposed to international market pressures as opposed to companies which are shielded from the global economy, specifically when it comes to wage-setting mechanisms and the costs of labour turnover. This division at the company level also affects the status and employment security of the employees which can differ greatly across these two sectors and leads to a dualisation of labour markets consisting of two groups of employees, labour market insiders and labour market outsiders.[3] Building on the work by labour economists and taking the dualisation of labour markets further, political economists took on board the political implications of this increasing labour market dualisation (Rueda 2005, 2007). Based on the increasing dualisation of labour markets, this literature assumes that labour is no longer a homogeneous political actor exhibiting similar preferences regarding social policies and labour standards, but rather that the political interests of labour market participants differ significantly. The key determinant affecting the policy preferences of labour market participants is their individual exposure to labour market risks, such as job loss, which is influenced by individual level characteristics (education, skills) but also by the extent to which the employer is exposed to the world market. Whether an employee benefits from the changing macroeconomic environment remains unaffected or experiences negative implications has an impact on their political preferences and party choice. The increasing heterogeneity of labour market participants thus leads to a similar diversity in policy preferences on the part of the labour force.

The preferred policies of insiders are social policy reforms that strengthen their position in the labour market and protect their already-existing rights. They, for example, advocate for the continuation of existing protection against dismissal and generally support policies which secure their standing in the labour market and maintain their social status by means of fairly generous temporary unemployment insurance benefits. Policy measures aimed at protecting jobs are not necessarily directly related to classical social policies but nevertheless can have an impact on a company's competitiveness and hence indirectly benefit employees. Governments, for instance, can pay subsidies to companies in order to protect jobs in an import-competing sector which is under threat from international competition, or help to increase the competitiveness of an exporting company on the international market. An example of the former strategy is the immense government expenditure on the coal mining sector in Germany. This is a highly organised sector and has defended its interests very successfully even though it has been unprofitable for decades. An example of the latter strategy is the grant of high subsidies in high-technology sectors, for example, the aircraft industries in Europe and the United States. Alternatively, governments can also help specific industrial sectors in times of economic downturn by financing short periods where the employees work reduced hours.[4] All these measures guarantee that jobs continue to exist in these areas and that the country can maintain a specific industrial sector and its associated knowhow. However, these are very costly measures which can be considered to arise from the social concern that members of the labour force in these industries – who can be classified as insiders – not be made unemployed. These policies are thus related to a wider range of social policies that governments can design and implement to compensate specific groups among the labour force.

In contrast, labour market outsiders are more likely to prefer social policies that offer them the possibility to re-enter the labour market after spells of unemployment or which compensate them if they accept employment where job insecurity is high. Measures to assist the re-entry into the labour market of outsiders are often related to professional training and up-skilling. Since many outsiders have very little initial vocational training, the training measures should increase the marketable skills of these individuals and ideally allow them to find regular employment. So-called active labour market policies, which often consist of a mix of setting incentives for people to shorten their period of unemployment along with measures to help them update their skill set, have become popular instruments of labour market policy-making over recent decades and are said to particularly help labour market outsiders (Bonoli 2010; Rueda 2006). In contrast to insiders, who are very well organised and represented by powerful interest groups, mainly labour unions, outsiders have hardly any powerful lobbying groups which play a major role in the policy-making process. Although labour unions often raise the problems of the low-skilled workforce in public debates, their primary lobbying activities naturally concern the interests of their main constituents and members, who are mostly insiders.

Table 3.2 presents the division of the labour force into labour market insiders and outsiders based on their work logic and skills.[5] The cells shaded in dark grey represent occupational classes with a potentially high proportion of labour market outsiders working in the industrial or the service sector. They hold jobs which are often characterised by low wages, short-term

**Table 3.2. Labour Market Insiders and Outsiders in a Globalised Economy**

| *Self-Employed* | *Employees* | | | |
|---|---|---|---|---|
| *Independent Work Logic* | *Technical Work Logic* | *Organisational Work Logic* | *Interpersonal Work Logic* | *Marketable Skills* |
| **Large Employers and Self-Employed Professionals** | **Technical Experts and Technicians** | **Higher and Associate Managers** | **Socio-cultural (semi) Professionals** | *Managerial* |
| **Small Proprietors with and without Employees** | **Blue Collar** Labour market insider with predominantly stable employment relations, often unionised | **White Collar** Predominantly labour market insiders, stable employment relations | **Skilled Service** Mostly insiders, though many professions with a majority of women who often work part-time and enjoy less social insurance coverage | *Vocational* |
| | **Routine Operatives and Agriculture** Labour market outsiders with fixed-term, precarious employment relations | **Routine Office** Often precarious, part-time employment; many women | **Routine Service** Often precarious, part-time employment; many women | *Low Skilled* |

Source: Based on Oesch (2006b, p. 68) and adapted.

contracts, or which offer only part-time employment. The cell shaded in light grey is characterised by occupations that are often dominated by female employees working part-time. Depending on the national legislative framework, members of this group also have an increased probability of being categorised as labour market outsiders due to the configuration of social rights.

## 3.2 THE ROLE OF SOCIAL POLICY IN POLITICAL COMPETITION

The ongoing structural changes increase the need for protection from labour market risks and also have an impact on preference formation at the individual level with regard to social and redistributive policies. Recent scholarly evidence shows that the support and demand for social policies is strongly determined by and associated with people's status in the labour market (Cusack, Iversen and Rehm 2006). People who are afraid of losing employment and income are significantly more in favour of redistributive policies than employees in secure positions. Furthermore, the extent to which an individual is exposed to unemployment and other labour market risks is significantly influenced by someone's occupation (Rehm 2009, 2011), with unskilled people working in the manufacturing or service sector experiencing more labour market insecurity than highly skilled people. Figure 3.1 supports this evidence. Assessing to what extent different occupational groups support the government's involvement in limiting income inequality (which can be taken as a proxy for their support of redistribution), we see that these preferences differ greatly across occupational classes.[6]

The graph offers two key take-away points: first, it shows that support for redistribution differs significantly across occupational classes, with occupational groups that are most threatened by the changes that affect the global economic structure and production processes most in favour of redistributive policies. Typical blue-collar workers and people with jobs that require few marketable skills are significantly more in favour of redistribution than white-collar workers, the self-employed and people in technical and engineering positions, as demonstrated by the larger share of the 'strongly agree' category. This is in line with other research that finds that social policy institutions still enjoy a very high level of approval and trust among the public (Brooks and Manza 2007; Kenworthy 2009; Kenworthy and McCall 2008; Rehm 2005). Second, the figure also shows that redistributive and social policies continue to be important for other electoral groups which indicates that such policies are salient among a potentially large proportion of the electorate and for a number of political parties and hence have

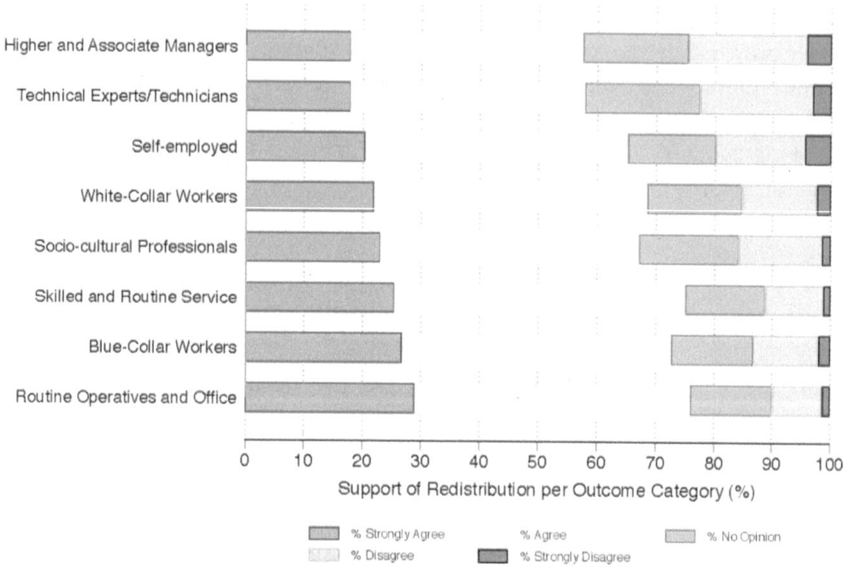


**Figure 3.1. Preferences for Redistribution Based on Occupational Class**

the capacity to shape party competition and electoral campaigns. Research shows that there is a strong linkage between redistributive preferences, partisan support and government policies (Cusack, Iversen and Rehm 2006, p. 366).[7] This implies that economic cleavages and government partisanship continue to matter for public policy-making. In short, constituencies expect an elected government to formulate distinct social policies with respect to redistribution.

## 3.3 PARTY GOVERNMENTS, POLITICAL CONSTRAINTS AND WELFARE STATE REFORMS

The aforementioned paragraphs established how structural changes affect labour markets and also provide evidence about the continuing popularity of social and redistributive policies which are important building blocks of the welfare state. The tensions and developments caused by structural changes which reverberate across society also highlight that social and labour market policies still have the potential to shape party competition and electoral outcomes. Moreover, the continuing salience of redistributive issues implies that political parties seeking to win elections and office cannot simply ignore topics related to social policy and redistributive issues but rather have to position themselves and offer policy solutions that echo the preferences of their core constituency. Figure 3.2 shows how the position of four distinct party families on the traditional left-right dimension has evolved between 1970 and 2013. The plotted positions are based on the well-known left-right scale included in the Comparative Manifesto database (2016), where lower values represent more left-wing electoral programmes and higher values more conservative, right-wing positions.[8] As we would expect, the political space covered by these four party families is defined by the parties of the conservative right, which represents one end of the left/right spectrum, and the group of socialist and green parties, which demarcate the political space at the left-winged of the spectrum.

While the programmatic space covered by political parties has narrowed somewhat over the past forty years, the programmatic offerings of left-wing and conservative/right-wing parties are still sufficiently different to offer real policy alternatives and different policy solutions to contemporary policy problems. In addition, throughout the period covered by the data, the programmatic offerings from the four party families are by and large distinct and only occasionally overlap. This shows that party positions in general, and policy positions on social policies more specifically, can still be taken

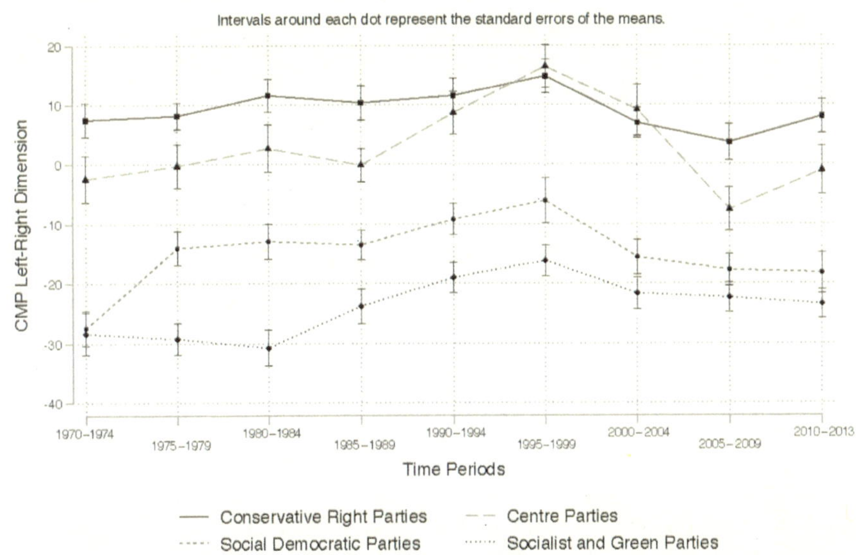


**Figure 3.2. Development of Electoral Platforms for Four Party Families, over Forty Years**

as important pointers regarding a party's political programme. Taking into account the differences in their electoral platforms and the diverging preferences of their relative constituencies, political parties are still likely to design differing reform proposals. Recent research has also shown that the policy agendas of ideologically different political parties differ with regard to the way scarce financial resources are to be spent and allocated (e.g. Kenworthy and McCall 2008; Kwon and Pontusson 2010). Whereas the Right has always advocated smaller government with a low or non-existent budget deficit, and continues to do so, the Left may be willing to accept a higher deficit to support the welfare state.

Looking at the programmatic differences, party and policy competition still seem to play a role in Western democracies, contrary to contributions published within the wider literature on the impact of globalisation which have suggested a convergence of policy positions among traditional party families (Mishra 1999; Rodrik 1997; Ross 2000a). Scholarship specific to the reform of welfare states and social policy in times of globalisation has also started to question the influence of distinct ideological profiles on the design and reform of social policies and policy outcomes. The 'New Politics' literature, an influential strand of welfare state research, has proposed that politics – in particular, party politics has ceased to influence welfare state policy-making, with political actors anxiously trying to avoid blame and risky reforms (Pierson 1996; Seeleib-Kaiser, van Dyk and Roggenkamp 2008). Other work by quantitatively oriented scholars has also suggested that economic and demographic pressures limit the room to manoeuvre for parties in office and consequentially lead to a convergence of policy outcomes (Huber and Stephens 2001; Kittel and Obinger 2003; Stephens, Huber and Ray 1999). These contributions stand in stark contrast to the traditional 'parties matter' literature, which proposes that political parties, once in office, will translate their policy programme into specific policies with the aim of responding to their electorate's preferences and attitudes (Cameron 1978; Schmidt 1996; Stephens 1980). Despite the fact that both right-wing and left-wing party governments are similarly affected by the internationalisation of the economy and the resulting pressure on their activity, research shows relatively little convergence across different welfare states over the past decades. Welfare state institutions prove to be resilient (Häusermann 2010a) with distinct reform paths that differ across countries. The role of party governments, however, has remained to some extent unresolved and neglected in research assessing welfare and social policy reforms during times of austerity. Only recently have welfare state scholars reintegrated party politics into their theories about welfare state change and started to critically question the underlying strategies and goals of parties in office (Häusermann, Picot and Geering 2013; Jensen and Mortensen 2014). The following paragraphs set out to scrutinise the role of party governments on the outcome of public policy-making by assessing how party governments, along with institutional constraints, shape policy outcomes.

As shown in the previous chapter, governments of all colours have been implementing budgetary cuts over the past decades to address fiscal deficits. In line with this, large parts of the welfare state-specific literature emphasise that governments have tried to contain social spending or attempted to roll back social security programmes (Green-Pedersen and Haverland 2002; Pierson 1996; Starke, Obinger and Castles 2008). While continuous economic pressure on party governments suggest that the room to manoeuvre for governments is declining, the evidently high level of public support for redistributive and social policies among the population indicates that rolling back social policies and retrenching the welfare state is likely to be very unpopular with the electorate at large (Hübscher and Sattler 2018). This suggests that parties in government can be expected to exploit both the salience of the topic and their capacity to strategically design reforms in a given institutional context in order to survive in office and maintain the support of their electorate.

Figure 3.3 illustrates how the preferences regarding redistribution are distributed across various occupational groups in Germany and Ireland. The

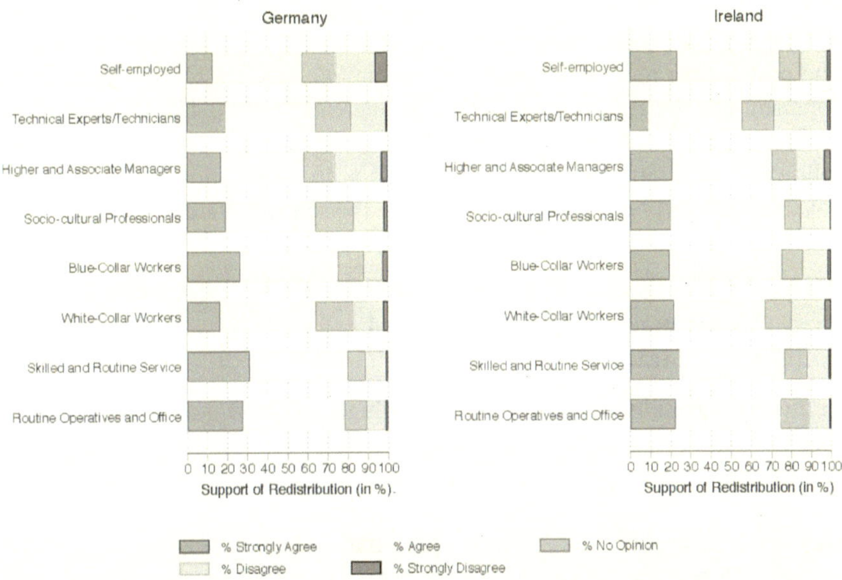


**Figure 3.3. Preferences for Redistribution Based on Occupational Class (in Germany and Ireland)**

two figures show that the extent to which different occupational classes support redistribution is very similar in both countries. Based on this preference structure, one might assume that similar policies would be implemented by a government trying to please a similar group of voters. However, when assessing the situation on the ground, it very quickly becomes clear that this is not the case.

The direction and extent of policy reforms, however, is not only influenced by the ideology of the parties in government and the policy preferences of their overall electorate but also shaped by constraints which manifest themselves through checks and balances that are rooted in the institutional settings of a country and which governments face in some countries but not in others (Immergut 1990). Although institutional analyses of social policy-making are popular, they often do not take into account that the impact of the constraints inherent in a political system may vary for ideologically different party governments.[9] Whether a particular party government is able to have a significant impact on the further development of core social policy programmes and its reform not only is contingent on the state of the economy and demographic factors but also depends on the institutional setting of a country. In line with Immergut's (1990) logic of veto points, reforms proposed by the government can be blocked by independent branches of government with veto-power over the governments' reform proposal. Constraints, as they are understood here, consist of institutional constraints (e.g. federalism and bicameralism) and their interaction with the changing political majorities and the way the interests of parties in power are enmeshed with those of organised interest groups. The presence or absence of such constraints in a country enables or hinders opponents to the reform and organised interests (mainly labour unions) to pressure the incumbents to alter the design of the reform proposal.[10] The following paragraph develops the different scenarios of how different party governments can be expected to influence the reform outcomes in countries with low and high levels of institutional constraints.

## Party Governments and Varying Levels of Political Constraints

Left party governments in countries with high levels of political constraints may have to accept higher cuts in spending than in situations where political constraints and pressure from the opposition are low. In order to ensure that any proposed reform passes the legislative process, the left-wing government has to accommodate their partisan opponents with greater expenditure cuts. However, when the amount to be cut increases due to the presence of open veto points, such as an upper parliamentary chamber with a majority from the opposition parties, the core workforce, which is the Left party's main constituency, may call for compensation for any potential losses in economic and social security. Furthermore, planned cuts in core social security programmes may create public outcry and open opposition by the organised workforce, which would massively damage the reputation and future public and electoral support of the left-wing governments.[11] Left-wing governments thus are severely restricted in their possibility of dismantling core social security programmes but may escape the reform gridlock by compensating labour market insiders. The compensation of the core constituency, however, comes at the expense of labour force participants who do not enjoy full coverage by core social security programmes, such as workers in the low-wage sector and people with part-time or contracted jobs. In other words, when the Left is in government but its room to manoeuvre is constrained through open veto points such as an upper parliamentary chamber dominated by the conservative opposition, it is forced to adjust its policies in a twofold manner. First, the government has to meet the demands of the opposition with regard to the size of spending cuts in order to overcome the veto point. Second, in order to retain good relations with societal groups that are well organised and could politically harm the government in future elections, the government will leave core social security programmes which benefit the core constituency unaltered or reform them only at the margins. Tailoring reforms in such a way as to please the core workforce is also relatively easy as their interests are well known and forcefully represented by the respective organisations. Labour market outsiders, however, are a heterogeneous group with a wide variety of preferences (see Finseraas 2009; Pontusson and Rueda 2010) and also lack organisational representation. Overall, the outcome in such a situation is a clientelistic reform benefiting the core workforce which enjoys coverage from major social insurance schemes and which is represented by well-organised and networked interest groups.[12]

The situation for left-wing governments is different when political constraints are low, that is, when potential veto points are closed and their reform proposals cannot be blocked during the legislative process and hence the opposition parties cannot force the government to accept a compromise in their favour. There is evidence, however, that left-wing governments can convince the public that, due to the adverse economic circumstances, some retrenchment and reforms are necessary (Green-Pedersen, van Kersbergen and Hemerijck 2001; Ross 1997, 2000b).[13] However, since the government proposal cannot be blocked by an additional independent branch of government, the deficit can remain higher than the right-wing parties would generally accept. Without accommodating the opposition, a left-wing government can engage in more egalitarian reforms which benefit not only the core workforce but also the so-called losers of globalisation, or 'labour market outsiders', and core programmes will be sustained at a level acceptable by the core workforce. Furthermore, offering a broader range of policies and reforms which are not only targeted at the core workforce may also help the party to reach out to different electoral segments.[14]

The presence or absence of political constraints also conditions the reform logic of conservative governments. If confronted with high levels of political constraints, the conservative government will accommodate the opposition to a certain extent as it needs to overcome the resistance of the political opponent. The conservative government is likely to compromise on the reform of core social security programmes, as these are in the core interest of left-wing parties. This strategy may also aid in preventing a situation where left-wing parties and organised labour are given grounds to mobilise against the conservative government and diminish their future electoral prospects. With the conservatives in government, left-wing parties that have the possibility to block government proposals through open veto points can present themselves as the advocate of all groups facing various social risks, that is, both the core workforce and labour market outsiders. The policies demanded by left-wing parties in the opposition therefore take a broader and more egalitarian approach, at least in the public debate. When political constraints are high, we should therefore observe little impact of conservative governments on either welfare state programme generosity or social spending as the left-wing parties can oppose and block legislative proposals that demand unacceptably high cuts. When political constraints are low, however, the right-wing parties in power will cut social expenditures and the generosity of core social security programmes as this is in line with their overall partisan preferences (Amable, Gatti and Schumacher 2006; Korpi and Palme 2003).

However, the Left also wants to be able to accuse the incumbent right-wing government of social injustice. Hence, public outrage and protest when organised labour loses social privileges is desired as the discontent with the planned reforms is directed towards the conservative parties in government. Left-wing parties are expected to benefit rather than suffer when outrage by well-organised labour receives public attention and may free-ride on unions' actions against reform programmes in the form of new votes in future elections. Similarly, to the situation when the Left in government does not face open veto points, left-wing parties will attempt to gain the support of the broader range of groups which are affected by the reforms proposed by the conservative government. As the left-wing party does not need to take the responsibility of implementing the policies that it proposes, it also has more freedom to demand a fair and equal distribution of burdens caused by economic globalisation. This logic implies that the organised workforce (the traditional electorate of left-wing parties) will receive less exclusive support from left-wing parties when a right-wing party is in power. Moreover, the right-wing party in power will in principle be less responsive to the demands of organised labour.

Two empirical implications follow from this argument. First, we should see an increase in welfare state generosity when a left-wing government attempts to reform welfare states in a situation of high political constraints. This is a direct result of the clientelistic character of the reform, which aims at accommodating the parliamentary opposition and compensating the core workforce. When political constraints are low, however, we should see comparatively little impact of left-wing governments on the redistributive generosity of core welfare state programmes. Table 3.3 summarises these mechanisms in a stylised manner.

Second, left-wing governments should attempt to retrench less than right-wing governments when they face few political constraints but should retrench to approximately the same extent as right-wing governments when constraints are high. This does not mean that left-wing governments do not retrench at all; however, the difference in social spending between Right and Left should diminish or disappear with higher levels of political constraints due to the conditioning effect of political constraints, resulting in different reform logics for left- and right-wing party governments. Table 3.4 summarises the hypotheses related to the spending dimension that will be tested in the subsequent empirical analysis.

**Table 3.3. Expected Effects of Partisanship and Political Constraints on Programme Generosity**

| | | ***Political Constraints*** | |
|---|---|---|---|
| | | *Low* | *High* |
| **Government Partisanship** | *Left* | Stability | Increase **(Clientelistic policy-making)** |
| | *Right* | Modest retrenchment | Stability |

**Table 3.4. Expected Effects of Partisanship and Political Constraints on Social Spending**

| | | ***Political Constraints*** | |
|---|---|---|---|
| | | *Low* | *High* |
| **Government Partisanship** | *Left* | Stability | Modest retrenchment |
| | *Right* | Significant retrenchment | Modest retrenchment |

The argument this book proposes is therefore grounded in the growing tension between changing demands for and constraints upon the supply of social policies in Western industrialised countries. The reorganisation of production due to economic globalisation and structural changes has created a more heterogeneous labour force with diverging needs which results in new demands for social security coverage. Broadly speaking, governments today face a workforce that is divided into well-trained workers with permanent contracts ('insiders') and low-skilled, part-time employees ('outsiders'). The former are generally well organised in labour unions, while the latter are often not represented by interest groups in the political arena. When governments design social policy reforms, they have to take these diverging needs into account while at the same time being under pressure to cut social spending. How a government reforms social policies then depends on its partisanship in combination with the institutional constraints that it faces. Institutional constraints determine whether a party government has to gain support from opposition parties (e.g. in a bicameral system) to implement a reform, and the extent to which interest groups can access the policy-making process and block a reform proposal.

In a nutshell, a right-wing government that does not face high institutional constraints will mainly cut social spending without offering any compensation for the losers of the reform through redistribution. The situation is different for a right-wing government in a country where institutional constraints are high. These governments tend to end up with social policy reforms that bring little change in terms of either retrenchment or redistribution because of the pressure which interest groups – mainly labour unions and employers' organisations – exert on the government. Labour unions demand compensation for their constituencies, while employers, who are closely connected to the conservative party in power, oppose this. The result is a failed reform or one with little impact on social policies. However, the reform outcomes will differ when a left-wing government is in power. Left-wing governments in countries with few institutional constraints tend to implement welfare state reforms that reduce spending and at the same time compensate workers through greater redistribution. Both labour market 'insiders' and 'outsiders' benefit in a similar manner from the compensation measures. When a left-wing government faces high institutional constraints, however, it has to accommodate conservative forces and thus must offer greater retrenchment to reach an agreement. The left-wing government also has to ensure that 'insiders', represented by labour unions, are not overly negatively affected by the reform. At the same time, compensation cannot come from the wealthy because this would provoke resistance from the right-wing parties. The solution is a disproportionate retrenchment on the part of 'outsiders' in order to satisfy the needs of the 'insiders' and, simultaneously, achieve a sufficient reduction in social expenditure to accommodate the opposition.

The theoretical framework that has been presented in the previous pages is rigid in the sense that it proposes causal mechanisms and processes leading to clear-cut predictions about the policy choices of different party governments in different institutional settings. An encompassing empirical test of these theoretical propositions makes great demands on the data and the empirical material in general. The empirical analysis presented in this work aims at approximating this rigorous framework, and the discussion of the results in each chapter is based on the same. The concluding chapter, however, critically challenges and scrutinises the collected evidence and also provides alternative explanations, pointing at deficiencies of the collected empirical evidence and the theoretical framework.

The following empirical chapters consist of two complementary parts. The first focuses on the macro level and examines the correlations between party governments and redistributive generosity and expenditure, and whether government partisanship and constraints have the effect on the 'insider'-'outsider' divide predicted by the theoretical model. The second consists of two country case studies concentrating on labour market reforms under various party governments. The in-depth analysis of labour market reforms will on the one hand substantiate the macro-level evidence and on the other hand focus more closely on how labour market 'outsiders' are affected by these reforms.

## NOTES

1 In continental and conservative welfare states, such as Germany and Switzerland, the core workforce consisted of the male population. In other countries, for example, those of Scandinavia, welfare states attended to the needs of women who participated in the labour force more often than did the traditionally conservative countries.

2 This is particularly apparent in countries with mass unemployment, such as Germany. Even during times when unemployment peaked in the late 1990s and early 2000s, employers were unable to fill a substantial number of positions that required very specialised skills and a high level of training.

3 Lindbeck and Snower (1988, 2001) defined 'insiders' as 'experienced incumbent employees whose positions are protected by various job-preserving measures that make it costly for companies to fire them and hire someone else in their place'.

4 Reduced working hours for a limited time period are a tool that is used in a number of continental European countries (e.g. Germany, Austria and Switzerland) which helps firms in the industrial sector to overcome periods with a low workload due to decreasing orders. Usually, firms can apply for subsidies from the state which allow them to reduce the working hours of their employee while maintaining full pay. This measure permits employers to hold on to their skilled workforce and swiftly move back to pre-crisis production levels as soon as the economy recovers.

5 Table 3.2 presents only a rough categorisation of insiders and outsiders. Whether an individual falls into one or the other category is also dependent on the institutional context and the structure of the labour market. The Netherlands, for example, has a large share of part-time employees (46.8 per cent of the total labour force in 2007), who enjoy the same social rights as full-time employees. This, however, is not the case in Germany. The same is true for women, who more often work part time, with the consequence that their status within the labour market is dependent on the legislation and the social rights concerning part-time employees. It is also important to note that the literature discusses different dimensions of 'outsiderness'. People can be outsiders with regard to their ability to participate in the labour market, but they can also be outsiders in the light of their chance of being represented in the political sphere. However, often these dimensions correlate, as is the case for the unemployed or foreign workers (Davidsson and Naczyk 2009; Kalleberg 2000; Palier 2005).

6 The graph is based on the European Social Survey 2008 and includes the following thirteen countries: Belgium, Denmark, Finland, France, Germany, Great Britain, Ireland, the Netherlands, Norway, Portugal, Spain, Sweden and Switzerland. To approximate people's preference for redistribution, the following question was used: 'Whether governments should take measures to reduce income differences?' The exact wording of the question in the survey is 'To what extent do you agree with the following statement: The government should take measures to reduce differences in income levels?.' The coding of respondents into different occupational groups is based on Oesch (2006b) and Häusermann (2010b) who make use of the ISCO-88 codes suggested by the International Labour Organization (ILO).

7 Their analysis shows that redistributional preferences are excellent predictors of partisan affiliation. Whereas individuals voting for right-wing parties prefer less redistributive policies, individuals voting for left-wing parties prefer more redistributive policies (Cusack, Iversen and Rehm 2006, p. 378).

8 Figure 3.2 is based on data from the Comparative Party Manifesto Project (2016). The graph is based on the same eighteen countries that are also included in the following quantitative analysis. The parties coded as nationalist in the original data set as well as parties from the 'ethnic and regional' party family were excluded from the calculations. Liberal parties were grouped together with conservative parties and labelled 'conservative right', and Christian Democratic parties are labelled 'center parties'. Agrarian parties were recoded into either centrist or conservative-right parties based on their own characterisation (i.e. the Swiss People's Party, originally an agrarian party, was coded as 'conservative right', whereas the Finnish Centre Party has been recoded into a 'center party'). To simplify matters, the original data set has been reduced to a data set that includes the mean position of a given party family for specific (five-year) time periods. While this is an admittedly crude approximation to how political parties in a specific country context reposition themselves over time, the method chosen here still drives home the point that the party landscapes in post-industrial democracies offers reasonably different policy solutions.

9 Exceptions are Green-Pedersen (2001b, 2002) and Bonoli (2001), who offer both a partial framework of contingent effects of particular party governments and the institutional framework for the politics of retrenchment. The present contribution builds on this tradition and develops the framework further.

10 This pressure through organised interests can take different forms, either through close linkages with the relevant political parties represented in government or through independent veto points such as popular referenda in Switzerland, which significantly influences the reform pace and content of major social security schemes.

11 An illustrative example of the proposed mechanism is the impact of the German Bundesrat on the legislative behaviour of the German executive. In cases where the government is divided, it already anticipates a potential veto from the Bundesrat and hence drafts the law in such a way as to avoid the veto (Manow and Burkhart 2007).

12 Germany serves as a good example illustrating the strong connection between left-wing parties and labour unions: During the twelfth legislative period (1990–1994), over 70 per cent of the Social Democratic members of the German parliament were also union members. Despite the fact that overall union membership is decreasing, this figure even increased to over 80 per cent during the fourteenth legislative period (1999–2003). The share of Christian Democratic members of parliament who are also members of trade unions is significantly smaller and decreased from 7.5 per cent to 1 per cent between the twelfth and the fourteenth (Trampusch 2003, p.92).

13 The ability of left-wing governments to convince the public about the necessity of welfare state reforms is also based on the fact that left-wing parties are considered to be more trustworthy when it comes to reforming the welfare state (a phenomena sometimes called the 'Nixon Goes to China Effect') (Ross 2000b). In addition, left-wing parties are the traditional 'owners' of the welfare state issue and are not expected to dismantle social security schemes (Bélanger and Meguid 2008; Budge and Farlie 1983; Petrocik 1996).

14 The incentive for left-wing governments for a more egalitarian approach to welfare state restructuring is influenced not only by their different ideological background but also by the desire to attract a broader electorate if the political circumstances allow them to do so. Recent research by Brady and Leicht (2008) and Boix (1998) shows that left-wing governments still aim at implementing more egalitarian policies and try to decrease inequality within society if they have the possibility of doing so.

# *Chapter 4*

# Austerity, Party Governments and Welfare State Output

This chapter quantitatively assesses the theoretical claims discussed in the previous chapter. It thus analyses the joint impact of government ideology and political constraints on two output measures of public policy, in particular, welfare state programme generosity and social spending.

## 4.1 ESTIMATION TECHNIQUE AND BASIC EMPIRICAL MODEL

The following analysis is based on a panel data set which includes eighteen open post-industrial economies from 1971 to 2002.[1] This allows for a maximum of 551 observations (country-years) for the welfare state generosity model and 373 for the social expenditure model. The substantially lower number of observations for the expenditure model is due to the fact that the availability of social expenditure data is limited. There are a minimum of six and a maximum of thirty-two observations per country in each of the presented regressions, with an average of twenty-eight observations per country. In the following sections, the determinants of welfare state generosity and social expenditure will be statistically examined using pooled cross-section time-series analysis.

A performed 'Levin-Lin Chu' test and an 'Im-Pesaran-Shin' test for panel unit roots indicate that at least some of the time series included in the model are non-stationary. This study therefore primarily relies on models that are estimated in first differences. Conceptually, the use of first differences is appropriate because, controlling for the impact of structural factors, changes in social policy measures should reflect reforms (or changes), which is the focus of this analysis. I follow Beck and Katz (1995, 1996) in the way the standard errors are computed to account for panel-specific heteroskedasticity in the residual structure. To account for serial correlation, the models are estimated using Prais-Winston regressions, which correct for first-order serially correlated errors.[2]

As indicated later, a full set of country dummies (N-1 country dummies) is included in some of the models to account for country-specific characteristics. The country dummies allow the intercept to vary across the different units. However, the inclusion of fixed effects also leads to certain problems. Country dummies are non-theoretical variables and increase the explained variance without adding substantive insights. In addition, the coefficients of fixed-effects models take into account the within-country variation only. I therefore estimate my model with and without country dummies and report the coefficients of both models.[3] Models with two different dependent variables are estimated, welfare state generosity and social spending. Each of the two dependent variables is regressed on the same set of explanatory variables. This allows me to analyse how the influence of the variables changes across the two dimensions of social policy-making and makes it possible to test the mechanisms proposed in the theory chapter.

I expect that structural factors play a more important role in the spending equation than in the programme generosity equation, whereas government ideology and institutions should be more important in the generosity model than in the spending model. The core explanatory variables of interest are government ideology and the political constraints that the incumbent faces. The basic empirical specification thus takes the following form:

$$\begin{aligned} \Delta DV_{i,t} = {} & \beta_0 + \beta_1 \times Government\,Ideology_{i,t-1} + \beta_2 \times \Delta Actual\,Flows_{i,t} + \beta_3 \\ & \times Financial\,Flows_{i,t} + \beta_4 \times \Delta Econ.Growth_{i,t} + \beta_5 \times \Delta Unemployment_{t,i} \\ & + \beta_6 \times \Delta Deindustrialisation_{i,t} + \beta_7 \times \Delta Elderly_{i,t} + \beta_8 \\ & \times Political\,Constraints_{i,t} + \left( \sum_{i=1}^{n} \times \beta_{i-1}\,Country\,Dummy_{i,t} \right) + \epsilon_{i,t} \end{aligned}$$

where $DV_{i,t}$ is either Programme $Generosity_{i,t}$ or Social $Expenditure_{i,t}$ as indicated for the different analyses.

## Dependent Variables

To capture the impact of party governments and institutional constraints on the redistributive generosity of core welfare state programmes benefiting the well-integrated workforce, I use the welfare state generosity index by Allan and Scruggs (2004).[4] The index covers information about regulative and institutional characteristics of three major, predominantly insurance-based, welfare state programmes. In particular, the duration, eligibility and level of benefits paid in public pension schemes, unemployment insurance schemes and sick pay schemes. This measure thus captures well the overall generosity of the main social security schemes, or the extent to which they make an individual independent from gainful employment. The degree of generosity is highest if an individual without employment earns as much as he or she would earn while having a job. This index thus mainly reflects how generous welfare states are towards members of the core workforce who regularly contribute to these schemes and hence earn social rights in terms of benefits. For instance, pension schemes are most beneficial for those people who have been integrated into the labour market and were gainfully employed during most of their working age. Similarly, to be eligible for unemployment insurance benefits, workers are required to have contributed to the insurance scheme for a certain period. Having a stable contributory period often goes hand in hand with regular and long-term employment. The same applies to the third scheme – sick-pay – which is included in the index. The welfare state generosity index thus primarily captures generosity towards people who are part of the active workforce or who have been integrated in the labour market in earlier stages of their lives. The generosity index is particularly well suited for this analysis because it captures to what extent a welfare state is redistributing resources within specific groups, particularly the members of specific social insurance schemes. Unlike horizontal redistribution, which aims at redistributing resources across different social strata, this so-called vertical redistribution tends to reproduce and reinforce existing class structures. In this sense, the generosity index primarily indicates how welfare states favour 'insiders' and how dense the safety net for labour market 'insiders' is.

The amount of social spending, which is the second dependent variable used in the following analyses, is measured as the share of total social expenditure as a percentage of GDP. The data are available from the OECD Social Expenditure database. This measure is commonly used in welfare state research (e.g. Castles 2002; Kittel and Obinger 2003; Kwon and Pontusson 2010). It captures how much states spend on social policies. This measure has been available only since 1980, and some countries have longer periods of missing data (for Austria, 1980–1989 is missing; for Norway, 1980–1987 is missing). This significantly diminishes the number of observations in the spending models. Social spending covers all types of social policy programmes funded by the state.

## Independent Variables

This study operationalises government ideology by making use of a measure proposed by Kim and Fording (2002). Their index is based on two components: on the one hand, the position on the left-right dimension of political competition provided within the Comparative Party Manifesto data; and on the other, the relative share of votes held by each party in the government.

The RILE measure is an index taking into account twenty-six issue categories on various topics relevant to determine a party's position on this dimension. The information on issue salience and the policy preferences of individual political parties is based on electoral platforms. Kim and Fording's measure of government ideology has the advantage that it combines a measure of partisan strength in government (e.g. the percentage of left-wing parties in power) with its relative position on the left-right dimension, the most important dimension of electoral competition. The variable was transformed to range from 0 to 10 where higher values indicate a more left-wing government and lower values refer to more right-wing/conservative governments. For the sake of this analysis, Kim and Fording's original index has been updated using the data set from the Party Manifesto Research Group (Klingemann et al. 2006), as well as the yearly 'Political Data' update from the *European Journal of Political Research* to extract the information about the composition of the government cabinets.

To account for the varying political constraints present in the countries included in the analyses, I include Henisz's index of political constraints (Henisz 2006). Henisz's measure of political constraints is based on information about the number of independent branches of government with veto power over policy change, and the degree of alignment across branches of government based on the party composition of each branch. The measure also takes into account situations where the executive is in a minority position. In such cases, the constraints index rises to a level comparable to situations where a majority government faces an open veto point in an independent branch of government, such as the upper parliamentary chamber in Germany.[5] Hence, the index adequately captures the concept of veto points and the constraints that arise for governments when they face obstacles during the legislative process. Henisz's measure of political constraints is more comprehensive than the additive indices consisting of various institutional features because it is based on a spatial model of political interaction with the aim of deriving the likelihood of policy change. As opposed to the additive indices on institutional constraints, which are time invariant, Henisz's measure of political constraints also accounts for changes in the power constellation across the different branches of government over time.[6]

To operationalise the control variables, the previous literature is followed. Economic globalisation is measured using a measure of actual trade and capital flows from the KOF index of globalisation (Dreher 2006). In addition to measures of international economic openness, I include variables that capture structural changes in the domestic economy and society, such as deindustrialisation, economic growth, unemployment and demographic change. Deindustrialisation is measured as the percentage of people working in the industrial and agricultural sectors as a percentage of the total labour force, while demographic

**Table 4.1. Summary Statistics**

| *Variable* | *Mean* | *Std. Dev.* | *Min.* | *Max.* | *N* |
|---|---|---|---|---|---|
| Δ Redistributive generosity | 0.137 | 1.016 | −4.168 | 10.673 | 526 |
| Δ Social expenditure | 0.163 | 0.900 | −3.700 | 5.1 | 357 |
| Government ideology | 0.529 | 0.179 | 0.079 | 0.941 | 526 |
| Constraints | 0.464 | 0.26 | 0 | 1 | 526 |
| Δ Trade flows | 1.188 | 3.816 | −20.88 | 20.98 | 526 |
| Δ Financial flows | 0.062 | 0.291 | −1.297 | 2.231 | 526 |
| Δ Economic growth | −0.096 | 2.419 | −9.2 | 9.2 | 526 |
| Δ Unemployment | 0.115 | 1.013 | −2.96 | 5.06 | 526 |
| Δ Deindustrialisation | −0.65 | 0.656 | −5.998 | 2.919 | 526 |
| Δ Elderly | 0.125 | 0.161 | −0.71 | 0.67 | 526 |

change is operationalised as the percentage of the total population that is sixty-five years and older. Table 4.1 presents the summary statistics.[7]

## 4.2 DISCUSSION OF THE RESULTS

The results for both dependent variables – welfare state generosity and social spending – will be presented in the following paragraphs. The presentation and discussion of the results is split into three sections: the first establishes the baseline model, the second adds the conditioning effect of political constraints and the last assesses the relationship between party government and the two dimensions of aggregate welfare state output for two different time periods.

Table 4.2 presents the coefficients of the basic model for both dependent variables, welfare state generosity (columns 1 and 2) and social spending (columns 3 and 4). The table includes two different specifications for each model: columns 1 and 3 show the models which include fixed effects (country dummies), and columns 2 and 4 show the coefficients which were obtained estimating the model without country dummies. The base model shows a statistically significant and positive impact of government ideology on redistributive generosity. The estimated parameters of the models are robust, and are similar for those both with and without country dummies. This means that governments with a higher score on the ideology scale carry out reforms of social policy in order to bring about higher programme generosity. In other words, when the share of left-wing parties in a government is higher, the welfare state is more redistributive and greater financial means are allocated to people covered by core social insurance programmes such as pension schemes and unemployment insurance. More specifically,

**Table 4.2. Regression Estimates for Determinants of Δ Generosity and Δ Social Spending**

| | *Dependent Variable* | | | |
|---|---|---|---|---|
| | *Δ Programme Generosity* | | *Δ Social Expenditure* | |
| | *FE* | *No FE* | *FE* | *No FE* |
| Government ideology$_{t-1}$ | 0.946*** | 0.740*** | 0.769** | 0.422 |
| | (0.291) | (0.283) | (0.315) | (0.266) |
| Constraints$_{t-1}$ | −0.728 | 0.054 | −1.314 | 0.054 |
| | (0.790) | (0.174) | (0.932) | (0.099) |
| Δ Trade flows$_t$ | −0.019 | −0.021 | −0.038*** | −0.037*** |
| | (0.013) | (0.014) | (0.012) | (0.012) |
| Δ Economic growth$_t$ | 0.040** | 0.040** | −0.116*** | −0.115*** |
| | (0.019) | (0.019) | (0.023) | (0.023) |
| Δ Unemployment$_t$ | −0.026 | −0.023 | 0.334*** | 0.337*** |
| | (0.049) | (0.050) | (0.056) | (0.056) |
| Δ Deindustrialisation$_t$ | −0.122 | −0.111 | −0.114* | −0.107* |
| | (0.076) | (0.076) | (0.061) | (0.060) |
| Δ Elderly$_t$ | 0.132 | 0.105 | 0.127 | 0.164 |
| | (0.306) | (0.256) | (0.281) | (0.241) |
| Constant | 0.241 | −0.333* | 0.893 | −0.138 |
| | (0.643) | (0.181) | (0.742) | (0.158) |
| $R^2$ | 0.05 | 0.04 | 0.36 | 0.33 |
| $\chi^2$ | 69.83 | 20.49 | 173.5 | 101.18 |
| p-value | 0 | 0.005 | 0 | 0 |
| P | 0.009 | 0.003 | 0.065 | 0.091 |
| N | 551 | 551 | 373 | 373 |

Table presents Prais-Winsten regression estimates accounting for serially correlated errors; panel-corrected standard errors are in parentheses below coefficients; results for country dummies are not presented. FE = Fixed-Effect model (includes country dummies). * = $p < 0.10$, ** = $p < 0.05$, *** = $p < 0.01$.

if government ideology changes from 0 to 1, that is, from a fully right-wing to a fully left-wing government, the change in redistributive generosity on average increases by around 0.95 (when country dummies are included). If we assume that a government is in office over a standard legislative period of four years, the cumulative change in redistributive generosity during the legislative term is an increase of almost 4 (when country dummies are included) when a left-wing party is in government. The effect of government ideology on social expenditure is statistically significant at a 90 per cent level and positive for the fixed-effect model but not statistically significant when fixed effects are excluded.[8]

This result confirms the proposition that left-wing governments still have an impact on welfare state generosity despite the pressure to retrench social security systems due to the various domestic and internal economic constraints they experience. Assessing the mixed results for the impact of party government on social expenditure implies that the long-standing claim that left-wing governments lead to an increase in (social) spending holds within some countries, although the coefficient of the pooled model (without fixed effects) would suggest that this long-standing relationship does not hold for all countries for the time period covered by this study.[9] This finding is in line with the theoretical framework presented in the previous chapter and the general literature on government partisanship relating to its impact on the expenditure dimension in times of fiscal austerity and economic interdependence. According to the 'room to manoeuvre' thesis, the impact of party governments, particularly of left-wing governments, should have waned in more recent years. This question will be examined in more detail in the next section, where the period of analysis is divided into two sub-periods. The results of the variable capturing political constraints are mixed. The coefficient never reaches statistical significance at conventional levels and the direction of the influence varies between the fixed-effect model and the models that exclude country fixed effects. The models excluding country fixed effects, however, have the sign in the correct direction, implying that increasing levels of political constraint lead to an increase in both programme generosity and social spending. The counterintuitive result for the fixed-effects models can be explained by the fact that fixed effects and institutional variables often capture similar effects because both are time-invariant (country fixed effects) or exhibit very little variance over time (political constraints/institutional settings).

The variable capturing globalisation (measured by trade openness) shows signs that point in the expected direction and vindicate the hypothesis that greater economic openness has a negative impact on the overall redistributive generosity of core welfare state programmes. However, the association between yearly change in trade openness and redistributive generosity does not reach conventional levels of statistical significance. The direction of influence is the same for the social spending models and the effect is also statistically significant. This supports the argument that globalisation has, at least in the short run, a negative effect on social spending. Hence, the sign of the coefficients points in the expected direction, implying that more trade and economic openness leads to a downward pressure on expenditure and generosity. The coefficient is consistent with the fixed-effect models as well as the models where fixed effects are excluded. By and large, this finding is in line with Dreher, Sturm and Ursprung (2006) and Iversen and Cusack (2000), who conclude that the various forms of globalisation have not affected the configuration of government expenditure. The coefficients capturing the effect of economic growth on welfare state generosity and social spending have the signs in the expected direction and are statistically significant for both model specifications. Economic growth thus leads to an increase in welfare state generosity and to a decrease in social spending. Change in unemployment has a significant and positive effect on social spending, implying that an increase in unemployment leads to more social spending. This finding is consistent with the work by Kittel and Obinger (2003) and Kwon and Pontusson (2005). The strong positive effect is intuitive and confirms the expectation that higher unemployment rates lead to greater expenditure on unemployment benefits and other related active labour-market policies (training, public employment measures, wage subsidies, etc.). These measures are often cost-intensive. Welfare state generosity, however, is not affected by changes in unemployment. These results are not contradictory but rather confirm that changes in social spending are significantly exposed to general macroeconomic trends and conditions. This is less the case with programme generosity, which is more exposed to political decisions changing eligibility, contributory rates, and the duration benefits are paid. The design of such reforms is ideologically motivated and differs across party governments.

The coefficient on deindustrialisation is negative and insignificant for the generosity models and negative but statistically significant at the 90 per cent level for the social spending models. This implies that a larger share of people working in industry and agriculture suppresses the redistributive generosity of core welfare state programmes such as pension, unemployment insurance and sick pay, and also diminishes social spending. This counter-intuitive result is in line with the work by Burgoon (2001), who also finds a negative association between deindustrialisation and government expenditure in the short term. One possible explanation for this result might be that some countries heavily subsidise the traditional industrial sector (e.g. Germany still subsidises coal mining and most OECD countries finance certain industrial sectors to some degree). With the expansion of the service industry, concurrently with the decline of the industrial sector, the volume of these subsidies may decrease as well. Furthermore, the proportion of elderly people has a negative, statistically insignificant impact on redistributive generosity and social spending. The negative sign for the generosity model can be theoretically justified, since, in a manner similar to the negative sign for the unemployment variable, the bigger the share of retired people in a society, the more resources the state requires in order to redistribute wealth. However, the redistributive generosity of the programme does not necessarily increase when more people have to rely on it; in fact, rather the opposite may be true.

Based on these first analyses, we can draw a preliminary conclusion and confirm the hypothesis derived from the theoretical framework, namely that left-wing governments have a positive and significant impact on redistributive generosity. The ongoing structural changes are only partly related to redistributional outcomes – measured as redistributive generosity – on the macro level. This is true despite domestic and international constraints. This result hints at a more general development, namely that the existing core social security schemes, such as pension and unemployment insurances, remain an important pillar of social policy-making and that left-wing governments in particular pursue different paths to those followed by right-wing governments. The finding that left-wing party governments have a significant and positive impact on core programme generosity, however, also implies that the attention left-wing governing parties devote to the support of core welfare state programmes, which predominantly cover labour market 'insiders', may come at the cost of more inclusive social policies reaching out to the so-called losers of globalisation and labour market 'outsiders'. The results for the social spending model, however, are inconclusive and tend to confirm a broader discussion in the comparative welfare-state literature, which on the one hand centres around the adequacy of spending measures in order to assess the impact of politics on public policy outcomes, and on the other hand proposes that the room to manoeuvre for governing parties has significantly declined due to macroeconomic constraints.

## 4.3 THE MODIFYING EFFECT OF POLITICAL CONSTRAINTS

The institutional setting in which political processes take place has an important impact on the policy outcomes, and thus the impact of party governments varies across institutional systems. This study therefore evaluates the effects of political constraints (veto points) on welfare generosity and social expenditure by estimating an interaction model. As discussed in the previous chapter on theory and in line with a broad literature, this analysis proposes that political constraints and political institutions significantly influence the ability of political actors to shape policy outcomes. In many policy-making processes, political constraints act as 'transmission belts' (Birchfield and Crepaz 1998) between various political actors and their preferred policies, or alternatively they slow down government activities and plans. I therefore argue that the impact of government partisanship on welfare state output varies significantly between countries where institutional constraints are low and those where institutional constraints are high. Specifically, this book proposes that political constraints condition the effect party governments have on welfare state output, particularly the generosity of core welfare state programmes. In political settings with high levels of constraints, left-wing governments will resort to clientelistic policy-making by compensating the groups whose support they deem indispensable. The underlying hypothesis that will be tested is the following: *A left-wing government is more likely to increase the redistributive generosity benefiting the core workforce when political constraints are high.* The rationale behind the hypothesis is that the presence of greater political constraints also implies that more compromises among political actors must be made. This eventually leads to higher redistributive generosity/expenditure.

Technically, the inclusion of interaction effects does not affect the econometrics of the empirical model. However, it is crucial to bear in mind that the interpretation of the coefficients in an interaction model is not as straightforward as the interpretation of simple regression coefficients. In an interaction model, the effect of a particular variable *X* is conditioned on the value of *Z*. Hence, the coefficients of multiplicative terms do not reveal whether variable *X* has a meaningful conditional effect on the dependent variable (*Y*) when the conditioning variable (*Z*) is different from zero. In order to show the impact of *X* on various values of *Z*, it is necessary to present more than just the regression coefficient. The conditional logic of the multiplicative interaction term is illustrated by means of graphs displaying the marginal effects. To illustrate the conditional effects is additionally important due to the fact that a seemingly statistically insignificant coefficient – which is not significantly different from zero on a 95 per cent significance level – captures the coefficient of the multiplicative term at a single value of the variable. However, the significance of the coefficient is conditional and varies when the conditioning variable changes its value, and this is not captured by the coefficient demonstrated in the regression table. The following section examines the modifying effects of political constraints, based on the theoretical discussion in the previous chapter.

$$\Delta DV_{i,t} = \beta_0 + \beta_1 \times Government\ Ideology_{i,t-1} + \beta_2 \times Political\ Constraints_{i,t} + \\ \beta_3 \times \left(Government\ Ideology_{i,t-1} \times Political\ Constraints_{i,t-1}\right) + Controls_{i,t} + \varepsilon_{i,t}$$

where $DV_{i,t}$ is either Redistributive $Generosity_{i,t}$ or Social $Expenditure_{i,t}$ as indicated for the different analyses.

Based on the theoretical propositions, the expected joint impact of government ideology and constraints on the dependent variables would imply that the coefficients on the ideology variable, the constraints variable and the interaction term would have the following values: the coefficient on government ideology ($\beta_1$), which indicates how the ideology of the government affects redistributive generosity when constraints are low, should be greater than zero; the coefficient on political constraints ($\beta_2$) describes how political constraints influence redistributive generosity when government ideology is right-wing (ideology = 0), and is expected to be zero; lastly, according to the theoretical argument, the coefficient on the interaction ($\beta_3$), indicating the effect of a more left-wing government on redistributive generosity when constraints increase, is expected to be greater than zero. For the expenditure model, the respective coefficients should have the following values: contrary to the earlier literature examining the effect of left-wing governments, the coefficient on government ideology ($\beta_1$), which captures the effect of ideology on the size of spending, should be zero; the coefficient on constraints ($\beta_2$) is also expected to be zero; similarly, the coefficient on the interaction terms ($\beta_3$) should be close to zero.

Table 4.3 shows the regression coefficients for the model capturing the impact on the core programme-generosity dimension. The results for the specifications with the interaction term for the programme-generosity models largely correspond to the theoretical expectations. The coefficient on government ideology is greater than zero but not statistically significant. This

**Table 4.3. Conditioning Effects of Political Constraints: Estimates for Determinants of Δ Generosity and Δ Social Spending**

| | *Dependent Variable* | | | |
|---|---|---|---|---|
| | *Δ Programme Generosity* | | *Δ Social Expenditure* | |
| | *FE* | *No FE* | *FE* | *No FE* |
| Government ideology$_{t-1}$ | 0.341 | 0.193 | 1.426** | 0.928** |
| | (0.549) | (0.517) | (0.599) | (0.473) |
| Constraints$_{t-1}$ | −1.352 | −0.59 | −0.508 | 0.635 |
| | (0.928) | (0.508) | (1.022) | (0.418) |
| Government ideology$_{t-1}$* Constraints$_{t-1}$ | 1.44 | 1.298 | −1.501 | −1.219 |
| | (1.051) | (0.958) | (0.984) | (0.839) |
| Δ Trade flows$_t$ | −0.019 | −0.021 | −0.038*** | −0.037*** |
| | (0.013) | (0.014) | (0.012) | (0.012) |
| Δ Economic growth$_t$ | 0.041** | 0.041** | −0.116*** | −0.116*** |
| | (0.019) | (0.019) | (0.023) | (0.023) |
| Δ Unemployment$_t$ | −0.027 | −0.025 | 0.338*** | 0.340*** |
| | (0.048) | (0.049) | (0.055) | (0.056) |
| Δ Deindustrialisation$_t$ | −0.128* | −0.115 | −0.106* | −0.102* |
| | (0.076) | (0.076) | (0.062) | (0.061) |
| Δ Elderly$_t$ | 0.147 | 0.118 | 0.131 | 0.156 |
| | (0.306) | (0.256) | (0.280) | (0.239) |
| Constant | 0.504 | −0.059 | 0.462 | −0.381 |
| | (0.684) | (0.279) | (0.775) | (0.250) |
| $R^2$ | 0.05 | 0.04 | 0.37 | 0.34 |
| $\chi^2$ | 64.91 | 23.26 | 178.18 | 104.63 |
| p-Value | 0 | 0.003 | 0 | 0 |
| P | −0.01 | −0.001 | 0.053 | 0.08 |
| N | 551 | 551 | 373 | 373 |

Table presents Prais-Winsten regression estimates accounting for serially correlated errors; Panel- corrected standard errors are in parentheses below coefficients; Results for country dummies are not presented. FE = Fixed-Effects model (includes country dummies). * = $p < 0.10$, ** = $p < 0.05$, *** = $p < 0.01$.

indicates that purely left-wing governments do not allocate more resources to policies which are beneficiary for the core workforce if political constraints are small. The coefficient on constraints is negative, which suggests that high constraints have a negative effect on programme generosity if a right-wing government is in power. This is consistent with the theoretical argument implying that conservative party governments do not aim at increasing the generosity of core social security programmes. As expected, the joint effect of ideology and constraints, as represented by the coefficient of the interaction term, is greater than zero, which indicates that the impact of more left-wing governments on programme generosity increases as political constraints become larger in the pooled model. In the expenditure models, the coefficient on government ideology is greater than zero and statistically significant, which means that left-wing governments that face no political constraints cut socials spending to a lesser degree. Based on the previously presented theory, one would expect that the joint effect of a left-wing government and high levels of political constraint would be negative. The significance of the coefficient on the constraints variable and the interaction term thus point into the expected direction. To facilitate the interpretation of the interaction terms, Figures 4.1 and 4.2 visualise the effect of government ideology on policy-making conditioned by the level of political constraints for both dependent

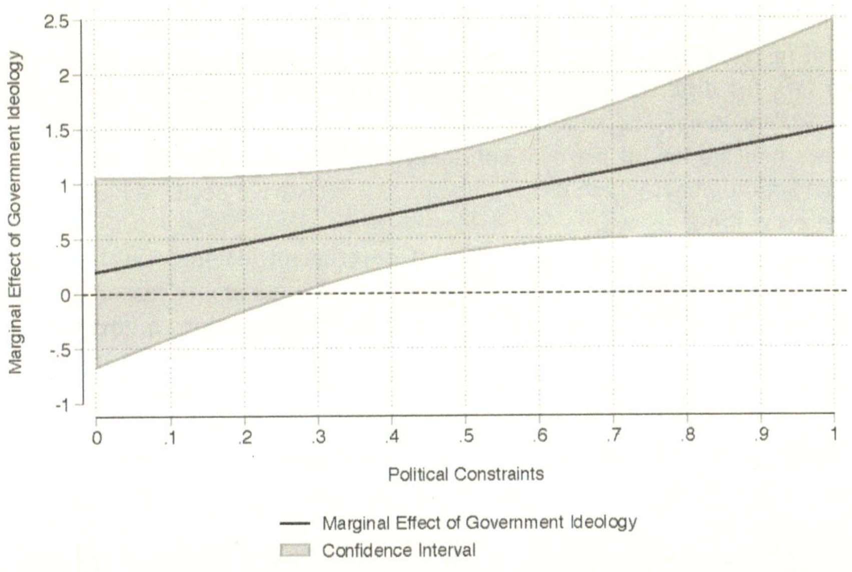


**Figure 4.1. The Modifying Effect of Political Constraints on the Redistributive Generosity of Welfare State Programmes**

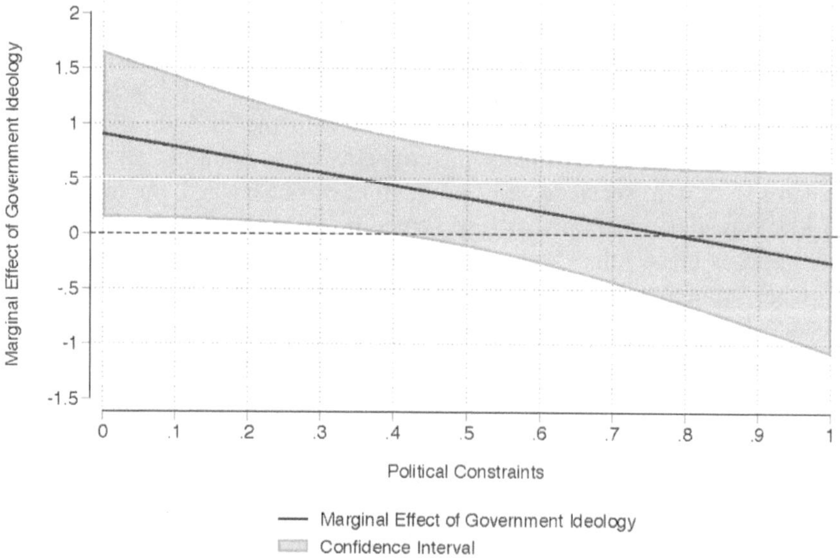


**Figure 4.2. The Modifying Effect of Political Constraints on Social Spending**

variables: programme generosity (4.1) and social spending (4.2). The graphs show the marginal effect of government ideology, that is, the effect of a one-unit increase in ideology or, equivalently, a government change from right to left, for different values of political constraints, welfare generosity and social spending. The solid line plots the estimated marginal effect; dashed lines indicate the 90 per cent confidence interval. The plot is based on the interaction model where the country fixed effects have been excluded from the estimation.

Figure 4.1 implies that the effect of government ideology on the redistributive generosity of the core social insurance programmes increases with political constraints. When political constraints are very low, a government change from a right-wing to a left-wing government does not have any effect on redistributive generosity directed towards the core workforce or labour market 'insiders'. If political constraints increase, the impact of a government change on the dimension capturing programme generosity increases as well. However, the confidence interval includes zero for values below approximately 0.4 on the political constraints scale.[10] This means that the marginal effect is statistically insignificant for low levels of constraints. When political constraints are at their maximum value, a government change from right to left leads to an average increase of around 1.5 in the index capturing redistributive generosity towards labour market 'insiders'. Over a four-year legislative period, this effect accumulates to about 6. This impact is approximately one and a half times as large as the unconditional effect of ideology presented in table 4.2.

These results are consistent with the theoretical framework outlined in chapter 3. The overall design of reforms proposed by left-wing governments together with the general support and trust that a left-wing government enjoys when reforming social policies enables the government to implement the reforms in the first place. A left-wing government, however, is constrained in two ways. First, the conservative parties in opposition have some leverage over the policy-making efforts of the government when constraints are high. Second, political constraints in the form of organised interests with strong ties to the left-wing government demand additional compensation when the government cuts spending more than expected in order to accommodate the conservative opposition. Therefore, left-wing governments in countries with high political constraints are obliged to engage in greater redistribution of the available resources among people represented by strong interest groups, mainly 'insiders', that is, skilled people who are well integrated into the labour market.

When we examine the graph visualising the modifying effect of political constraints on social expenditure (figure 4.2), we see that the two-tailed confidence interval of 90 per cent is above zero at low levels of political constraint, and the effect is only marginally statistically significant. This implies that a change from a left-wing to a right-wing government with low levels of political constraint would have a negative effect on social spending. This result would confirm the work by scholars who propose that left-wing governments are more successful in cutting social expenditure because they enjoy a higher level of trust in society when reforming social security institutions (Levy 1999; Ross 2000a).

The observed mechanism between high levels of political constraint and the strategies of governing parties on both programme generosity and social spending is worth further examination. Figures 4.3 and 4.4 thus show the predicted values of change in programme generosity or social spending while holding all but the 'economic openness' variable at their mean level for fully left-wing or fully right-wing governments. The predicted values were generated by bootstrapping the predicted size of change for right-wing (ideology = 0) and left-wing (ideology = 1) governments mediated by political constraints holding all other variables, except the measure for 'trade and capital flows' at their mean level. The variable 'trade and capital flow' was set to its maximum level to simulate a situation with a fully open economy. Figure 4.3 shows that programme generosity significantly increases for a left-wing government when constraints are high, which confirms the logic of the argument discussed in the theory chapter. The predicted size of change

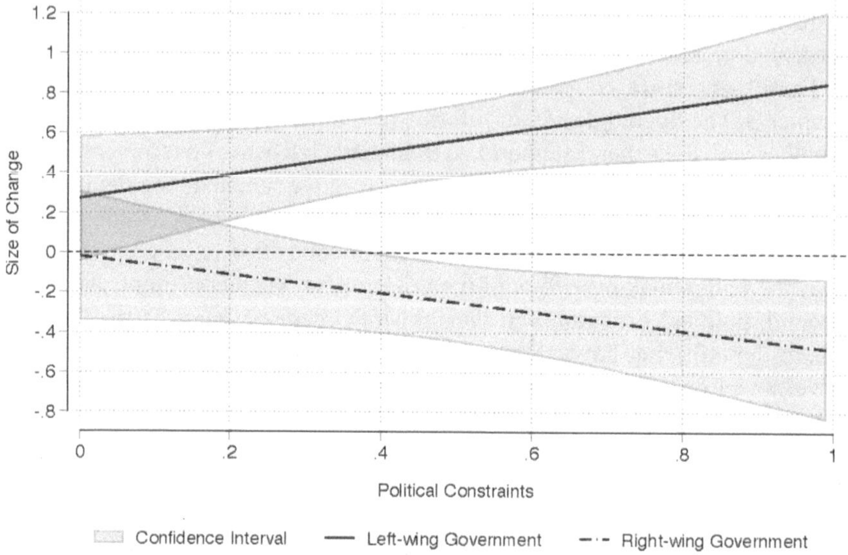


**Figure 4.3. Predicted Changes for Left- and Right-Wing Governments (Programme Generosity)**

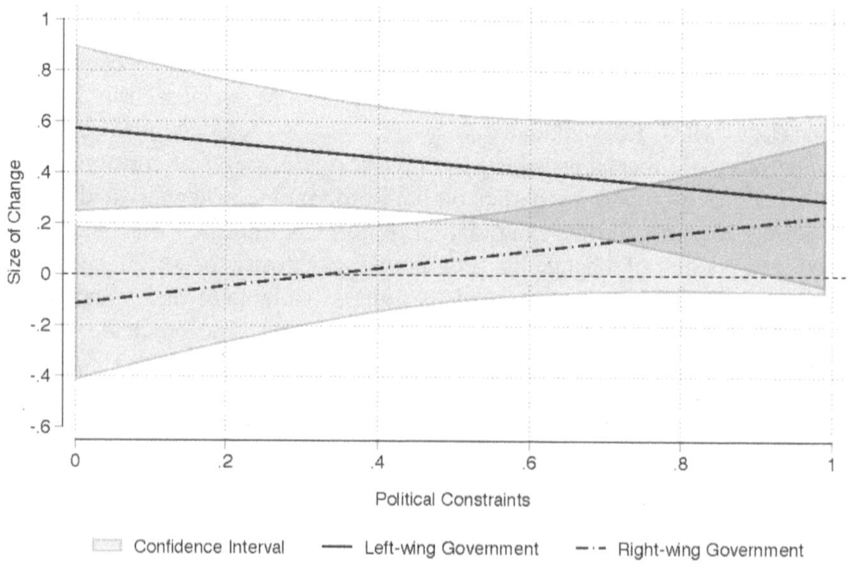


**Figure 4.4. Predicted Changes for Left- and Right-Wing Governments (Social Spending)**

in programme generosity for right-wing governments is not significant at low levels of political constraint but significant and negative at high levels of constraint. However, the overall size of cuts in programme generosity of right-wing governments when facing high levels of constraint is smaller than the increase in generosity by left-wing governments at the same level of constraint (which is indicated by the varying steepness of the slope).

When examining the size of predicted changes of social expenditure under purely left-wing and right-wing governments (see figure 4.4), we see that left-wing governments tend to increase social spending when political constraints are low. As constraints increase, the predicted change in social spending by left-wing governments decreases, which is because the conservative opposition that is in the position to block the reform needs to be accommodated. Most important, under high constraints, changes in spending are almost equivalent to those of a right-wing government. This is indicated by the fact that the predicted size for change for both a left-wing and a right-wing government are almost identical at highest levels of political constraint, thus confirming the implications of the theory. For right-wing governments, the opposite can be observed.[11] Right-wing governments cut spending when constraints are low but have to accommodate the left-wing opposition when political constraints are high.

## 4.4 CHANGING PATTERNS OF PARTISAN EFFECTS OVER TIME?

The question remains whether these results hold for the whole period of analysis or with increasing economic interdependence and austerity, the room to manoeuvre for governments has become increasingly constrained. This was particularly argued by the proponents of the 'New Politics' literature who propose that the underlying mechanisms and rational of social policy-making have changed with the increasing economic openness and the fiscal austerity experienced in many industrialised countries since the 1990s (1994, 1996, 2001). In line with this literature, we would expect the phenomenon of clientelistic policy-making to have emerged only recently. In order to examine this important claim of the 'New Politics' literature, the marginal effects for two time periods (1980–1991 and 1992–2002) are assessed at both low and high levels of political constraint for both dependent variables.

The results presented in table 4.4 show that the mediating effect of political constraints and left-wing government on programme generosity was not statistically significant during the first period (as indicated by the confidence interval including zero). It is only during the second period (1992–2002) that the level of political constraint has become an important factor in shaping the

**Table 4.4. Marginal Effects of Programme Generosity and Social Spending for Two Time Periods and Different Levels of Political Constraints**

| | Time Period | | | |
|---|---|---|---|---|
| | *1980–1991* | | *1992–2002* | |
| | *Low Constraints* | *High Constraints* | *Low Constraints* | *High Constraints* |
| Programme generosity | −0.158 [1.599/-1.294] | −0.163 [0.726/-1.052] | 0.426 [1.344/-0.491] | 1.301 [2.143/0.458] |
| Social spending | 0.881 [1.531/0.230] | 0.008 [0.830/-0.815] | 0.428 [1.319/-0.463] | −0.036 [0.911/-0.984] |

The marginal effect for 'low' levels of political constraint represents the effect when political constraints take the value of 0.25. The marginal effect for 'high' levels of political constraint represents the effect when political constraints take a value of 0.75. Numbers in brackets represent the 90 per cent confidence interval.

policies offered by governments of differing political hue. This finding is in line with the theoretical expectations as it is mostly during the latter period when pressures on welfare states increased such that left-wing governments needed to appease their core constituency. In times where the economy was less interdependent and left-wing governments had more freedom to choose supply-side policies, a broader and more comprehensive approach to social policy-making was still possible. The marginal effect for the second period is strong and statistically significant despite the fact that the estimation is based on fewer observations. The results for the second dependent variable (social spending) are also consistent with the theoretical argumentation. During the first period, left-wing governments in an unconstrained context had a large and statistically significant positive impact on social spending. This impact vanished during the later time period as indicated by the size of the effect (close to zero) and the fact that the effect is not statistically significant. The evidence further supports the reform mechanisms proposed in the theoretical section and points to new strategies parties in government pursue when facing permanent austerity and economic crisis. The results presented in the empirical section lead to the conclusion that despite greater economic interdependence and fiscal austerity, governing parties still partially translate their programmes into policies. However, the policy design of the reforms has changed.

## 4.5 CONCLUSION

This chapter analysed reform outcomes of party governments in times of fiscal austerity and economic interdependence. The theoretical framework suggests that party governments alter their strategy for reforming welfare state policies depending on the level of political constraint. The results show that left-wing governments that need the consent both of a strong conservative opposition in parliament and of influential and well-organised labour unions outside parliament choose a clientelistic way of reforming social policies. This strategy includes on the one hand the accommodation of the opposition through higher cuts in social spending, and on the other hand the protection of the core workforce through increasing or sustaining the generosity of core welfare state programmes. The results further show that the degree of clientelistic policy-making used by parties in government has increased and mostly occurred after 1990. The study thus confirms that the politics of retrenchment and welfare state cuts are different from the politics of welfare state development, but the analysis also points to the conclusion that party politics still matter. The manner in which party governments influence public policies, however, has changed, an observation that is particularly true for left-wing governments.

My analysis corroborates the findings by Jensen and Mortensen (2013, p. 161), who conclude that the Left and the Right still entertain distinct policy agendas. The way these different agendas come into play, however, is mediated by political constraints or the way policy responsibility is attributed in the system. Overall, the results support the claim that we need to update and adjust our conception of party politics and who political parties really represent. In addition, and as suggested by Häusermann et al. (2013), the days when party governments could linearly transfer their preferences into policy output are over and our understanding about how the specific groups among the electorate are linked to and represented by specific political parties needs to be updated. The findings are also in line with recent contributions by Beramendi and Cusack (2009) and Beramendi and Rueda (2007), which indicate that left-wing governments are not necessarily successful in creating egalitarian policy outcomes, especially in the presence of corporatist arrangements. Furthermore, the previous empirical analyses also confirm and expand Korpi and Palme's (1998) 'paradox of redistribution'. In their 1998 contribution, Korpi and Palme showed that it is the middle class, which to a large extent consists of labour market 'insiders', that benefits most from core social insurance schemes, such as unemployment insurance schemes, pensions and sick pay.

The theoretical argument also makes some implicit assumptions concerning the behaviour of labour market 'outsiders' and the impact of the policies implemented by governments on marginalised groups in the labour market. However, the scope of this chapter does not permit an assessment of how different party governments affect labour market 'outsiders' and whether other policies of benefit to losers of globalisation but not captured by the aggregate measures of policy reform used in this chapter were introduced. Further research is needed to determine the political and institutional configuration that leads to policy changes that are more directly related or targeted at those who lose out from globalisation. Also, this (and most other) research on welfare state changes and social policy reforms is at least implicitly based on assumptions and implications for coalition building in legislatures and the impact such coalitions have on the meso-level or the actual drafting and legislative processes going on in parliament and parliamentary committees. To further explore the link between reform strategies of party governments and the social policy reforms implemented in open economies, a more direct measure of policy change would be useful. Large parts of the comparative welfare state literature are based on highly aggregate measures of policy change, mainly aggregate spending data. Data on spending, whether it be general public outlay or social spending, to a large degree reflects developments and changes that are unrelated to social policy choices as influenced by party ideology and politics. A more finely grained measure of policy reforms would help to better explore how politics influences social policies in post-industrial democracies. For instance, data examining legislative decisions and social policy reforms on various dimensions would improve and advance our insight.

## NOTES

1 The following countries are included: Australia, Austria, Belgium, Canada, Denmark, Finland, France, Germany, Ireland, Italy, Japan, the Netherlands, New Zealand, Norway, Sweden, Switzerland, the United Kingdom and the United States.

2 An alternative way to account for serial correlation would be the inclusion of a lagged dependent variable (LDV). However, there is little theoretical reason to estimate a model whose dependent variable should capture change, since a change in year 't' is not necessarily related to a change in the subsequent or previous year. In other words, a change in the DV at year 't' is unlikely to be explained by a change in the dependent variable at t-1. Nevertheless, for sensitivity analyses, I also estimate the model using a LDV (for the models excluding fixed effects). The results of the alternative specifications are substantially the same. For an in-depth discussion of dynamic panel models and LDV, see for example, Wilson and Butler (2007), Achen (2000), Keele and Kelly (2006) and Beck and Katz (2004).

3 Dummy variables absorb explained variance, which could be explained by the variables which are of theoretical interest. In addition, they highly correlate with other variables (mostly institutional variables) which vary little over time. For a recent critique on whether to include country fixed effects in a pooled cross-section time-series model, see Plümper and Troeger (2007) and Plümper, Troeger and Manow (2005). In a related paper, Kittel and Obinger (2003) explicitly

excluded country-fixed effects and justified this choice by asserting that one of their core explanatory variables was institutional rigidity which does not vary over time.

4 The index, which was initially generated by Scruggs and Allan, is modelled after the concept of de-commodification, which essentially measures to what extent workers depend on market forces or to what extent their income is dependent on labour. The greater an individual's dependence on labour, the less decommodified he or she is. De-commodification is greatest if a person's income is not linked to employment. The concept originally goes back to Polanyi (1954) and was subsequently further developed by Offe (1984) and Esping-Andersen (1985, 1990). Esping-Andersen suggested an initial operationalisation of the concept. The measure by Scruggs and Allan used here borrows from these seminal works.

5 For a more comprehensive overview of the underlying model, see the codebook provided by Henisz and the discussion of the index by Hoffmann (2010).

6 For robustness checks, I also used the CHECKS variable included in the 'Database of Political Institutions' by Keefer and Stasavage (2003); the results were essentially the same.

7 Economic growth and unemployment are taken from the OECD Main Economic indicators. The variable representing demographic change is included in the OECD labour force statistic.

8 Country fixed effects allow for different unit intercepts. This means that the estimation of the coefficients is mainly based on the variation of the variables *within* the units. This implies that the association between the variables within a particular unit is the same as the association between the variables of the pooled model. The coefficients, however, only reflect a combined estimate over time and across all countries.

9 Due to the fact that the social expenditure series starts only at 1980, the number of observations is considerably smaller than in the redistribution models discussed earlier. Sensitivity analyses show a consistent difference between the models, including the country dummies and the models without fixed effects. Whereas the fixed-effect model shows a statistically significant effect of government ideology on social spending, the 'government ideology' coefficient never reaches statistical significance in the models without fixed effects.

10 For ease of presentation, the variable for political constraints in the interaction model is multiplied by ten.

11 Note that the level of predicted change depends on the values of the other independent variables.

## *Chapter 5*

# The Mechanisms of Clientelistic Politics – Case Study Framework

The quantitative analyses presented in the previous chapter generally support the expectations that were formulated on the basis of the theoretical framework. Political constraints tend to mediate the impact party governments have on policy output. In particular, the joint effect of political constraints and left-wing party government results in more clientelistic policies which compensate the core workforce rather than improving the situation of labour market outsiders. This is shown by a statistically significant and positive effect of the interaction term on programme generosity. The statistically non-significant effects of the interaction term and the stand-alone government variable in the expenditure model complement and further support these findings. The more substantive interpretation of this finding implies that no party government, whether conservative or left-wing, can significantly affect the spending on social security schemes. This finding is independent of the level of political constraints present in a given country, which is in line with the general wisdom that the room to manoeuvre for party governments has declined with the increasing economic interdependence experienced by industrialised economies.

The quantitative analyses, however, do not reveal the underlying mechanisms of social policy-making and labour market reforms. Nor do the statistical analyses show how parties in government tailor reforms in order to compensate their core electorate. The case studies therefore are conducted with the aim of further substantiating the findings established on the macro level by means of a thorough analysis of specific labour market and social security reforms. This resonates with the fact that qualitative analyses of the politics of dualisation are missing in the literature (Davidsson and Naczyk 2009). The reforms analysed in the subsequent chapters took place in two countries which differ with regard to their levels of political constraints. The policy changes which were proposed in the light of these selected reforms will be analysed with a focus on their consequences for labour market insiders and outsiders, respectively. This chapter presents a rationale for the case selection and lays out the analytical framework that is used for the analyses of the specific reform processes.

## 5.1 SELECTION OF COUNTRIES

The previous cross-section time-series analysis particularly focused on the mediating effects of institutional constraints. This is why the countries selected for the case studies need to show variation on the key independent variable, which is the level of institutional constraints present in a country (Geddes 2003). In addition, and in line with Bennett and Elman (2006), the complex interplay between various variables cannot be captured by relying on statistical methods only. Furthermore, the countries need to show variation in the type of parties in charge of government, particularly during the last period covered by the quantitative analysis, the period during which 'clientelistic' policy-making was most acute. Party government should not simply show some variation but show a specific turn from a conservative to a left-leaning party government (or the other way around) as – based on the theoretical propositions – the difference in policy design should be greatest between conservative governments and left-wing governments. This variation in party government should occur during the second period of the analysis (covering the years between 1992 and 2002) because, as the results of the statistical analysis show, the joint impact of party government and political constraints is statistically significant only for the second period.[1]

Of the eighteen countries included in my quantitative design, Germany and Ireland fulfil these criteria. In Germany, the level of political constraints is particularly high because the country combines federalism with a powerful second chamber of parliament that is formed by the representatives of the *Bundesländer*. In situations where the majority of the *Bundesländer* are governed by parties which constitute the opposition at the federal level, the *Bundesrat*, which is the parliamentary chamber which represents the *Bundesländer* at the federal level, is dominated by parties which form the opposition in the *Bundestag*. This particular institutional setting allows opposition parties and lower-level state authorities to influence or block the government's policy proposals. Moreover, influential interest groups can access the policy-making procedure in various ways. Two channels of interest representation are particularly important in the context of this study. The first channel is linked to personal contacts of representatives from interest groups to members of parliaments or people working in the administration of key ministries.

These strong personal ties guarantee interest groups an indirect access to the policy-making process (Streeck 2003; Trampusch 2003). The second, and more direct channel of influence, interest groups can use is their participating in hearings organised by the respective ministries. These hearings predominantly serve to present and discuss reform proposals with stakeholders. Usually, these hearings are used by peak organisations to feed back their evaluation of the proposed changes and suggest amendments.

Unlike in the German system, the legislative processes in the Irish political system face hardly any political constraints rooted in institutionalised features (Chari and McMahon 2003; Connolly and O'Halpin 1999). Even though Ireland also has a bicameral system, the competences of the Seanad (the second parliamentary chamber) during the legislative process are very limited. Moreover, the Taoiseach (prime minister) has the right to appoint eleven members of the Seanad, which means that the governing coalition always has the majority in the second chamber of parliament. Unlike in Germany, where the chamber representing the *Bundesländer* has the power to block legislative proposals, the Irish Seanad does not have the power to block bills and can only delay the final vote on a given legislative proposal by a maximum of three months. In terms of interest representation, the channels in the Irish system are less established than in Germany, this in spite of the fact that the government established so-called social partnerships between key interest organisations and the government in 1987. The key aims of these partnership programmes were to improve organisational and economic performance (Roche 2007). For a limited period of time, the government also established a number of working groups which were to contribute to the development of social policies. However, this initiative did not prove to be effective, and the working groups were dissolved (Hardiman 2006). This shows that the government has considerable room to manoeuvre when it comes to influencing policy development and changes related to labour market and social issues.

## Party Governments in Germany and Ireland between 1992 and 2002

The following graphs visualise the political spectrum in Germany and Ireland by plotting the positions of the political parties using the left-right measure proposed by the Comparative Manifesto Project. Lower values indicate a more left-wing position and higher values a more right-wing position. A red party label indicates that the party was part of a coalition during the legislative period following the general elections. In Germany, two types of coalition governments dominated the thirty-year period covered in the quantitative analysis: a coalition between the Social Democrats and the Liberal Party on the one hand, and a coalition between the Christian Democrats and the Liberal Party on the other. Except for the last legislative period, when the Green

Party for the first time entered a coalition with the Social Democrats at the national level, the Liberal Party was always part of the government and often served as an important intra-governmental veto player.

By looking at figure 5.1 we can observe that – according to the Comparative Manifesto measure of party ideology – the Social Democrats became considerably more centrist between 1990, which marks the first general election in the newly unified Germany, and 2002, which marks the end point of the present study. This move towards the centre of the Green Party coincided with an increase in vote shares and culminated in the formation of the governing coalition between the Social Democrats and the Green Party in 1998. The overall party landscape and the character of political competition thus changed significantly after German unification. In addition to the Green Party, another leftist competitor entered the political stage in the mid-1990s. After the unification of Germany, the former Socialist Party of the GDR merged with the relatively minor leftist party present in old *Bundesländer*. While the electoral success of the PDS/Linke was relatively small in the old *Bundesländer*, the party has been more successful in the *Länder* of the former

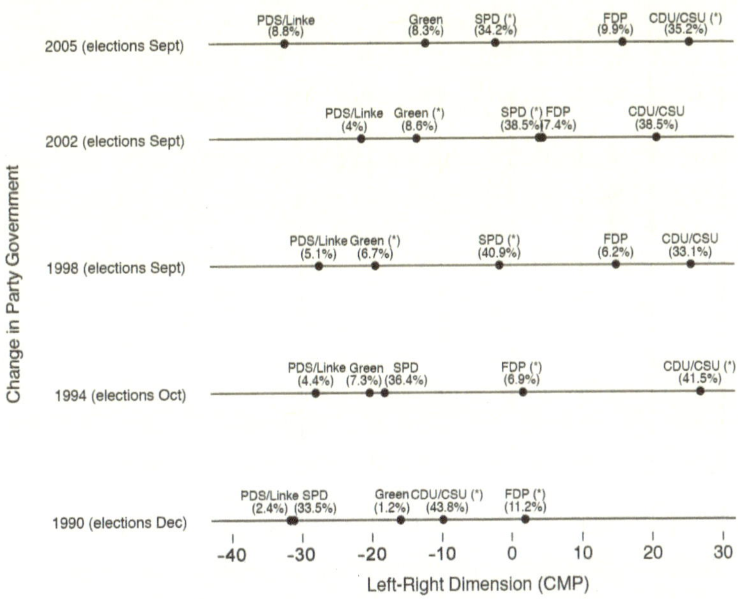


**Figure 5.1. Political Spectrum Germany**

Notes: SPD = Sozialdemokratische Partei Deutschland (Social Democrats); Greens = Bündnis 90/Die Grünen (Green Party), PDS/Linke = Leftist Alliance (between the former Socialist Party of the GDR and the leftist party of former West Germany), FDP = Freie Demokratische Partei (Liberal party), CDU/CSU = Christlich Demokratische Union (Christian Democrats). The graph visualises the positions of the German political parties on the CMP left-right dimension for four consecutive elections. Lower values indicate more left-wing positions, higher values a more right-wing election platform. The numbers in brackets indicate the percentage of votes for the respective party. * party is part of the coalition government.

GDR.[2] However, despite the relative success of the PDS/Linke in the East, the party only surmounted the 5 per cent threshold necessary to enter the *Bundestag* in 1998 and 2005. In the 2005 general elections, the PDS/Linke was even able to significantly increase their share of votes, which made a renewal of the SPD/Green coalition impossible and also excluded the possibility of a revival of a coalition between the CDU/CSU and the FDP.[3] In this sense, the electoral success at the national level of the PDS/Linke paved the way for the grand coalition between the CDU/CSU and the SPD that has been governing Germany since 2005.

As opposed to Germany, where alternations in government followed a relatively predictive pattern, Ireland experienced a considerable diversity of governing coalitions between 1973 and 2002. Except for relatively short periods during the 1970s and 1980s when the country was governed by a single party Fianna Fáil government, Ireland has been governed by various types of coalition government.[4] Most of them were based on cooperation between Fine Gael and Labour. However, the period between 1992 and 2002, which is decisive for the labour market reforms which will be assessed in the following chapter, was characterised by a number of government changes and a couple of unusual government constellations, in particular the one-off coalition between Fianna Fàil and Labour (1993/1994) and the so-called Rainbow coalition between Fine Gael, Labour and the Democratic Left, which took over government after the break-up of the Fianna Fáil/ Labour government in 1994. Characteristically, for the Irish party system, Fine Gael and Fianna Fáil occupy similar positions on the traditional left-right dimension. In addition, and also specific to the Irish political landscape, left-wing forces are significantly weaker than in other European countries. The combined vote for the Left (taking together the votes for Labour and the Worker's party, or the Democratic Left) usually hovers around 10 per cent and came close to 20 per cent only in the 1992 general elections. While the 1992 elections marked an unprecedented electoral success for Labour, the outcome for both centrist parties, Fine Gael and Fianna Fáil, marked an all-time low in electoral support. The outcome of the 1992 elections gave way to a turbulent legislative period with several changes in government. Figure 5.2 shows that the two biggest political parties in the system occupy very similar positions on the general left-right dimension. Overall, the electoral platforms of Irish political parties broadened the space covered, with the Progressive Democrats taking a pronounced right-wing/ conservative position in the general elections of 1992 and 1997. In 2002, the electoral platforms of all political parties appear to move more towards the centre-left. However, taking into account the electoral platform focusing on economic issues, the Progressive Democrats and Fianna Fàil pursued a distinctively liberal agenda emphasising further tax cuts and deregulations of the financial sector.

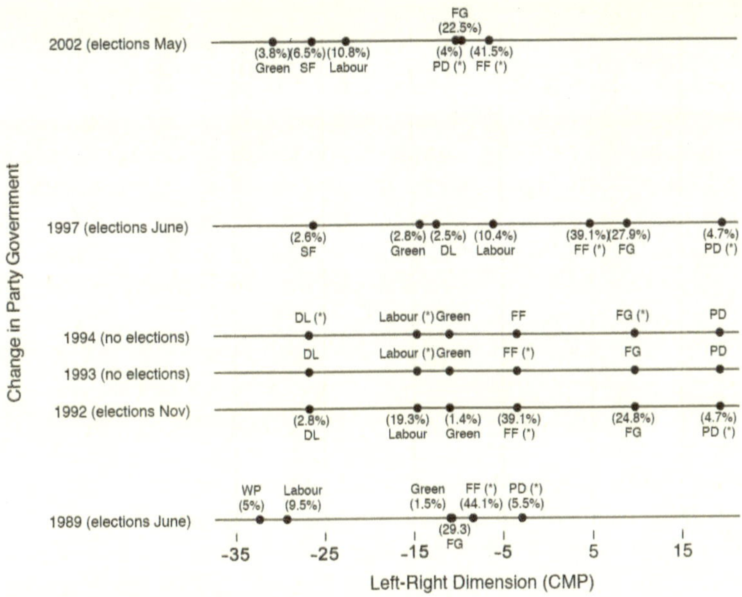


**Figure 5.2. Political Spectrum Ireland**

Notes: SF = Sinn Fein (republican party, pro-unification), Green = Ecological/Green Party, Labour = Labour Party, PD = Progressive Democrats (market liberal party), FF = Fianna Fàil (centrist, republican party), FG = Fine Gael (liberal-conservative/centrist party), DL = Democratic Left (successor of the Workers Party), WP = Workers Party. The graph visualises the positions of the Irish political parties on the CMP left-right dimension for four consecutive elections. Lower values indicate more left-wing positions, higher values a more right-wing election platform. The numbers in brackets indicate the percentage of votes for the respective party. * party is part of the coalition government.

## 5.2 SELECTION OF REFORMS

To examine the underlying mechanisms which generate the macro-level policy outcomes presented in the third chapter, it is important to tie the case studies to the preceding quantitative analyses. For substantive and theoretical reasons, I focus on labour market reforms and reforms relating to the unemployment insurance schemes. An analysis of changes in labour market policies and policy changes which affect the status of the unemployed workforce in the labour market is meaningful for theoretical and substantive reasons. Due to the forces of globalisation, labour markets in advanced industrialised democracies experienced significant pressure during the 1990s and many countries implemented significant reforms which affected both passive and active labour market policy schemes.[5] How party governments affect changes in passive labour market policy-making (reforms of unemployment insurance schemes) has been established in the preceding quantitative analysis. The subsequent case studies will therefore broaden the view and reconcile how different types of party governments shape passive and active labour market policies with a specific emphasis on how labour market outsiders are affected by these reforms. In addition to focusing on the policy preferences of the government, the case studies assess the interventions and reform preferences of key interest groups, such as trade unions and employer organisations. The reform processes within this policy field involve similar actors across countries and are therefore amenable to a cross-national comparison. Finally, changes related to unemployment insurance schemes and the labour market in general are highly visible and often intensively debated in the public sphere because the reforms affect most people of working age. Therefore, political parties and party governments should be sensitive to the preferences of their electorate and exploit the opportunity to gain a distinct political profile.

For each of the two countries, I have selected two reform processes, one that was implemented by a conservative government and another by a left-wing government. For Germany, I will analyse the 'Beschäftigungsförderungs' legislation and the 'JobAQTIV' legislation in 1994 and 2001, respectively. The first reform in Germany was implemented by a conservative coalition government of the Christian Democrats (CDU/CSU) and the Liberals (FDP) led by Helmut Kohl. The second reform was designed by the coalition government of the Social Democrats (SPD) and the Green Party under Chancellor Gerhard Schröder. For Ireland, I chose the Financial and Social Welfare Bills in 1996 and 2001. The Irish Financial and Social Welfare Bill of 1996 was presented by a left-wing coalition government consisting of Fine Gael, Labour and the Democratic Left ('rainbow coalition'). Despite the fact that the existence of the classical left-right dimension has been contested in the context of Ireland, the 'rainbow coalition' can be labelled as left-wing because the Democratic Left, which had a significant impact on the government's policy-making, corresponds to traditional left-wing parties present on the continent. In 2001, the reform was implemented by a conservative government consisting of Fianna Fáil and the Progressive Democrats.[6] The aforementioned reforms were all implemented during the period that is covered by the quantitative empirical analysis. Each country chapter, however, concludes with an outlook which highlights the most important developments in terms of labour market changes and outsider-challenges in the subsequent years.

## Analysing Labour Market Policy Changes in a Qualitative Setting

The theoretical argument outlined in chapter 3 emphasises the importance of the multi-dimensionality of policies and policy-making for political actors. Whereas the post-war period was characterised by the gradual expansion of existing social security schemes (in particular, pension and unemployment schemes) in terms of eligibility and level of benefits and the implementation of new social policies (such as family policies), more recent decades have shown that resources are scarce and that politically motivated increases in spending on social policies and the welfare state are difficult to implement given the macroeconomic context.

Therefore, party governments find themselves under pressure to cut rather than expand expenditures or reallocate the available resources in a way that matches the demand of their core constituency. The quantitative analysis indeed showed that while party governments still have a statistically significant impact on the generosity of key welfare state schemes, they have lost considerable room to manoeuvre on the spending dimension, where changes in social expenditure are mostly driven by macroeconomic factors. However, this shift from expansion towards retrenchment and cuts also requires a shift in how the impact of party governments on policy changes is identified and examined.

By assessing comprehensive labour market reforms, the case studies take into account the policy preferences and proposals of political actors on a broader spending and generosity dimension than the one applied in the macro analyses. This is important because the macro-level analysis does not take into account more finely grained policy changes and also does not reveal the full picture of clientelistic policy-making. As an example, while we would expect a left-wing political party in office to aim at expanding the redistributive generosity of unemployment insurance schemes, we would probably not expect the same party to deregulate labour markets and hence negatively affect the employment security of workers who enjoy less protection from trade unions. In order to assess whether party politics in government still matters, the scope of the following analyses has been expanded to additional dimensions of government activity which equally affect the social rights and duties of labour market participants, such as changes of the regulatory aspects of labour markets, the implementation of new duties for unemployed people and the development of new training and up-skilling schemes which have an effect on individual level labour market risks. While such changes can significantly alter employment conditions, they are not directly linked to patterns of generosity and entitlement of classic unemployment insurance schemes.

In the case studies, the reform issues will be divided into issues that affect the generosity of labour market programmes, with a particular focus on how the policy changes affect the generosity of labour market institutions, both in terms of passive labour market policies, such as insurance schemes, and active policies that can be more or less inclusive regarding the targeted population. Table 5.1 lists a number of policy changes which are attributed to this particular dimension. Issues attributed to the spending dimension (see table 5.2) are either related to classical cuts in benefits (level or duration of unemployment benefits) or aim at minimising public spending on passive labour market policies in the long run by increasing the efficiency of the labour market through the implementation of active labour market policies and outsourcing services to private agencies.

A key aspect that is assessed for all reform issues is whether or not the policy change targets specific societal or occupational groups, that is, whether the policy change is expected to affect predominantly people with a certain

**Table 5.1. Generosity**

| Policy Issue | Description |
|---|---|
| *Eligibility:* | The inclusion or exclusion of specific groups from insurance schemes or other policy measures which aim at changing the distribution of social rights and how generous they are. Eligibility in the more narrow sense is related to unemployment insurance schemes and is influenced whether a given individual has accumulated the necessary contribution period. Eligibility in a broader sense is related to the question whether workers are entitled to participate in up-skilling measures or training programmes. |
| *Benefits relative to previous income:* | The level of individual unemployment insurance benefits usually depends on previous earnings. The level of benefits sets the rate to which extent the original income will be replaced by unemployment benefits in case of job loss. This is a matter of redistribution if low incomes get a higher percentage of their previous income than individuals with a high previous income. |
| *Contributions relative to income:* | The contributory rates (for unemployment insurance schemes) can be different for employees given a particular income. A related issue is how the contributions are split between employee and employer and whether there are different contributory rates for different income levels., |

**Table 5.2. Spending**

| Policy Issue | Description |
|---|---|
| *Duration of benefits:* | Unemployed people are eligible for unemployment benefits during a certain period only. Shortening or extending the duration of benefits influences the expenditure dimension. |
| *Public funding:* | Unemployment insurance schemes often receive some tax money in addition to the contributions from employers and employees. Higher/lower coverage by the state means more/less public expenditure. |
| *Active labour market policies (ALMP):* | Active labour market policies aim at re-integrating unemployed people into the labour market more efficiently. The aim is to unburden the insurance scheme and to cut down on expenditure. |
| *Outsourcing and deregulation:* | Establishment of regional (privately organised) placement centres with the aim of closer monitoring and lowering the costs of placing unemployed people. |

professional background or training, within specific income brackets, or with a particular type of employment contract. To target specific professional groups or workers with a specific type of employment contract can further support the proposed mechanisms of clientelistic policy-making, which is triggered by an increasing demand for increasingly scarce resources. The decision of party governments to privilege specific labour market participants over other groups, irrespective of whether these privileges are related to the level of benefits or changes in employment security, leads to an increasing polarisation within the workforce and hence a bigger divide between labour market insiders and labour market outsiders.

## Document Sources

I will predominantly rely on parliamentary minutes, policy documents and consultation processes to identify the policy preferences of the partisan and extra-parliamentarian policy actors. In addition to the parliamentary minutes, I add evidence from committee hearings (for Germany) and newspapers (Ireland) to include the policy positions of the relevant extra-parliamentarian actors. This is useful to substantiate the policy positions of the extra-parliamentarian actors because the committee stage of the legislative process in Ireland has very little impact on the design of the draft and, unlike in Germany, the committee system is less institutionalised, and the committees varied over time. For the German case study, the main sources of information to identify the policy preferences of trade unions and employer organisations are public hearings and written statements submitted to the parliamentary commission leading the reform, and, most important, the parliamentary minutes from the German Bundestag. The minutes from the German Bundestag are available online, while the minutes of the public hearings and consultations with key interest groups were obtained through the parliamentary archive ('Parlamentsarchiv').[7] The legislative process consists of three parliamentary readings of the proposal. Generally, the substantive debate of the proposal takes place during its second reading in parliament, while the first reading usually consists of identifying one or multiple suitable parliamentary committee(s) which prepare the proposal for the subsequent second and substantial reading in the parliament. During the third reading, a substantive discussion only takes place if a parliamentary party or a significant number of Members of Parliament (MPs) (5 per cent) ask to further debate the matter. In all other cases, the parliament takes a vote on the proposal during the third and final reading which concludes the parliamentary stage.

The policy-positions and statements for the Irish reform processes are based on minutes of the Irish parliament (Dáil Éirann).[8] Unlike in Germany, where the examined reforms exclusively address unemployment and labour market issues, policies affecting labour market changes and social policy changes are not proposed in specific legislative acts in Ireland. Social policy and labour market changes are included in two major legislative bills, the Financial Bill (the annual budget) and the Annual Social Welfare Bill. This is why I analyse the parliamentary debates following the presentation of these two bills. From these major bills, I single out the relevant issues related to labour market and unemployment policy-making. The budget debate follows a strict order. At the beginning, the respective minister announces the content of the bill. The second speech is always made by the official spokesperson of the opposition parties, followed by the spokesperson for financial matters of each parliamentary party. It is only later, usually on a separate day, that the prime minister (Taoiseach) comments on the budget. This speech is followed by speeches from party leaders, after whose contribution, the floor is opened to other members of the governing parties and the opposition. The budget debate usually takes place over several meetings. The debate of the Social Welfare Bill follows a similar choreography and is also spread over various parliamentary meetings. The budget for the next fiscal year is usually announced in December (for the next fiscal year). The presentation and debate of the Social Welfare Bill usually takes place during the spring.

Since the committee stage of the legislative process has very little impact on the design of the legislation and trade unions cannot comment during the actual drafting process of the budget and the welfare state act, I relied on the *Irish Times*. I used this source to derive the policy preferences and arguments of key interest groups, such as trade unions, employer organisations and other third- party actors, concerning the budget and welfare state bill proposed by the government and discussed in parliament. To select the articles I used a set of key words: 'unemployment AND insurance', 'social AND welfare', 'labour AND market', '(Name of key trade union) AND budget', '(Name of key employer organisation) AND budget', (Name of key trade union) AND welfare' and '(Name of key employer organisation) AND welfare'. I selected articles that were published up to two months before the respective bill was discussed in parliament and articles published during the period of discussion in the Dáil. Since the discussion of both the annual budget and the annual welfare bill takes place on several dates, the search of the articles covers a good part of the year.

## NOTES

1 During this period, the effects of economic globalisation, which were already visible in the 1980s, became more apparent and severe. The importance of dimensions other than expenditure on social policy-making, as for example redistributive

generosity, became particularly important for parties reforming welfare state institutions from the mid-1990s onwards.

2 Between 1999 and 2014, the party even was the second-largest political force in three states (Saxony, Saxony Anhalt and Thüringen).

3 Since the general elections in 2005, the PDS/Linke has always been represented in the *Bundestag*.

4 In the early days of the Republic until the mid-1980s, Fianna Fáil, which has always been the biggest party in the Irish political system, was governing on its own. It is only since the late 1980s that Fianna Fáil had to build a coalition government.

5 Some prominent and well-researched examples are the reforms implemented in Denmark and the Netherlands, which led to a significant liberalisation of the labour market and a decline in social protection.

6 Because the reforms analysed in this study should be related as closely to the precedent quantitative analysis, I chose reforms that were designed and implemented before 2002.

7 The historical record of the German parliament is available on the following website: http//dip.bundestag.de.

8 The historical records of the Irish parliament are available on the following website: http//historical-debates.oireachtas.ie/index.html.

# *Chapter 6*

# Germany

This chapter assesses the underlying mechanisms that lead to more clientelistic welfare state policies in countries with a high level of political constraints. In doing so, the chapter focuses on Germany and starts with a short introduction to the German political economy before delving into the in-depth analysis of German labour market reforms.

## 6.1 WELFARE SYSTEM AND LABOUR MARKET

Germany, according to Esping-Andersen's (1990) well-known typology of welfare states and social security systems, represents the prototype of a continental welfare state, with the terms Bismarckian welfare state or 'social insurance' state used synonymously to characterise the way different types of social security schemes and labour market institutions complement each other. In the German welfare state, the key social security programmes (e.g. pension, sick-pay and unemployment insurance) are organised as insurance schemes, and although membership is compulsory for all these schemes, they cannot be considered universal, and eligibility and benefits are to a great extent linked to regular employment and previous contributions. The origins of the social insurance schemes which, to a great extent, still exist today go back to the late nineteenth century, a time when Germany was moving very quickly from being an agriculturally dominated country towards being an industrialised nation, soon to be on a par with the leaders in industrial development at the time, Britain, Belgium and France.

The first social insurance scheme, implemented in 1883, aimed at protecting blue-collar workers against sickness, thereby cushioning some of the newly emerging social risks triggered by the industrial revolution. Schemes insuring workers against industrial accidents (1884) and old age (1889) were implemented shortly after. In 1911, these three individual legislative acts were combined in a single document which led to the first National Insurance Code ('Reichsversicherungsordnung'). A contributory unemployment insurance scheme was not added to the system until 1927. However, the relatively late introduction of this contributory unemployment insurance scheme was not unique to Germany; indeed, most other industrialising European countries also implemented pension and sickness schemes first (see Mares 1997, 2000).

From the very beginning, the emphasis of the implemented insurance schemes was on cash benefits with equal contributions from workers and employers. The clearly stated aim of the schemes was to maintain the income of the worker or – putting it in Esping-Andersen's words – to decommodify individuals from the labour market and break the strong cash-labour nexus that had been established ever since industrialisation took hold of national economies (see Alber 1986, 1987; Bleses and Seeleib-Kaiser 2004). Although financial contributions by the state were minimal, the parliament and the government were always responsible for the design and the reforms of the legislative acts. It is interesting to note that the relatively advanced social security schemes in Germany remained largely intact during the Second World War, and some aspects of welfare state policy were even expanded. For instance, compulsory pension insurance was extended to self-employed people and policies targeting families were implemented. The most important reason why the National Socialist regime did not dismantle the welfare state was because it was dependent on the public support of the workforce, and the maintenance and partial expansion of the social insurance schemes was one way to stabilise the regime (see Reidegeld 2000 and Alber 1986, p. 10f). However, the formerly autonomous and self-administrated insurance bodies were abolished by law in 1934, and the system was run by the state authorities during the war. After the defeat of the regime, the pre-war status quo was restored and consolidated by the implementation of the Social Insurance Adjustment Law in 1949 ('Sozialversicherungs Anpassungsgesetz'). This law, though heavily amended, is still in use today. The post-war years were the most successful period for the German economy and welfare state, with the insurance schemes all benefiting from the fast economic recovery and very low unemployment rate (between 1964 and 1973), the mean unemployment rate was 0.7 per cent (see Bleses and Seeleib-Kaiser 2004, p. 22).

The funding principles, such as compulsory membership, equal contributions by workers and employers and the strong relationship between earlier contributions and eligibility, have significantly shaped the development of the social security system and the functioning of the welfare state up until the present day. Even though social policies in most mature welfare states are in flux, scholars agree that, at its core, Germany continues to be a typical proponent of a continental welfare state. Until the early 2000s, the benefits provided by the insurance system ensured that the living standard of the insured person could be maintained in case of unemployment, sickness/disability and retirement, leading to the preservation of the existing class system. Furthermore, the strong focus of the social insurance system on the male breadwinner was due to the dominant role Christian Democratic parties played in the development of the welfare state. Their view of the 'ideal standard family' was based on a single (male) wage earner with a partner fulfilling the role of carer for the children or elderly people in the household.[1] The strong impact of a family vision based on Christian values led to the relatively late development of child and elderly care policies, and, more importantly within the framework of this contribution, a comparatively low level of female participation in the labour market.

## 6.2 INSTITUTIONAL FRAMEWORK AND POLITICAL ACTORS

The institutional and political landscape of post-war Germany is characterised by a horizontal and vertical dispersion of power, a competitive party system and a stable relationship between politics, labour unions and employer organisations. In order to understand the German institutional framework and the interactions between the various political actors, it is important to keep in mind that the Federal Republic is a relatively young state whose political institutions were reconstructed following the Second World War. They have been designed to ensure that a single political actor can accumulate only limited power.[2] The distinct horizontal fragmentation of political power results in multiple veto points and political constraints for policy-making at the national level.

The 'Bundesländer' are represented in the second chamber of parliament ('Bundesrat').[3] Originally, the second chamber was thought to represent the interests of the 'Länder', but nowadays, it has become an additional forum for national party politics and competition over issues and policies. Nonetheless, although the second chamber ('Bundesrat') has the power to block legislative processes, this happens only occasionally.[4] Still, the 'Bundesrat' is important in shaping legislation and is also able to draw out the legislative process, especially when the opposition has a majority in the second chamber, as was the case during the following periods: 1972–1982, 1991–1998 and 1999–2005.

Social policy-making, however, mainly takes place at the national level, something that is common to all three countries included in the second part of the empirical analysis. The national character of social policy is also emphasised by the role that the 'Bundestag', the lower chamber of the parliament, plays in social policy-making, with most of the legislative action taking place within this chamber. The fact that the lower chambers are functional equivalents in each of these three countries facilitates the task of comparing policy-making processes across them.

## Partisan Actors

It is mostly through political parties that the political will and policies are shaped in representative parliamentary democracies. According to the theoretical framework, the reform processes that I will analyse should be influenced by party preferences and party politics and it is therefore useful to highlight the most important features of the country's party system. According to the German constitution, party competition plays an essential role in the development of policy programmes. The notion of 'Germany as a party state' ('Parteienstaat') describes the important role that was granted to political parties by the German constitution.[5]

Historically, the political landscape was dominated by the Christian Democrats ('Christlich Demokratische Union', CDU) and the Social Democrats ('Sozialdemokratische Partei Deutschlands', SPD), which took turns in governing or occasionally governed together in a 'grand coalition'.[6] The third major party, the Liberal Party ('Freie Demokratische Partei', FDP), has been acting as a pivotal player between the two largest parties (Schmidt 1987, p. 163). According to Blondel's categorisation of party systems, which takes into account the number and importance of parties, Germany has a 2 1/2 party system, with the FDP being the 'half-party' (Blondel 1968, p. 184f).[7] Both the CDU and the SPD are 'Volksparteien', or so-called mass parties, whose constituencies are not merely class-based.

The first success of the Green Party at the national level in 1983 slightly changed the post-war party system and the balance between the different parties, and fragmentation of the party system increased further after the first elections in the unified country were held in 1990. Due to exceptional rules, the former Communist Party ('Partei des Demokratischen Sozialismus', PDS), entered the 'Bundestag' without having to achieve 5 per cent of the popular vote, instead winning the minimum number of direct mandates required. In the 1994 national elections, the PDS successfully defended these mandates and was able to stay in the parliament. The increasing support for the Green Party, together with a revitalisation of the party system after reunification, increased the number of parties competing for seats and the variety of policies espoused at the national level. Even though the PDS enjoys strong support in the eastern part of Germany, its success in the old 'Bundesländer' is very limited. Limited support in the West and a pronounced leftist manifesto are the reasons why the PDS is considered unsuitable for coalition at the national level.[8] Therefore, it is mainly the Green Party that is considered to be a viable left-wing coalition partner for the SPD at the national level.[9] Due to the gradual transformation of the party system, the FDP lost its role of pivotal player and the power to make or break a government.[10] Since 1998, it is the SPD that has had the most options to form a coalition government at the national level. In many ways, the development of the German Party system resembles changes in other Western European party systems, with the number of parties represented in parliament increasing over the past decades in many European countries.

## Industrial Relations

While party politics is crucial in shaping the design of public policies, organised interests also have a significant role in influencing reform paths and the drawing up of new policies. Germany has a long history of corporatism, and industrial relations in the post-war era were extremely robust and stable with powerful and independent trade unions and employers' organisations. Unlike in other corporatist countries, such as Sweden and Austria, collective agreements in Germany are usually negotiated at the sectorial level between the peak organisations without the intervention of the central government. The coverage of these sectorial agreements has been broad and stable even when union membership and density started to decline.[11] Even though the agreement of peak organisations is not formally needed to reform social policies in Germany, unions and employers' organisations are considered important and powerful actors during reform processes, particularly because their exponents often have close ties with political parties or have a political function themselves.[12] The relatively close relationship between peak interest organisations and political parties and the broad coverage of the sectorial agreements also led to relatively low levels of industrial conflict.

Generally, these institutions are still in place today but have recently started to show signs of decay (see e.g. Hassel 1999; Manow 1997; Streeck 2003; Streeck and Hassel 2003). With the increasing internationalisation of the economy, the German model of broad sectorial agreements came under pressure, mainly because companies are differently affected by globalisation and structural change. During the past decade, a trend towards the decentralisation of bargaining has been observed, with in some sectors, agreements reached at the plant level rather than at the sectorial level. Additionally, fewer workers' councils have been formed at the company level. These councils, however, are important to pass on company-specific interests to the unions.

They are also important in recruiting new union members. Even though union membership has been decreasing and the strong focus on sectorial agreements has weakened over the past years, unions and employers' organisations remain important political actors in social policy-making. Often members of peak organisations are invited to commission hearings in parliament to present their opinions on reform plans or to act as experts on behalf of the semi-sovereign unemployment insurance companies. The policy preferences of the peak organisations in the most important economic sectors will therefore be empirically analysed in this work.

## 6.3 ECONOMIC CONTEXT OF LABOUR MARKET POLICY-MAKING (FROM 1970s UNTIL THE MID-1990s)

Before the German economy was hit by the first oil crisis in 1973, the period after the Second World War was a story of success. The German economy was characterised by high economic growth rates and low (or literally non-existent) unemployment. The German 'Wirtschaftswunder' (economic miracle) benefited from several factors. First, the stable relationship between employers' organisations, trade unions and the government created an inclusive environment in which conflicting interests were channelled and pacified without leading to disruptive conflicts. Second, the decentralised political system, where the state has limited capacities to interfere, provided business with the necessary entrepreneurial freedom.[13] In addition to the favourable domestic institutional setting, the international economic environment was stable and the Bretton Woods system of fixed exchange rates provided an environment which facilitated the trading of goods but significantly limited the flow of capital between countries, thus enabling states to expand the provision of social security. This period of 'embedded liberalism' ended in the 1970s (Ruggie 1982) and gave way to globalisation and increasingly interdependent national economies which were not only competing for export markets but also trying to attract capital.

As indicated in figure 6.1, the steadily running motor of the healthy German economy began to falter in the early 1970s. One of the reasons for this was the breakdown of the Bretton Woods system in 1973. The first oil crisis and the end of the existing international monetary system negatively affected the industrial sector in most Western European economies.[14] At the beginning of the 1970s, economic growth declined sharply and even became negative in 1974. The German economy was able to recover quickly, however, but the second oil crisis in 1979 again led to a steep decrease in economic growth. After the second oil shock, the German economy did not fully

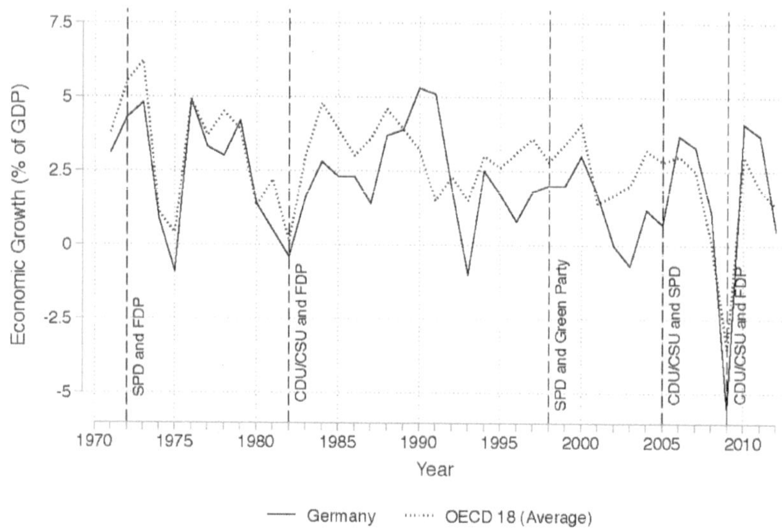


**Figure 6.1. Annual Economic Growth Rates in Germany: 1970–2012**

recover for years, and from 1977 growth rates remained below the OECD average for ten consecutive years. Several factors explain why the German economy faced increasing problems from the mid-1980: the German industrial sector, which was heavily focused on the export market, was one of the key beneficiaries of fixed exchange rates under the Bretton Woods system, as the undervalued German currency (deutsche mark) helped the German export industry to maintain its competitiveness in the international market. However, with the combined effects of end of the era of fixed exchange rates and a central bank committed to restrictive monetary policy aimed at price stability and low inflation rates, the value of the German currency gradually increased, which in turn increased the price of German goods on the international market (see e.g. Manow and Seils 2000a; Scharpf 2000a; Schmidt 1987, p. 153).

Partially triggered by this development, the size of the industrial sector shrank significantly during the 1970s and 1980s and transformed Germany into a post-industrial society in which more than half of GDP was produced in the service sector. Although the service sector contributed a major share to the GDP, employment in this sector did not grow accordingly. The main obstacle to job creation in the low-wage sector is the relatively high non-wage labour costs that are characteristic of the German economy, and since most jobs in the service sector belong to the low-wage category, employers in this sector remained reluctant to create new jobs. Additionally, skill formation in Germany is strongly related to the respective industrial sector in which workers are employed and hence is not easily transferable to a different sector (see Hall and Soskice 2001; Thelen 2004). Thus, the relatively slow job growth in the service sector largely contributed to the rising level of unemployment.

Furthermore, employment relations in German industry were traditionally based on long-term (permanent) and full-time contracts, and the ability of employers to dismiss individual workers is heavily restricted. Hence, the rigid German employment regulations did not allow businesses to adjust to the rapidly changing economic conditions and the increasing importance of technological innovation (Kitschelt and Streeck 2003). In addition to the aforementioned factors, the decentralised political system and the federal veto points made it difficult to efficiently reform the relevant economic policies.

After a long period of near-full employment during which the German population considered full employment to be the norm rather than the exception (see e.g. Bleses and Seeleib-Kaiser 2004), Germany was taken aback by the sudden steep rise in unemployment.[15] As visualised in figure 6.2, by the mid-1970s, the level of unemployment reached 4 per cent and subsequently fell below this level only for a very short period at the beginning of the 1980s. During the late 1990s, unemployment rose again

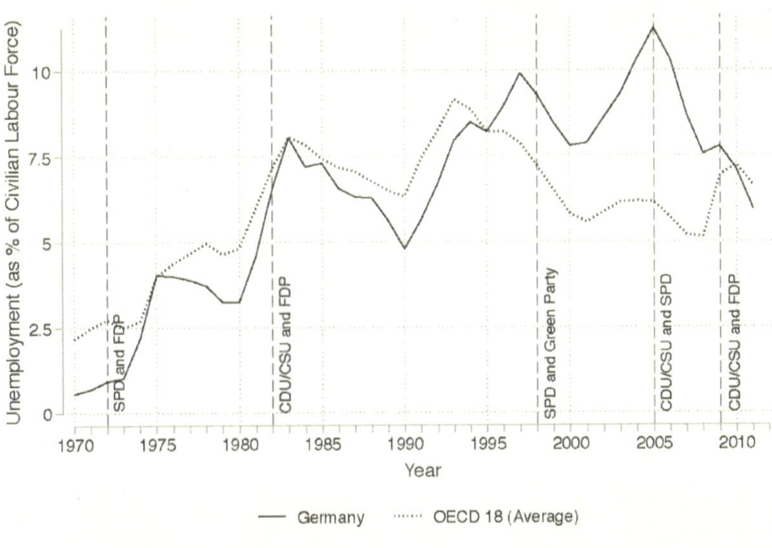


**Figure 6.2. Unemployment Rate in Germany (as Percentage of Total Labour Force)**

to unprecedented heights, with a spike of 9.4 per cent in 1997. Whereas the unemployment rate in most OECD countries started to decrease at the beginning of the 1990s, unemployment in Germany further increased and was significantly above the OECD mean until 2005. The high level of unemployment, which is influenced by rigid legislation, stands in stark contrast to the persistently positive performance of the German economy as a whole. In order to smoothen out and cushion structural change and help companies to downsize, German employers' associations and trade unions, under the aegis of the government, negotiated generous programmes to facilitate early retirement, a tool that had already been established during the economic crisis of 1929/1930 and has been frequently used to help companies in times of economic downturn in an otherwise-rigid labour market with very strong employment protection (see Ebbinghaus 2006; Trampusch 2005). By facilitating these negotiations, the government directly helped to cushion the structural change of the economy and helped the industrial sector to partially externalise the costs of structural adjustment (see Manow and Seils 2000b). The various early retirement schemes, however, constituted a heavy burden for the German pension scheme and only artificially lowered the official unemployment figures.

Apart from the increasing level of unemployment and slower economic growth caused by structural change (which affected all post-industrial societies), the German economy, compared to other OECD countries, was still prosperous and internationally competitive. Even the heavy financial burdens caused by the re-unification process with the former German Democratic Republic did not alter this picture. As figure 6.1 shows, the economy recovered surprisingly quickly after the reunification shock in 1991/1992. The overall economic success of German industry in an open economy mainly relies on a skilled workforce and a focus on producing high-quality products rather than low-cost goods.[16] The success of the social market economy ('soziale Marktwirtschaft'), as this interplay between the economy and politics in Germany is often called, has proved to be largely successful.[17]

## 6.4 ANALYSIS OF RECENT LABOUR MARKET REFORMS

Until 2003, the German unemployment insurance law was divided into two main tiers. The first included rules and regulations related to classical unemployment insurance, the second covered issues related to unemployment assistance. In 2003, in light of the encompassing reforms modernising the German labour market, the unemployment assistance scheme was abolished and essentially merged with the means-tested social assistance scheme. The analyses of specific reform processes in this chapter will mostly focus on reforms relating to the first tier of the unemployment insurance law, the unemployment insurance benefits ('Arbeitslosengeld'), rather than the unemployment assistance benefits ('Arbeitslosenhilfe'), culminating in the series of reforms at the beginning of 2000 that significantly changed the German labour market and individual career paths within it.

Table 6.1 gives an overview of the most important labour market reforms, including those directly related to the unemployment insurance

**Table 6.1. Reforms in Germany**

| *Year* | *Reform Title and Key Content* | *Government Coalition* |
|---|---|---|
| 1991 | Act of 21 June 1991: Amendment to the Employment Promotion Act (1969).Contribution Rate Adjustment Act; increase of unemployment insurance benefits. | CDU/CSU and FDP |
| 1992 | Decree on the period for the drawing of compensatory benefit for periods of reduced hours in case of structural unemployment. | CDU/CSU and FDP |
| 1993 | Amendment to the Employment Promotion Act ('Arbeitsförderungsgesetz', AFG); focuses on active labour market policies, but also includes issues related to the eligibility to and the duration of benefits. | CDU/CSU and FDP |
| 1994 | First 'Saving, Consolidation and Growth Program' ('Erstes Gesetz zur Umsetzung des Spar-, Konsolidierungs- und Wachstumsprogramms'); focus on active labour market policies, adjustment of unemployment benefits for target groups (bad weather benefits) and other changes affecting benefits. | CDU/CSU and FDP |
| 1994 | Employment Promotion Act 1994 ('Beschäftigungsgesetz, BeschfG'); labour market policies targeting part-time workers, implementation of short-term training programmes without loss of unemployment benefits. Measures targeting people older than fifty-eight years. Other minor adjustments to the SKWPG programme. | CDU/CSU and FDP |
| 1996 | Unemployment Assistance Reform Act; adjustments to parts of the Employment Promotion Act, that is, introduction of old-age part-time work (allowing for gradual retirement). | CDU/CSU and FDP |

*(Continued)*

**Table 6.1. (Continued)**

| *Year* | *Reform Title and Key Content* | *Government Coalition* |
|---|---|---|
| 1997 | Amendment to the Third Book of the Social Code ('Drittes Sozialgesetz Buch'); amends provisions of the Third Book of the Social Code regarding payment of unemployment benefits and other laws. Reform of the 'Employment Promotion Act' ('Beschäftigungsförderungsgesetz'). | CDU/CSU and FDP |
| 1998 | Reform of Employment Promotion; employment promotion is integrated into the 'Third Book of the Social Code' ('Sozialgesetzbuch'). Changes related to the contributory system, and new assessment periods for eligibility. | CDU/CSU and FDP |
| 1999 | Amendment to the Third Book of the Social Code (second act); changes in calculating unemployment benefits, introduction of employment creation measures. | SPD and Bündnis90/Die Grünen |
| 2000 | Act to improve the cooperation between labour offices and welfare institutions (organisational reform); increasing the efficiency and the cooperation between labour offices and welfare institutions that provide benefits and assistance to the unemployed. | SPD and Bündnis90/Die Grünen |
| 2001 | JobAQTIV Act ('Gesetz zur Reform der Arbeitsmarktpolitischen Instrumente'); implementation of measures to upskill employees and deregulates temporary employment. | SPD and Bündnis90/Die Grünen |
| 2002 | Hartz I and Hartz II ('Erstes und Zweites Gesetz für Moderne Dienstleistung am Arbeitsmarkt'); establishment of placement agencies, further liberalisation of temporary work agreements, introduction of 'Ich-AGs'. | SPD and Bündnis90/Die Grünen |
| 2003 | Hartz III and Hartz IV ('Erstes und Zweites Gesetz für Moderne Dienstleistung am Arbeitsmarkt'); merger of the unemployment assistance scheme with the social assistance scheme (Hartz IV), implementation of tighter eligibility criteria for unemployment benefits and stricter rules and duties for job seekers. | SPD and Bündnis90/Die Grünen |

National elections held in 1990 (first election after unification), 1994, 1998 and 2002. The table draws on information from the legislation data base of the German 'Bundestag' (http://dip.bundestag.de/), work by Ebbinghaus (2006), Aust et al. (2002) and the ILO NATLEX database (http://www.ilo.org/dyn/natlex/).

scheme (including active labour market policies, but not showing the various changes related to working hours and changes to the old-age part-time scheme, etc.). The large number of reforms during this period shows that the German labour market, and more specifically the unemployment insurance scheme, was under severe pressure due to the ongoing structural changes and the relatively sluggish growth of the economy. Both the Christian Democratic government under Kohl and the subsequent Schröder government expended much effort into restructuring the insurance scheme in an attempt to loosen the rigid labour market regulations, incentivise job growth and reintegrate the unemployed back into the labour market. Of the reforms included in table 6.1, the following reforms will be analysed in more detail: the 'Beschäftigungsförderungsgesetz' from 1994 (Employment promotion act), which took place under a conservative party government, and the 2001 JobAQTIV reform, which took place during the first term of the coalition between the Social Democrats and the Green Party. The 'Beschäftigungsförderungsgesetz' represents an early attempt to deregulate the German labour market and introduce more flexibility in terms of employment relations and part-time work. The reform marked a turning point in German labour market politics as, for the first time, the German government interfered in a previously unregulated area of employment relationships, namely part-time employment. While the reform had long-term implications for the further deregulation of the German labour market, the long-standing unemployment insurance institutions, securing the economic and societal status of regular employees, were not touched. While the 'Beschäftigungsförderungsgesetz' already indicated the direction of future labour market changes, the second reform process analysed in this chapter is often considered to mark a radical change of paradigm in labour market policy-making and social policy. Even though the JobAQTIV legislation was not as comprehensive as the 'Hartz reforms' which followed, the implications of which will be discussed at the end, it was the first reform to follow the principle of 'Fördern und Fordern', which established a more active labour market policy.

Each reform will be analysed as follows: first, the content of the reform proposal will be described in brief and located in the two-dimensional policy space. Second, the policy preferences and arguments of the involved actors will be analysed based on parliamentary debates and written documents prepared for the consultation process. Third, the legislation as passed by the parliamentary vote will be analysed using the same criteria, and lastly the differences between the reform proposals and the final reform will be discussed and linked to the wider context of this book.

## 6.5 BESCHÄFTIGUNGSFÖRDERUNGSGESETZ (BESCHFG1994)

The 'Beschäftigungsförderungsgesetz' (BeschfG1994), introduced by the conservative coalition between CDU/CSU and FDP, was one of the early legislative instruments that focused on active labour market policies aimed at setting incentives to bring people back into the labour market, rather than at strengthening and reforming so-called passive labour market policies. During this period, the discourse in labour market policy-making, not only in Germany but also in many other European countries, had indeed changed from a focus on passive labour market policies, such as the provision of benefits, towards policy measures aimed at the activation and reintegration of the unemployed into the labour market. There was also a move towards taking action to restructure the labour market in order to generate new jobs and towards increasing the flexibility of employment relationships and existing labour market institutions. The reform of the existing 'Beschäftigungsförderungsgesetz' was necessary to address the problematic situation of the German labour market, which was in a 'difficult economic transition period' (AfAS 1994), partly caused by German reunification, which had led to a significant increase in unemployment levels from roughly 5 per cent to 8.5 per cent in 1994. The parliamentary committee for work and social issues, which was in charge of drafting the bill, also stressed that the current situation made it 'necessary to exploit the existing room to manoeuvre in order to improve the conditions for the effective adjustment of supply and demand in the labour market' (Deutscher Bundestag 1994a, p. 1f).[18]

The reform process was accompanied by peak labour and employer organisations which participated in the public hearing and submitted written statements to the leading commission. Specifically, the most important voices covered in this analysis are, on the employer side, the policy preferences and arguments of the 'Bundesvereinigung der Deutschen Arbeitgeberverbände' (BDA), the 'Arbeitsgemeinschaft der selbständigen Unternehmer' (ASU), the 'Deutscher Industrie- und Handelstag' (DIHT) and the peak organisation of craftsmen (ZDH), while on the side of the labour unions, the role of the DGB ('Deutscher Gewerkschaftsbund'), the DAG ('Deutsche Angestelltengewerkschaft') and the ÖTV ('Gewerkschaft Öffentliche Dienste') are taken into account.[19]

In the light of the analytical framework applied in this study, the key issues of the reform can be assigned to the two overarching reform dimensions in the following manner: on the generosity dimension, the reform aimed at extending the period unemployed persons would receive unemployment benefits if they started their own business. This additional support was to be provided through the existing unemployment insurance scheme, and payments would match the benefits that the person had previously been entitled to based on his or her salary and contributions. The target groups of this specific policy change were skilled lower-middle class craftsmen and highly-skilled workers, as they were expected to have the necessary financial and educational background to successfully start their own business.

The second policy change affecting the generosity dimension was the promotion of part-time work. Employees who had given up a full-time position for part-time employment would continue to be entitled to unemployment insurance benefits based on their previous (full-time job) income. The right to receive full unemployment benefits would be limited to three years after changing from a full-time to a part-time position. Within the same scheme, and more importantly, unemployed people accepting a part-time job, while actually preferring a full-time position, would be compensated for the difference between the full- and part-time salaries. These compensatory payments would also be financed through the unemployment insurance scheme. According to the governing parties, the promotion of part-time positions would create additional jobs and increase labour market flexibility. The impact of this policy change would favour the less privileged in society, at least for the three-year period after accepting a part-time position. The government specifically emphasised that women and low-skilled workers would be the key beneficiaries of this scheme. Less privileged segments of the workforce would be encouraged to participate in the labour market and be offered better conditions by guaranteeing their entitlements, at least for a limited period. Overall, the reform would not affect the contributory scheme of the unemployment insurance; that is, employees with low and high income would still contribute the same percentage of their salary. This is largely in line with the preferences of the conservative party government which advocates a pure insurance design.

On the spending dimension, the major policy changes proposed by the government were related to the establishment of private placement centres. These job agencies were tasked with facilitating job searches and creating a more dynamic venue for people on the job market (the unemployed) to find future employers. The existing 'Bundesanstalt für Arbeit' was often criticised for its slow reactions to changes on the labour market and was therefore considered to be unable to efficiently help unemployed people. It was thought that inducing competition between private and public placement centres would revitalise the labour market and eventually help to reduce the number of unemployed people. The proponents of this policy change expected that private placement centres would be able to offer more flexible mentoring arrangements and work solutions than the public placement centres, a goal that was deemed necessary due to the structural changes of the economy. In addition, the market-oriented approach and the competition between the two

**Table 6.2. Key Policy Proposals Included in the 'Beschäftigungsförderungsgesetz, 1994'**

| *Generosity Dimension* | *Spending Dimension* |
|---|---|
| Adjustments for part-time workers (eligibility for unemployment benefits) | New regional placement agencies administered by private organisations |
| Improvement of social welfare of employees changing from full-time work to part-time work | Cutting salaries of jobs in (public) employment schemes |
| | Duration of benefits (target: people setting up their own business) |

service providers were expected to reduce expenditures and make the public job centres more efficient. The idea originated from the market-liberal Free Democrats, who were part of the coalition government. The second issue on the spending dimension was the implementation of a salary cap on salaries/ benefits for people employed in the so-called second labour market. This policy change targeted jobs subsidised through public money. More specifically, wages in this 'second labour market' were not to exceed 80 per cent of the salaries paid to employees in the main job market. The rationale of this reform, whose key policy proposals are summarised in table 6.2, was to increase incentives for people in the 'second labour market' to give up subsidised jobs and accept regular work relationships.

## Actor's Policy Preferences on the Generosity Dimension

The Employment Promotion act proposed in 1994 was clearly geared towards increasing the number of part-time jobs and making German labour market institutions more flexible, a change that became increasingly necessary due to the ongoing structural changes at the European and global levels. It was on the basis of this goal that the government at the time decided to use resources from the traditional unemployment insurance scheme to finance and support policy changes aimed at boosting part-time employment. While all parties agreed that the existing number of part-time jobs was insufficient and the German labour market was in need of more flexible arrangements, the views on how to support the creation of part-time jobs and incentivise employees to accept part-time work, however, widely diverged. The pressure for more part-time jobs was particularly strong from the FDP, which was *convinced that there [were] enormous reserves [for part-time jobs].* The party also claimed that a 'more flexible allocation of labour [would make it possible to] include more people into the labour market' (Gisela Babel, parliamentary minutes, 12. Wahlperiode, 219. Sitzung, 14.04.1994b, p. 18932).

The parliament as a whole clearly admitted the need for more part-time jobs also because Germany, at that time, was among the countries with the lowest percentage of part-time jobs in the OECD. Despite the general agreement over the need for reform and more part-time jobs, the Social Democrats and the Green Party critically evaluated the government proposal and heavily criticised the plans during the parliamentary debate. The most important criticism was that the job creation programme would simply turn out to be a measure to help companies to create part-time jobs that are not, or not fully, protected by social security schemes. They were particularly sceptical about the idea that one full-time job would be transformed into two or more part-time jobs, thereby increasing the total number of people included in the workforce. The reality, according to the Social Democratic MP Gerd Andres, was 'that more and more protected full-time jobs [would be] converted into unprotected part-time jobs' (parliamentary minutes, 14.04.1994b, p. 18943).

The Green Party added that the promotion of part-time jobs was a reasonable plan and also welcomed the way the government planned to modify the calculation of benefits for part-time employees for the suggested three-year period, but also made the criticism that 'an overall concept to promote part-time employment and particularly provide social security for part-time employees [was] missing from this reform' (parliamentary minutes, 219. Sitzung, 14.04.1994b, p. 18938). Similar to the Social Democrats, the Green Party also expected that the creation of part-time jobs, as proposed by the 'Beschäftigungsförderungsgesetz', would mainly create jobs that were unprotected by social insurance schemes, as the eligibility to benefits and coverage was generally tied to a regular full-time work relationship. As expected, the Left was the most critical of the government proposal and suggested a new way of distributing work by drastically reducing working hours and regulating overtime (parliamentary minutes, 219. Sitzung, 14.04.1994b, p. 18936). These measures, leftist MP's claimed, would lead to the creation of over two million new jobs, with a potential loss of income for people with low and average incomes to be mitigated through compensatory measures. Overall, more part-time jobs without concurrent major changes of the core social insurance system would, in the end, lead to a reduction of redistributive generosity and the exclusion of specific segments of the workforce from the social insurance scheme.

The social partners also agreed that part-time jobs should be more strongly promoted and that more flexibility to create part-time jobs would help the German labour market in the long run. However, the organisations disagreed with the means proposed by the government. The organisation representing craftsmen (ZDH) voiced the criticism that 'the improvement of unemployment benefits for people accepting a part-time rather than a full-time job is inconsistent with the insurance principle and will manipulate the entitlement scheme' ('Ausschuss für Arbeit und Soziales'). On the union side, the union representing public sector employees (ÖTV) stated that 'the measures are insufficient. In order to generate a significant impact, better social security measures for part-time employees are necessary' (written statement to the 'Ausschuss für Arbeit und Soziales').

The second issue on the generosity dimension concerned the twenty-six weeks of additional unemployment insurance benefits for people starting their own business and changing their status from being salaried to self-employed. This additional support was meant to encourage entrepreneurial people to set up their own business in the first place and hopefully create new jobs in the future. Again, the increase in redistributive generosity was to be temporary and directed at a very specific segment of the overall workforce. Volker Kauder (CDU/CSU) from the government coalition stressed that 'we need a huge self-employment offensive. All experience shows that the self-employed create new jobs within very short periods of time. Unlike in the US and other European states, we have too few unemployed people willing to take the risk of starting their own business' (parliamentary minutes, 219. Sitzung, 14.04.1994b, p. 18942). Again, the general aim of the proposal was met with support, although the actual implementation and the range of the reform was said to be insufficient and half-hearted.[20] One of the key criticisms from the Green Party was that the extent to which the new law would change the status quo was minimal, and benefiting from additional twenty-six weeks of unemployment insurance benefits was not considered enough to establish a small and stable business. The employers' organisations criticised the proposal for different reasons. The union representing German employees (DAG) mentioned in its comment that 'the allocation of financial means for start-up companies and self-employment is not a core task of unemployment benefit insurance and contributors to it' (written statement to the 'Ausschuss für Arbeit und Soziales'), thereby defending the privileges and rights of employees and employers contributing to the scheme. A similar argument was made by the peak organisation of the German trade and crafts industry. Table 6.3 illustrates whether the different actors were supportive or critical about the suggested changes on the generosity dimension.

In a nutshell, the expected impact of both proposed changes is an increase in redistributive generosity for a limited number of years, or months (in the case of the second proposal). However, after this initial period, people with involuntary part-time positions, who only accepted such an employment opportunity in the hope of finding a full-time position within the proposed three-year period, will lose this entitlement and are likely to face financial difficulties or the pressure to accept another part-time job with limited social protection and rights. This will also apply to people who decide to take the step towards self-employment. The support offered through the

**Table 6.3. Policy Proposals Affecting the Generosity Dimension, BeschfG 1994**

| | *Critical of Government Proposal* | *Supportive of Government Proposal* |
|---|---|---|
| **Part-Time Jobs** | SPD | CDU/CSU |
| | Green Party | FDP |
| | PDS/Die Linke | BDA |
| | ZDH | ASU |
| | DGB | **DAG** |
| | ÖTV | |
| **Self-Employment** | SPD | CDU/CSU |
| | Green Party | FDP |
| | PDS/Die Linke | BDA |
| | ZDH | ASU |
| | DGB | |
| | ÖTV | |
| | DHIT | |
| | **DAG** | |

ASU = Arbeitsgemeinschaft Selbständiger Unternehmer (organisation of independent entrepreneurs), BDA = Bundesverein Deutscher Arbeitgeber (employer organisation), DAG = Deutsche Angestelltengewerkschaft (white-collar union), DGB = Deutscher Gewerkschaftsbund (blue-collar union), DIHT = Deutscher Industrie und Handelstag (peak organisation for trade and industry), ÖTV = Gewerkschaft Öffentliche Dienste (public sector union), ZDH = Zentralverband des Deutschen Handwerks (craftsmen organisation).

unemployment insurance scheme will be valid for roughly six months, after which the business is expected to be self-supporting. The main beneficiaries of this measure are the well-educated and skilled people (the core workforce) who had lost their jobs and decide to start something on their own. This view is also supported by research evidence evaluating start-up programmes which shows that only a small percentage of people in need start their own business (Wolff and Nivorozhkin 2008). Despite the fact that the German self-employment programmes have been positively evaluated, studies show that a large percentage of the recipients are male and have qualifications and skills which are above average (Caliendo et al. 2007).

## Actor's Policy Preferences on the Spending Dimension

The implementation of private placement centres was to help decrease costs and increase efficiency in the job market. These privately organised centres were to compete with the public placement centres and be run for profit rather than be supported and financed by the tax payer or the unemployed. The service of the private placement centres would not be paid by the unemployment insurance scheme or by tax money but rather companies seeking new employees would pay for the services placement centres offered. While the proposal to implement privately run placement centres was met with scepticism and criticism by the opposition parties in parliament (see table 6.4),

**Table 6.4. Policy Proposals Affecting the Spending Dimension, BeschfG 1994**

| | *Critical of Government Proposal* | *Supportive of Government Proposal* |
|---|---|---|
| **Placement Centres** | SPD | CDU/CSU |
| | PDS/Linke | FDP |
| | Green Party | DIHT |
| | DGB | ASU |
| | DAG | ZDH |
| | ÖTV | **BDA** |
| **Salary Cap** | SPD | CDU/CSU |
| | Green Party | FDP |
| | PDS/Linke | DIHT |
| | DGB | ASU |
| | DAG | ZDH |
| | ÖTV | |
| | **BDA** | |

ASU = Arbeitsgemeinschaft Selbständiger Unternehmer (organisation of independent entrepreneurs), BDA = Bundesverein Deutscher Arbeitgeber (employer organisation), DAG = Deutsche Angestelltengewerkschaft (white-collar union), DGB = Deutscher Gewerkschaftsbund (blue-collar union), DIHT = Deutscher Industrie und Handelstag (peak organisation for trade and industry), ÖTV = Gewerkschaft Öffentliche Dienste (public sector union), ZDH = Zentralverband des Deutschen Handwerks (craftsmen organisation).

the CDU/CSU, together with the FDP, argued that private placement centres would bring jobs and the unemployed closer together and therefore increase the chances for the unemployed to find jobs more quickly. The FDP especially claimed that private placement centres were necessary to act as a role model for inefficient public institutions and that private actors were significantly more interested in offering these services (parliamentary minutes, 219. Sitzung, 12. Wahlperiode, 14.04.1994b, p. 18933). In addition, private placement centres were more flexible and better able to establish closer ties with companies, which would help them to fill open positions more quickly. Similar arguments were made by the employers' organisations, which mostly welcomed the proposal and argued that the creation of private placement centres was long overdue (written statement by the BDA to the 'Ausschuss für Arbeit und Soziales').

The opposition parties from the Left doubted that this change would have any effect on the number of jobs available or have a positive impact on the placement statistics as a whole. In addition, the SPD feared that private placement centres would mainly increase the headhunting capacities of bigger companies (see parliamentary minutes, 12. Wahlperiode, 14.04.1994b, p. 18930), whereas unemployed people with low levels of education and skills, the elderly and also women seeking jobs would not benefit from this change. Generally, the proposal was criticised as further deregulating and destabilising the labour market while offering a handful of new service agencies the opportunity to make a profit from the high levels of unemployment.[21]

The PDS/Linke Liste also made the criticism that the groups targeted by the proposal were the highly educated and skilled workers and that 'unemployed people who are hard to place will be left behind, dependent on the public placement centres, whereas unemployed people with more options will be placed through private centres' (Gregor Gysi, parliamentary minutes, 219. Sitzung, 14.04.1994b, p. 18936). The DGB argued in the same vein, making the criticism that the labour force would be traded like goods ('Beschlussempfehlung und Bericht des Ausschusses für Arbeit und Soziales', 1994a, p. 30).

The other key proposal related to the spending dimension concerned a decrease by 20 per cent in the support and payments of employees in public job-creation schemes. People working in public employment schemes would only get up to 80 per cent of the salary that an employee in the first labour market would earn.[22] The government framed this reform issue as an incentive for unemployed people working in the 'second labour market' to enter the first labour market again and stressed that more people would benefit despite cuts in individual earnings. The emphasis on job creation was to be placed in the main labour market and subsidised jobs should be a temporary solution only. The plan to cut compensation for people in job-creation schemes ran up against strong opposition by the Social Democrats and the Green Party. The attempt to compensate people in employment schemes at a ratio of 80 per cent was considered an attack on the tariff autonomy of the social partners and an effort to circumvent social partnership. In a contribution to the parliamentary debate on this issue, an SPD MP claimed that 'it becomes obvious that the government is trying to suspend tariff autonomy and to establish low-wage jobs by law . . . . This is dangerous, especially now that the unions are willing to negotiate new collective agreements in some sectors' (parliamentary minutes, 12. Wahlperiode, 219. Sitzung, 14.04.1994b, p. 18944).

The peak German labour union (DGB), together with other smaller unions, suspected that this measure would decrease the chances for people in the second labour market to be re-integrated into the normal labour market (see written statement to the 'Ausschuss für Arbeit und Soziales'), thereby further contributing to the creation of two classes of labour market participants. Members of parliament from the government parties, however, replied that 'it is time to finally bury the fiction that subsidised jobs, created as a social-policy measure, are worth as much as jobs in the real labour market' (Heinrich Kolb, FDP, parliamentary minutes, 219. Sitzung, 14.04.1994b, p. 18946). This statement is a strong sign that the governing coalition was not actively seeking to prevent a further division of the workforce into less and more privileged groups, by acknowledging and accepting that public employment schemes may ostracise specific groups from the first labour market and that the measure was mostly aimed at allowing the government to cut costs associated with these schemes. The government's plans were supported by employer's organisations and the represented interests of craft organisations, which were lobbying for even stronger pressure to be placed on people in the second labour market. The DIHT thus suggested an even greater decrease in payments to people working in job-creation schemes ('Arbeitsbeschaffungsmassnahmen') (50 per cent rather than the proposed 80 per cent). In fact, some exponents criticised the government for not exploiting the full room to manoeuvre.

## Mediating Effects of Political Constraints

At the time when the 'Beschäftigungsförderungsgesetz 1994' was debated in the two chambers, the SPD-led opposition had the majority in the 'Bundesrat', the most important veto player in the legislative process. Nine of the sixteen 'Länder-representatives' represented SPD-led Bundesländer. The bill, which was heavily criticised by the SPD, the Green Party and the PDS/Linke Liste in the 'Bundestag', would therefore not have passed the SPD-dominated 'Bundesrat'. However, there was disagreement as to whether the law in fact needed the approval by the 'Bundesrat' to pass. Whereas the governing coalition, which had the majority in the 'Bundestag', claimed that the reform proposal did not need the approval of the upper chamber, the majority in the 'Bundesrat' insisted that some of the proposed legislative changes touched on the competencies of the states and thus required the approval of both chambers. The part of the reform on the basis of which the 'Bundesrat' claimed to have the right to approve/disapprove the bill is not examined in this case study as it concerned a passage aimed at fighting illegal employment, which would have required the 'Länder' to collaborate with the border police. This detail was overlooked by the drafting committee and initially offered the 'Bundesrat' some leverage to block the law. Consequently, and in line with the criticism the bill faced in the lower chamber, the reform proposal was rejected. After the defeat of the legislative proposal in the 'Bundesrat' in the first round, the 'Ausschuss für Arbeit und Soziales' quickly redrafted the reform and eliminated the paragraphs that needed the approval of the states. These issues were integrated into a separate bill in order to proceed with the reform process. The 'new' reform proposal contained the same key measures described in the previous paragraph and allowed the government to increase the flexibility of the German labour market while avoiding an unavoidable veto from the upper chamber. Although the SPD-led 'Bundesländer' and the opposition parties in the 'Bundestag' heavily criticised this strategic manoeuvre, their hands were tied and the reform was approved by the majority of the parliament after the fourth reading of the bill. While in general such mistakes rarely happen, the overall pattern of drafting legislative proposals in such a way that they do not need the approval of the upper parliamentary chamber is well established and documented. Despite the relatively strong veto power of the 'Bundesrat', divided governments in which the opposition dominates the second chamber do not usually lead to blockage or legislative stalemate (Manow and Burkhart 2007; Manow and van Kersbergen 2008). The process described earlier well illustrates this finding. Indeed, in most cases, governments anticipate a veto and draft the bill in such a way that no consent is needed or seek compromise on conflicting issues before the bill is presented. Due to this mechanism of legislative self-restraint (Vanberg 1998), less than 3 per cent of all bills requiring the consent of the 'Bundesrat' are blocked.

## Discussion

The conflicting lines taken in the debates during this reform process are clear and correspond well with the assumptions discussed in the theory and also reinforce, and in more detail, the results of the quantitative section. The overall dire situation on the labour market contributed to the fact that the government was under great pressure to reform the labour market in order to stabilise the social insurance scheme and ameliorate conditions in the labour market. The main policy proposals and measures included in the 'Beschäftigungsförderungsgesetz' clearly aimed at cutting expenditures for labour market policies, in particular subsidised jobs, and were also geared at reducing the generosity of labour market policies, in particular the remuneration of people in the second labour market. Most measures indirectly affected unemployed people negatively and made it more difficult for people with little education and professional skills to find a new job and to live on their unemployment insurance benefits or unemployment assistance. The leader of the PDS/Linke Liste Gregor Gysi's final verdict of the reform reveals the core criticism the Social Democrats, and particularly the Left, had during the debate and also points out who suffers most from these changes. In his speech, he specifically said that 'I do not criticise the fact that the government aims at cutting expenditure or the opening up of new sources of income. I criticise that this reform comes mainly at the expense of the weakest members of our society while the wealthy are always treated with care' (parliamentary minutes, 219. Sitzung, 12. Wahlperiode, 14.04.1994b, p. 18935). Not all issues were contested outright by the opposition, but most of them, and especially the proposals affecting the redistributive generosity of the existing social security schemes, were strongly criticised. Moreover, the legislation that was finally implemented only offered superficial solutions to the more complex problem of the rigidity of the German labour market which had difficulties coping with the ongoing structural changes in the German economy.

Table 6.5 offers a summary and an overview of the most important reform issues implemented through the 1994 employment promotion law and also indicates how labour market 'insiders' and 'outsiders' were affected.

**Table 6.5. Reform Issues and Direction of Changes 'Beschäftigungsförderungsgesetz, 1994'**

| | | *Effect on* | |
|---|---|---|---|
| | *Reform Issues* | *'Insiders'* | *'Outsiders'* |
| **Generosity** | Promotion of part-time work (three-year top-up if the person takes a part-time job after being unemployed or changes from full-time to part-time employment) | + | – |
| | Start-up help ('Überbrückungsgeld'): additional six months of unemployment benefit if the person starts a business | + | – |
| | Immediate eligibility to participate in qualification and training measures | + | –/+ |
| **Spending** | Reducing the salaries for participants in public employment schemes | + | – |
| | Private placement centres | + | (+) |

*Legend*: + implicates that the implemented measure had a positive effect for the group indicated; – implicates that the reform negatively affected 'insiders'/'outsiders'.

The reform as a whole certainly did not dismantle the unemployment insurance scheme, and only minor changes were made to the contributory scheme of unemployment insurance and also to the levels of entitlement for people in standard employment. The overall redistributive generosity of the German unemployment scheme thus remained intact, and (skilled) workers with regular employment relationships were not negatively affected. One reason why the government coalition of the CDU/CSU and the FDP did not draft a reform with a more radical impact on the redistributive generosity of the scheme might have been the fact that the government could not count on the support of the 'Bundesrat'. This argument will be further examined in an analysis of an additional reform process that took place under the Schröder government (coalition between the SPD and the Green Party). This government had a majority in both chambers and did not need to fear the potential defeat of reform proposals in the 'Bundesrat'. Another reason the reform was not as far-reaching as it might have been could be that even within the governing coalition, support for more radical changes with a clear negative effect on the core workforce also would have been difficult to mobilise, as the CDU in particular draws its support from a large number of salaried workers who would have strongly disapproved of measures radically reforming the unemployment insurance scheme.

## 6.6 GESETZ ZUR REFORM DER ARBEITSMARKTPOLITISCHEN INSTRUMENTE 2001 (JOBAQTIV)

In common with the preceding conservative government, the coalition between the Social Democrats and the Green Party experienced significant pressure from high unemployment and a high budgetary deficit. When the government took office in 1998, the level of unemployment was at 9.3 per cent. The reform of the labour market was thus a central issue in the Social Democratic election campaign and was also a cornerstone of the coalition treaty and the government's programme. In fact, the labour market was the absolute top priority and was the first point referenced in the coalition treaty, which mentioned in the first section that 'the high number of unemployed people is the most difficult political heritage from the former government. The new government will do all it can to step by step lower the unemployment figures during the upcoming legislative period'. However, before the government presented its own strategies and policies to address the condition of the labour market, it cancelled some of the most recent measures by the conservative Kohl government, specifically measures that were intended to deregulate the labour market, such as reducing elements of dismissal protection ('Kündigungsschutz'). The reversal of these laws was in line with traditional Social Democratic labour market policy-making in Germany that closely reflected the interests of the major labour unions. Nonetheless, the general direction of the Schröder government was more unconventional in the sense that it aimed at integrating business preferences into Social Democratic social policy in an attempt to increase labour market efficiency.

At the beginning of the left-wing government regime, conflicts between Oskar Lafontaine representing the traditional left wing of the German Social Democrats, and Gerhard Schröder, pursuing a reform-oriented 'Third-Way' approach, inhibited the development of a clear social-policy path and reform strategy. However, with the sudden, if not completely unexpected, resignation of Lafontaine from his post in March 1999, the internal opposition the modernising reform course had been facing disappeared. This opened up new room to manoeuvre for the chancellor to plan and implement reforms that were more in line with the popular 'activation' paradigm in labour market policy-making. Soon after Lafontain's resignation, Schröder, together with the British prime minister Tony Blair, published a position paper that underlined his willingness to embark on a liberalising reform path.[23] After the resignation of Lafontaine as Minister of Finance in March 1999, the government's plan to reform the labour market took shape and, in line with the promises made during the election campaign and the announcement made in the coalition treaty, the government as a first step re-established the 'Alliance for Jobs' ('Bündnis für Arbeit, Ausbildung und Wettbewerbsfähigkeit').[24] After Lafontaine resigned, the government's labour market policy shifted from a focus on income protection towards activating the unemployed, increasing the flexibility of the labour market, and the reform of the unemployment insurance and assistance schemes. The JobAQTIV legislation was the first step in this direction by the newly elected left-wing government and is therefore a relevant policy reform for this project. In addition, at the time of the reform opposition parties had a majority in the second parliamentary chamber, the 'Bundesrat', which means that institutional constraints for social policy-making were high.

The major goal of the JobAQTIV reform was to lower the duration of unemployment by increasing labour market flexibility through greater efforts in training and education for people with and without work.[25] In addition, and in a manner similar to the 'Beschäftigungsförderungsgesetz' (1994), the reform aimed at increasing the efficiency of the job placement centres by establishing and improving reintegration procedures after people lose their jobs. Overall, the JobAQTIV legislation, whose key policy proposals are summarised in table 6.6, indicated the new direction of labour market policies

**Table 6.6. Key Policy Proposals Included in the 'JobAQTIV Law, 2001'**

| *Generosity Dimension* | *Spending Dimension* |
|---|---|
| Measures targeted at elderly employees and young people | 'Profiling' of newly unemployed people (increasing efficiency) |
| Job rotation (temporary jobs for long-term unemployed if employed people participate in qualification measures) | Job rotation (subsidies and financial support [between 50 per cent and 80 per cent of the salary] for employers/ firms if they temporarily employ long-term unemployed people) |
| Increased support for long-term unemployed (more rights for qualification measures) | Increase of the duration temporary employment is allowed ('Leiharbeit') |
| No decrease in unemployment assistance if unemployed person participates in qualification measures | Decrease in unemployment insurance/ assistance if person refuses job offers |
| Facilitates the combination of family and work | Financial support for employers who offer jobs to long-term unemployed |
| Immediate rights for unemployed to participate in job creation and qualification measures | |

under the left-wing coalition government. The emphasis was on activating the unemployed rather than offering a broad social security net through insurance schemes. The slogan of the reform sequence was 'Fördern und fordern', which can be translated as 'empowering and challenging people'. This shift, initiated with the JobAQTIV reform, was further pronounced and fleshed out in the subsequent series of so-called Hartz reforms.[26] In line with the overall goals of the coalition government, the new policies were also aimed at strengthening the integration of women in the labour market and helping people with lower skills and little education. The focus on women and low-skilled people is in contrast to traditional labour market policies in Germany, which were mainly directed towards the core labour market force, that is, the unionised and skilled male population.

On the generosity dimension, the government proposed to increase support for the long-term unemployed by creating new employment and training opportunities. Easier access to training and qualification schemes for the long-term unemployed and people with little professional experience should help them to improve their skills and future job prospects. Formerly imposed waiting periods or bans prohibiting unemployed people from entering into training schemes were reduced or cancelled completely. These bans essentially meant that people without employment were forced to stay home for a period of six months without having any external structure to their days. These waiting periods punished people and made it more difficult for some of them to be reintegrated into regular work and also negatively affected their readiness to participate in further training. The right to participate in qualification schemes immediately after losing a job was therefore at the heart of the new policy of activation. The principle that people first have to 'earn' the right to participate in skill enhancement schemes by waiting for a certain period was not compatible with the newly established principle of empowerment ('Fördern und Fordern'). Two reform proposals with a generosity aspect targeted specific groups of labour market participants. First, a reform aimed at encouraging older employees to participate in professional training and qualification schemes. The intention of this specific measure was to reduce the risk of older people losing their job. Second, and in a similar vein, a reform aimed at young employees who had just finished their vocational training or were unable to secure an apprenticeship would allow them to benefit from similar schemes offering them further qualifications. Special attention was paid to such cases in order to prevent situations in which they would need to postpone or give up their professional career due to youth unemployment and a lack of qualifications.

On the expenditure dimension, the government proposed to subsidise employers giving jobs to the long-term unemployed. In addition, financial support was offered for companies participating in the proposed job-rotation programme. Although these measures would not immediately lower the costs for social insurance payments, the government hoped that greater financial support for employers would be balanced by lower unemployment in the long run. The government also cut spending by implementing new and more rigorous rules for the payment of unemployment assistance.[27] The principle of 'activation' demanded that unemployed people be obliged to accept job offers that were 'reasonable', that is, jobs within a certain distance from the domicile and requiring a lower level of qualification than the person actually had. If a person were to decline such a job offer or refuse to participate in qualification schemes, unemployment assistance payments would be reduced.[28] Some of the proposed measures had an impact on both the generosity and the expenditure dimension. While the job-rotation measure offered the long-term unemployed the chance to be reintegrated into the first labour market, it also financially rewarded employers for employing them. The same logic applied to activation issues proposed to help young people. The general theme of the reform was to improve the employment structure and to increase the employability of individuals by means of specific measures and training. Particularly important for the improvement of the employment structure was the focus on mothers (or parents in general) and the attempt made to improve their chances of re-entering the labour market.

## Actor's Policy Preferences on the Generosity Dimension

By and large, the central idea of improving the professional qualifications of employees was generally well received. The opposition parties in parliament and the organised interest groups acknowledged that measures targeting older people and younger labour market participants were necessary given the state of the German labour market and the high levels of unemployment. The speaker for social policy and labour market issues of the SPD in parliament, Andrea Nahles, emphasised that 'by implementing this legislative change, for the first time in history, job centres will be given the opportunity to take over qualification and education schemes and therefore enable people to maintain their employability before they lose employment' (parliamentary minutes, 2001b, p. 19513). Any criticism centred mainly on the government's proposal of how the additional vocational training schemes would be financed. The intention was to finance the qualification schemes through the unemployment insurance system, which is financed through contributions from employers and employees. This suggestion met criticism from different sides, but all had in common that the different parties disagreed with the financing mechanisms. The Liberal Party (FDP), for instance, accused the government of 'socialising' qualification schemes while at the same time weakening the social insurance scheme (parliamentary minutes, 14. Wahlperiode, 27.09.2001a, p. 18519). The fact that employers, owners of small- and medium-sized businesses who constitute the core electorate of the party, would need to finance qualification schemes through their contributions to the unemployment insurance scheme did not meet with a lot of sympathy, particularly since the beneficiaries of these qualification schemes would be – to a large degree – labour market outsiders who themselves hardly contributed to the insurance scheme and were often supported by unemployment assistance, a scheme that is financed through tax money. The conservative CDU echoed the point that the biggest injustice was to burden the community of solidary contributors to the unemployment insurance scheme with such a nonsensical policy (Deutscher Bundestag 27.09.2001a, p. 18514).

The labour unions and employers' organisations that were consulted before the second reading of the bill generally welcomed the intention to reform the labour market, although the proposed changes did meet with some criticism, particularly the way the government intended to use resources and finance the re-qualification and up-skilling measures for older employees in small- and medium-sized enterprises. Whereas the government planned on financing the additional training measures through the unemployment insurance schemes, the labour unions would have preferred the resources for this initiative to come from tax money.[29] The demand of the DGB to finance additional training measures for elderly employees through taxes rather than the social insurance scheme clearly demonstrates an intention to protect the interests of 'insiders'. People benefiting from this particular legislative change were still part of the workforce, but the likelihood that they may lose their job was increased due to their age. Therefore, financing the qualification schemes through the unemployment insurance scheme made intuitive sense. However, the peak labour union feared that the money spent on qualification schemes would in the end increase the pressure to lower unemployment insurance benefits or lead to an increase in contributory rates for employees. Whereas the labour unions called for qualification schemes to be financed through taxes, the most important employers' organisation (BDA) also opposed the plan to finance the measures through the social insurance scheme. Unlike the labour unions, the BDA called for more self-responsibility on the part of employees and employers (written statement to the 'Ausschuss für Arbeit und Soziales', 10.10.2001, p. 3) rather than financing the expansion of qualification schemes with the unemployment insurance scheme, particularly because the organisation also expected that this would require an upward adjustment of the contributions.

The proposed job-rotation scheme would give the long-term unemployed the opportunity to get 'on-the-job training'. Meanwhile, the principal holder of the position being rotated would have the possibility to participate in further professional development. The up-skilling measures for older employees were intended to adjust and update their qualifications in order to meet the requirements the changing production processes in the industry demanded from workers. This measure was positively evaluated. The exponents of Bündnis90/Die Grünen emphasised that the implementation of the job-rotation principle had the potential to establish a bridge between the long-term unemployed and the first labour market (parliamentary minutes, 199. Sitzung, 9.11.2001, p. 19517). The possible re-integration of the long-term unemployed into the first labour market was one of the most important concerns of the liberal, market-oriented FDP, mainly because they opposed a further increase of the second labour market and a further expansion of the state's involvement in job-creation schemes. Their main concern was that the job-rotation scheme would not be attractive for small- and medium-sized enterprises because of the bureaucratic costs involved.[30]

As also indicated in table 6.7, the BDA (peak employers' organisation) strictly opposed all aspects of the job-rotation scheme for the long-term unemployed, both the proposed financing mechanism through the unemployment insurance scheme and the administration by the public employment agency financed by the unemployment insurance scheme. The main reason for the BDA's opposition was the concern that the unemployment insurance scheme and the employment agencies would have to engage in tasks and duties for which they were not intended. According to their written statement to the committee for 'Labour and Social Order' (p. 5), 'It needs to be clearly

**Table 6.7. Policy Proposals Affecting the Generosity Dimension, JobAQTIV 2001**

| | *Critical of Government Proposal* | *Supportive of Government Proposal* |
|---|---|---|
| **Qualification** | **FDP**<br>BDA<br>ZDH<br>**DGB** | SPD<br>Green Party<br>CDU/CSU |
| **Job-Rotation** | BDA | SPD<br>Green Party<br>CDU/CSU<br>**FDP**<br>**DGB** |

ASU = Arbeitsgemeinschaft Selbständiger Unternehmer (organisation of independent entrepreneurs), BDA = Bundesverein Deutscher Arbeitgeber (employer organisation), DAG = Deutsche Angestelltengewerkschaft (white-collar union), DGB = Deutscher Gewerkschaftsbund (blue-collar union), DIHT = Deutscher Industrie und Handelstag (peak organisation for trade and industry), ÖTV = Gewerkschaft Öffentliche Dienste (public sector union), ZDH = Zentralverband des Deutschen Handwerks (craftsmen organisation).

stated that the job-rotation scheme should help the long-term unemployed to be re-integrated into the labour market. Targeted re-qualification schemes benefiting existing employees need to be avoided. We strongly oppose that the job-rotation scheme is framed as an instrument for empowerment and qualification'. This statement emphasises that the peak employer organisation would prefer reforms that allowed for a more sustainable, less interventionist improvement of the employment situation in Germany.

## Actor's Policy Preferences on the Spending Dimension

Despite the fact that the establishment of private placement centres provoked much criticism from the left-wing opposition in 1994 (when the 'Beschäftigungsförderungsgesetz' was discussed in parliament), the JobAQTIV legislation drafted by the Schröder government aimed at further strengthening the role of private placement agencies. In addition, the legislation proposed the development of systematically 'profiling' people when they first entered unemployment. The profiling measure was to enable agencies to more efficiently match unemployed people with the needs of companies seeking new employees. As table 6.8 indicates, the opposition parties, particularly the Liberal Party, generally welcomed this change. The Greens, although part of the governing coalition, asked that the measures be accompanied by improved quality control and rules to be followed by the private agencies. They argued that the long-term unemployed in particular and those with a precarious standing in the labour market, furthermore, needed qualified personnel to help them to re-enter the labour market. This was also the request of the peak labour unions, which were still critical of private placement agencies and did not approve of the plan to further strengthen the role of private actors in helping to address labour market problems.

Even though Ursula Engelen-Kefer (DGB) mentioned during the hearing that past experiences with private placement agencies had not all been exclusively positive and that it would be important to establish quality control and standards similar to those in place for the public placement agencies (hearing of the 'Ausschuss für Arbeit und Sozialordnung', 10.10.2001), she acknowledged that 'profiling' could possibly be a helpful tool in ensuring that unemployed people found a new job quickly. The employers' organisations especially welcomed the fact that the 'profiling' would take place immediately after someone lost his or her job, this being seen as an important step to prevent long-term unemployment.

The plan to subsidise those employers participating in the job-rotation scheme (by taking on a long-term unemployed person while regular employees were participating in additional vocational training) was not subject to as much in-depth debate as the previously discussed measure. The labour unions merely positively acknowledged that the government had included an issue in

**Table 6.8. Policy Proposals Affecting the Spending Dimension, JobAQTIV 2001**

| | *Critical of Government Proposal* | *Supportive of Government Proposal* |
|---|---|---|
| **'Profiling'** | | SPD<br>Green Party<br>CDU/CSU<br>FDP<br>DGB<br>BDA<br>ZDH |
| **'Job-Rotation II'** | PDS/Die Linke<br>IG Metall<br>DGB<br>BDA | SPD<br>Green Party<br>CDU/CSU<br>FDP |

ASU = Arbeitsgemeinschaft Selbständiger Unternehmer (organisation of independent entrepreneurs), BDA = Bundesverein Deutscher Arbeitgeber (employer organisation), DAG = Deutsche Angestelltengewerkschaft (white-collar union), DGB = Deutscher Gewerkschaftsbund (blue-collar union), DIHT = Deutscher Industrie und Handelstag (peak organisation for trade and industry), ÖTV = Gewerkschaft Öffentliche Dienste (public sector union), ZDH= Zentralverband des Deutschen Handwerks (craftsmen organisation).

the reform that had previously been raised and was also part of the discussions taking place within the 'Alliance for Jobs'. However, the practical application of the financial issues related to the job-rotation scheme was criticised by the peak labour union, mainly because the legislation did not exclude formerly long-term unemployed people who were placed in a company by a temporary employment agency. Including the long-term unemployed with temporary contracts into this scheme basically meant that fewer regularly employed workers, who constitute the core constituency of the labour unions, would benefit from the government programme. This criticism not only reveals the labour union's preferential treatment of the core workforce but also shows their general scepticism related to the increasing importance of temporary employment in general. The strong opposition towards temporary contracts was mostly based on the observation that temporary employees were paid less than the negotiated wage, thereby undermining sectoral agreements with the result that wages of the core workforce were exposed to ever-increasing pressure not only from the global market but also through domestic policy changes.[31]

The leftist opposition party, PDS, took a very similar to the peak labour union. They were particularly critical of the fact that employees working for temporary employment agencies would also be entitled to participate in the programmes subsidised by the state or the unemployment insurance scheme. The reason why both the PDS and the labour unions were fiercely opposed to temporary employees benefiting from subsidised 'on the job training' or extra vocational training is because they were paid less than normal employees. The key labour union representing industry ('IG-Metall') even complained that the new legislation would further increase the crowding-out of older skilled workers who were covered by negotiated agreements and therefore had higher salaries.

Strengthening the rights of temporary employment agencies by extending the period someone is allowed to work on a temporary contract was also highly disputed. This proposal would significantly contribute to the liberalisation of the rigid German labour market in which employees holding regular contracts enjoyed high levels of employment security. In individual cases of job loss, the liberalisation of the temporary employment agency market could lead to the development of a low-wage sector and make it difficult for people caught in this sector to get a regular employment contract. It was first and foremost the Green Party, also part of the government, which accused the government of establishing a low-wage sector through the back door (Deutscher Bundestag 27.09.2001a, p. 18518). Both the labour unions and the Green Party questioned whether extending temporary contracts would really serve as a bridge between unemployment and regular employment and the full reintegration into the first labour market (see Deutscher Bundestag [27.09.2001a, p. 18520] or the minutes of the hearing organised by the 'Ausschuss für Arbeit und Sozialordnung', 10. October, p. 17). The conservative opposition, on the contrary, called for a more encompassing and drastic reform of the labour market, including cuts in unemployment insurance benefits and contributions. Their main argument was that even though deregulating the labour market would have a negative impact on wages, overall employment security would increase. This was something that the FDP did not associate with the JobAQTIV legislation proposed by the government.[32]

One issue that was mentioned throughout the discussion but that was not included in the JobAQTIV legislation was the plan to merge the unemployment assistance scheme with the social assistance scheme. The conservative and liberal parties in particular called for this step, in response to hopes for a more powerful tool to promote employment by focusing on re-integrating people into the workplace without the frictions that the coexistence of the two schemes were causing. The combined scheme should be financed through tax money and guarantee a means-tested income independent from previous earnings.[33] The government was prepared to give in on this issue but decided that to present a reform proposal before the elections would be strategically unwise (see minutes of the 'Ausschuss für Arbeit und Sozialordnung', 103. Meeting, 10th October, p. 15). This was because on the one hand, this legislative change would have touched upon the responsibilities of the 'Länder', and on the other, both the labour unions and the exponents of the traditional Left were clearly against such a change.[34] During the public hearing, the representative of 'IG-Metall' said: 'We categorically oppose a combination of the unemployment assistance and the social assistance schemes. They follow a completely different logic: whereas unemployment assistance still aims at maintaining (to some extent) the standard of living, social assistance mainly aims at minimising frictions' (without mentioning what frictions he was referring to – EH) (minutes of the hearing of the 'Ausschuss für Arbeit und Sozialordnung', 103. Sitzung, 10. October 2001, p. 6).

In addition, the conservative and liberal parties in opposition asserted and re-emphasised that future reforms of the labour market should also aim at strengthening and increasing the low-wage sector and that the 630 Mark jobs (the so-called Mini-jobs) should be abandoned. These 630 Mark jobs had been created by the former government, initially to suppress the shadow economy. It was also a measure to allow women to take on part-time jobs that were subject to only minimal social insurance payments and not subject to income tax. While this was certainly an important issue and motivated women to re-enter the labour market, these jobs were not covered by social insurance and women therefore were not able to increase their pension rights unless they decided to contribute to the insurance scheme on a voluntary basis. The so-called 630 Mark jobs thus mostly contributed to the establishment of a two-class workforce in which women were to some extent locked in employment relationships that were characterised by low pay, low or no insurance coverage and little room for professional development. This was changed by the Social Democratic/Green Party government after the elections when they required employers to contribute to the social insurance schemes, which made the scheme for some employers less attractive.

During the parliamentary debate, Horst Seehofer (CDU/CSU) proposed to increase the low-wage sector by specifically subsidising unemployed people who accept a low-wage job by topping up their salary (parliamentary minutes, 14. Wahlperiode, 27.09.2001a, p. 18515). According to the parties in opposition, the government also missed the chance to make sure that people living on social assistance or unemployment assistance would not receive more money than someone with a job in the low-wage sector.[35] Apart from the degressive characteristic inherent within the unemployment assistance scheme, the duration or level of unemployment insurance benefits would not change. Even though this had been criticised, the government did not propose to cut either benefits or their duration period.

## Mediating Effects of Political Constraints

The coalition between the Social Democrats and the Greens only had a majority in both chambers during their first year in power. The first year of the new red-green coalition, however, was also overshadowed by internal disputes, particularly between Schröder and his finance minister Lafontaine, who represented the two wings of the Social Democrats. The quarrels during the first year slowed down their reform projects, and after the resignation of Lafontaine in March 1999, the government aimed for a fresh start. After a series of by-elections in various 'Länder', the power balance shifted and the government was soon faced with an opposition majority in the 'Bundesrat'. The additional fact that the government had no majority in the 'Länderkammer' might have had an impact on the design and content of the proposed legislation. None of the changes proposed in the JobAQTIV reform proposal touched on the competencies of the 'Länder'; therefore, the legislation did not need the approval by the 'Bundesrat', nor did the 'Bundesrat' appeal to the mediation committee to extend and prolong the process. Changes that would have been in the realm of the 'Länder' would have mainly affected the expenditure dimension (i.e. if the legislation had had an impact on the budget of the sub-national units). It can be argued that since the government was under pressure to cut expenditure, it might have tried to impose more of the financial burden on the sub-national units, for example, shortening the period of unemployment insurance benefits paid often leads to an increase in social assistance payments. Social assistance, however, is administered through the 'Länder' and therefore any change would have needed the support of the 'Länderkammer'.

The government additionally, at least during this first year in power, tried not to lose the support of the labour unions, a fact that was criticised and mentioned during the parliamentary debate. Irmgard Schwaetzer from the FDP accused the government of failing to initiate a proper reform of the labour market because it was 'in bed' with the labour unions.[36] The Liberal Party also mentioned the fact that the closeness between the left-wing government and the labour unions had catastrophic consequences for the unemployed. This indicates that the opposition was not convinced that the policy decisions and changes implemented by the government so far had had a positive impact on the long-term unemployed, who represent a large group of labour market outsiders. While keeping the support of the labour unions was one thing, trying to prevent the alienation of the coalition partner, the Green Party, at this stage of the electoral cycle might have been another reason for the relatively prudent start of the labour market reform process. However, the relative power of the Green Party within the coalition should not be overestimated. After the resignation of Lafontaine, which significantly weakened the impact of the traditional wing of the Social Democrats, and the clear commitment of Schröder to 'Third Way' policies, the Green Party had little potential to threaten the Social Democrats, firstly, because they also had internal disputes between different camps, and secondly, it became clear that Schröder would also be willing to govern with the FDP in order to implement the non-ideological economic policies and reforms promoted in the Blair/Schröder paper.

## 6.7 DISCUSSION AND OUTLOOK

The timing and content of the JobAQTIV law were constrained by several parallel developments and processes. First, the government had to signal that the announcements made during the electoral campaign in 1998 to reform the labour market and significantly decrease the level of unemployment were not only empty promises. In addition, the pressure on the government to cure 'the sick man of Europe', as the German economy had been labelled by the Economist in 1999, was constantly increasing. Even though the Social Democrats campaigned on lowering unemployment in Germany, six months into the legislation, 500,000 more people were added to the statistics (Der Spiegel, 11/1999, p. 26). Proposing some remedies to address the rigidity of the labour market in the run-up to the 2002 elections was therefore vital. Despite this combination of political, economic and international pressure, the government was facing significant internal constraints, which explains the reluctance of the government to engage in reform activities at an earlier stage or propose more encompassing reforms. One of the key reasons was that the labour unions would withdraw from the 'Alliance for Jobs'. This fear was due especially to the fact that the traditional Left was poorly represented in the government since the resignation of Oskar Lafontaine. At this stage, Chancellor Schröder was still reluctant to damage the relationship with the labour unions. However, towards the end of the first term of the Schröder government, the number of unemployed in Germany increased again and exceeded the level of four million, a serious problem for Schröder, who wanted to be re-elected and had promised to reduce unemployment to below 3.5 million during the previous electoral campaign.[37] It was with this background that the Job-AQTIV package was drafted.

The JobAQTIV legislation as implemented in November 2001 included attempts to re-integrate labour market 'outsiders' and help people with low levels of professional skills and education to get 'on-the-job training' and thereby acquire further professional education. However, these positive intentions directed at labour market 'outsiders' were significantly moderated by the concessions made towards labour market 'insiders'. These compensating measures happened mainly through the promotion of additional professional training for (older) employees in regular work relationships. The additional training was to be financed through the unemployment insurance scheme. This fact was criticised by both the labour unions and the employers' organisations. According to the government, the JobAQTIV legislation would finance itself during the first year and would lead to fewer payments in unemployment insurance benefits and unemployment assistance benefits in the future. Retrenchment should not happen through cuts in benefits but through increased efficiency in the placement of the unemployed. Even though the parties in opposition called for a more encompassing reform of the social insurance scheme (especially unemployment assistance and social assistance), which would open opportunities for more extensive retrenchment, the governing coalition between the Social Democrats and the Greens did not include these suggestions and for the time being avoided the topic.

Table 6.9 offers a summary of how the reform proposals are expected to have an influence on two broader groups of labour market participants, the

**Table 6.9. Reform Issues and Direction of Changes 'JobAQTIV Law 2001'**

| | | *Effect on* | |
|---|---|---|---|
| | *Reform issues* | *'Insiders'* | *'Outsiders'* |
| **Generosity** | Secure work for specific groups (elderly/young people) by offering them the opportunity to participate in training measures | + | +/– |
| | Subsidies for employers/firms for temporarily employing long-term unemployed people | – | + |
| **Spending** | Implementation of degressive aspect of the unemployment assistance scheme (if person declines a job, qualification measures) | neutral | – |
| | Increase of the maximum period allowed for temporary employment ('Leiharbeit') | neutral | +/– |
| | Job-rotation scheme (unemployed person – temporarily – takes the job of a person that participates in a qualification scheme) | + | + |
| **Neutral** | No more waiting period for newly unemployed wishing to participate in training/ qualification measures, 'profiling' of newly unemployed through private agencies | + | neutral |

*Legend*: + implicates that the implemented measure had a positive effect for the group indicated; – implicates that the reform negatively affected 'insiders'/'outsiders'.

'insiders', which are in the German context mostly skilled, male employees with regular employment relationships, and the 'outsiders', which in Germany are people who often combine long-term unemployment with low levels of skills. A second pool of potential labour market 'outsiders' in the German context are women.[38] A qualitative assessment of the summarised measures shows that, by and large, the benefits of this reform favoured labour market 'insiders' more than 'outsiders'. While the majority of the proposals helping labour market 'outsiders' were of a temporary nature (i.e. the subsidies for employers or the job-rotation scheme) and did not necessarily help 'outsiders' to secure regular employment, the same measures consolidated the positions of labour market 'insiders' (i.e. on-the-job training), or at the very least, their impact on people with a regular employment contract was neutral (i.e. the extension of temporary work or the implementation of unemployment assistance benefits, which were conditional on the fulfilment of specific requirements). This interpretation is in line with recent figures which show that despite the series of profound labour market reforms implemented by the Schröder government, Germany still has a considerable number of long-term unemployed (Spermann 2014), and the estimated impact the reforms had on overall unemployment was small (Launov and Wälde 2013).[39]

Despite its limited scope, the legislative change brought about by the JobAQTIV law is an important landmark in German labour market policy-making as it anticipated some of the debates that became more prominent in subsequent reform plans. It was a clear shift away from a passive system of guaranteeing income security and the maintenance of living standards towards a more active labour market policy which aimed at activating the unemployed. With this emphasis on activating people rather than reforming passive help through existing social security institutions, the law is generally viewed as one of the first legislative packages implemented in Germany which can be considered as part of the so-called Third Way reforms (Huo 2009). The JobAQTIV reform also paved the way for the subsequent Hartz reforms, which integrated a number of changes which were already on the table, particularly the reform of the unemployment insurance and assistance schemes. After implementing the JobAQTIV legislation, the government benefited from a window of opportunity to draft and implement more encompassing reforms. The window opened due to a scandal within the public placement agencies, which published inaccurate statistics on their performance. The figures on successfully placed people were consistently massaged and did not reflect reality. This scandal played into the hands of the FDP, which had always criticised the state-run job agencies of being inefficient. In the wake of this scandal, the government established the 'Hartz' Commission, consisting of business representatives, politicians and members of peak employer and labour unions. In early 2002, the commission started to work on reform proposals, subsequently known as the Hartz reforms. The commission presented its report to the government in August 2002, and already in December 2002, the first package of proposals based on the commission's report were adopted in parliament. Table 6.10 gives an overview of the key reform issues included in the Hartz reforms.

These reforms mark a turning point in German labour market policy-making as they had a profound impact on the structure of the formerly two-tiered unemployment insurance scheme. In essence, the four packages

**Table 6.10. Summary Hartz Reforms**

| | *Implemented* | *Key Reform Issues* |
|---|---|---|
| **Hartz I** | January 2003 | Establishment of placement agencies (personal service agencies) and job centres, operating as temporary agencies.<br>Further liberalisation of temporary work.<br>Programmes for further vocational education allowing for more flexibility in the use of qualification schemes.<br>Renewal of the definition of 'acceptable employment' that shifts the burden of proof of why employment offer is not acceptable to the unemployed. |
| **Hartz II** | April 2003 | Establishment of job centres.<br>New regulation of mini-jobs.<br>Implementation of subsidies for entrepreneurs (so-called Ich-AGs). |
| **Hartz III** | April 2004 | Tighter eligibility criteria for unemployment insurance benefits (in order to receive benefits, unemployed people had to contribute for at least twelve months during the previous past twenty-four months, as opposed to twelve months over a period of thirty-six months).<br>Implementation of provision to allow for a up to 30 per cent cut in benefits if person refuses to take up a reasonable/acceptable job offer. |
| **Hartz IV** | January 2005 | Merger of the social assistance and unemployment assistance scheme (implementation of `Arbeitslosengeld II).<br>Implementation of 'One-Euro' Jobs: Jobs in the public interest paid one Euro/hour (integrates long-term unemployed into the second labour market, while still getting the new form of unemployment assistance).<br>Shortening of the duration unemployment benefits are paid.<br>Implementation of new sanctions if 'acceptable' jobs are refused. |

strengthened the activation and liberalisation aspects of earlier reforms, leading to a significant increase in the number of people contracted with temporary employment agencies, and people holding precarious and low-paid jobs. Most important, however, the relatively generous unemployment assistance scheme was merged with the social assistance scheme, which provides means-tested minimum benefits. This significantly altered the system from being predominantly focused on status protection into one where people with irregular employment biographies and difficult perspectives in the labour market face a latent threat of downward social mobility. Overall, the merger of the social assistance and the unemployment assistance schemes negatively affected roughly 50 per cent of the long-term unemployed (Launov and Wälde 2013), and on average, people in long-term unemployment were financially worse-off than before the reform, meaning that these people received less support through the social insurance scheme after the implementation of the Hartz reforms.

Overall, the series of reforms led to the expected liberalisation of the labour market with the positive effect that the matching process between the unemployed and potential employers was improved with the newly established job centres and the better profiling of job seekers. Unemployment in general also significantly decreased, though this positive development can be attributed to a significant degree to the period of strong economic growth Germany experienced between 2004 and 2008. The positive unemployment figures, however, stand in contrast to the stagnation in the development of wages and the fact that workers – after spells of unemployment – often had to accept lower salaries (Engbom, Detragiache and Raei 2015). In addition, and as predicted by the previously discussed quantitative analysis of the JobAQTIV reform, the reforms did not affect all segments of the labour market equally. While figures show that the average duration of an employment relationship is longer now than right after the implementation of the reforms, people with irregular work histories and previous spells of unemployment are more likely to be caught in a vicious circle where temporary employment contracts alternate with periods during which the individual falls back on receiving the newly created unemployment assistance (vom Berge et al. 2015). This so-called revolving door pattern mostly affects people in the low-wage service industry or people with insufficient professional skills working in the industrial sector.

Although the aforementioned reform packages were contested during the drafting process and during the parliamentary debates, the actual implementation went relatively smoothly. However, the reform packages generated a backlash, and its impact and consequences were often at the centre of public debates. While it is still difficult to clearly link some of the more recent developments within Germany society and the labour market to specific reform packages, it is now widely accepted that the reforms placed more responsibility and duties upon job seekers and that not all segments of the labour market were equally affected by these reforms. Generally, it is now established that the prospects of low-skilled labour market participants and typical labour market 'outsiders' were negatively affected by this change of paradigm. The increased flexibility of employment patterns particularly affected low-skilled workers with jobs in the service economy. The new regulatory environment gave rise to temporary work agencies whose employees enjoyed significantly lower levels of employment protection. The proliferation of temporary and part-time employees went hand in hand with the growth of the service sector. For a long time, high non-wage labour costs endangered the competitiveness of the German economy, particularly the service sector (Manow and Seils 2000b, p. 138). However, the increased flexibility to employ people with temporary contracts was particularly beneficial for the German service sector.[40] Skilled labour market participants, the so-called insiders with permanent contracts, on the other hand, still enjoy a high degree of employment protection. Employment protection essentially remained largely unchanged during the latest labour market reforms, and Germany still features among the top countries when it comes to employment protection.[41] Despite the fact that over recent years, media and talk shows have often lamented the decline and disappearance of the German middle class; due to the aforementioned changes in the labour market and the accompanying changes in the social security schemes, the middle class has proven to be resilient and is able to preserve and consolidate its privileges, as recent research shows.

Still, the series of deregulating labour market reforms has had a significant impact on overall societal developments. While the German economy has been thriving and key economic and social indicators are positive, inequality has been increasing (see figure 6.3). Those with fewer skills and lower levels of education have been left behind and the opportunities available to them to move up the social ladder have decreased. While showing an upward trend in the aftermath of the war, recent scholarship shows that social mobility is declining for people born in the late 1970s and 1980s. One factor that affects this new downward trend in social mobility is the recent changes in the structure of the labour market which opened new pathways for downward social mobility (Pollak 2010, 2012). Recent studies show that poverty in Germany is increasing and that people who fall below the poverty line face more difficulties in overcoming poverty. In fact, during the 1990s, up to 50 per cent of people who were considered 'poor' were able to overcome this status within a time frame of five years. More recently (between 2003 and 2008), only 30 per cent of the poor were able to achieve this step, meaning that poverty in Germany has become more persistent (Groh-Samberg 2015). In addition, Germany is one of the few countries where

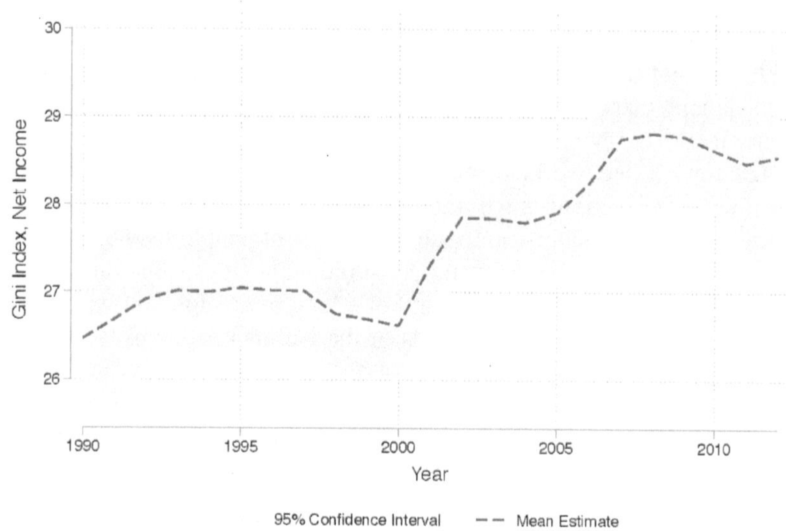


**Figure 6.3. Net Income Inequality in Germany (1990–2012)**

wage inequality has increased during the past decade rather than decreased (Fredriksen 2012).

While not all of these trends and changes can be attributed to the above-described labour market reforms and the merger of the unemployment assistance scheme with the generally means-tested social assistance, these processes worked as facilitators in a changing economic environment.

## NOTES

1 This view has its origins in the Christian/Catholic principle of 'subsidiarity', according to which the responsibility for providing help and care should always lie with the smallest unit (e.g. the family rather than the community or the state). Welfare state policies in Germany and other countries with strong Christian Democratic parties are heavily influenced by this principle. For a more detailed discussion of the impact of the subsidiarity doctrine, see van Kersbergen and Manow (2009) and Lewis and Oster (1994). Scholarly interest in the impact of Christian Democratic parties on welfare state development and policies has increased recently, and studies emphasise the importance of Christian Democratic parties in the development of various continental welfare states (see e.g. Manow and van Kersbergen 2008; Seeleib-Kaiser, van Dyk and Roggenkamp 2008; van Kersbergen 1995).

2 Two examples that greatly influenced policy-making in Germany are the independent and powerful central bank 'Bundesbank' and the strong federal constitutional court ('Bundesverfassungsgericht'). Both institutions have the capacity to either limit the government's room to manoeuvre or to alter/block legislative acts in retrospect. Compared with other Western countries, the 'Bundesbank' always enjoyed a high degree of autonomy and was considered to be the most powerful central bank in the west (Schmidt 1987, p.150). The impact that the constitutional court has on legislative action and politics has led scholars to coin the term governing with judges (see e.g. Stone Sweet 2000). The reason why both institutions are equipped with far-reaching competencies is related to past experiences with totalitarian regimes.

3 Since the reunification in 1990, Germany consists of the following sixteen 'Bundesländer': Baden-Württemberg, Bavaria, Berlin, Brandenburg, Bremen, Hamburg, Hesse, Mecklenburg-Vorpommern, Lower Saxony, North Rhine-Westphalia, Rhineland-Palatinate, Saarland, Saxony, Saxony-Anhalt, Schleswig-Holstein and Thuringia. The 'Bundesrat' consists of the members of the 'Länder' governments.

4 According to Brunner and Debus (2008, p. 235), only 66 out of 6,107 (1.1 per cent) legislative proposals requiring the consent of both chambers ('zustimmungspflichtige Gesetze') have been blocked by the 'Bundesrat'.

5 'Party state' mainly refers to the constitutional clause stating that the Federal Republic be governed by competing parties. The prominent role of political parties is additionally strengthened by the fact that parties are to a large extent financed by the state.

6 The first 'grand coalition' was led by Kiesinger (CDU) between 1966 and 1969, and the second by Merkel (CDU) between 2005 and 2009. 'Grand coalitions' occur more often at the state level (see e.g. Schniewind, Freitag and Vatter 2009; Shikano and Linhart 2010).

7 Between 1957 and 1983, these three parties (together with the CSU, the Bavarian sister party of the CDU) were the only ones represented in the 'Bundestag'. The major reason why small and niche parties are not represented in the national parliament is the 5 per cent hurdle that artificially limits the number of parties entering the 'Bundestag'.

8 However, Mecklenburg-Vorpommern and Berlin were governed by a coalition that included the PDS.

9 The Green Party has been part of a national government coalition only once, with the SPD. More recently, coalitions between the Christian Democrats and the Green Party have been formed at the sub-national level (e.g. in Hamburg 2004).

10 Until 1998 (with a short exception between 1966 and 1969 when Germany was governed by a grand coalition for the first time), the FDP was always part of the government.

11 Union membership and density in Germany was relatively stable between 1960 and 1980. However, union density started to decrease during the 1990s, a trend which was briefly arrested due to reunification, when the system of industrial relations was extended to the new 'Bundesländer'. The reunification of the

two Germanys did not profoundly affect the functioning of the German model (Manow and Seils 2000b, p. 137). However, after the peak in the early 1990s, union density started to decrease sharply (see e.g. Fitzenberger, Kohn and Wang 2006; Schnabel and Wagner 2005; Wallerstein and Western 2000).

12 The close connection between the Social Democratic Party and labour unions is best illustrated by the following numbers: During the twelfth legislative period (1990–1994), over 70 per cent of the Social Democratic members of the German parliament were also union members. Despite the fact that overall union membership has been decreasing, this figure even increased to over 80 per cent during the fourteenth legislative period (1999–2003) (Trampusch 2003, p. 92). More recent work corroborates this evidence and conceptualises unions as 'a group inside Germany's composite SPD' (Jacoby and Behrens 2016, p. 292).

13 Katzenstein (1987) described Germany as a semi-sovereign, weak state. According to Streeck (2003), the German economy and welfare state benefited from this weakness during the years of the economic miracle.

14 The collapse of the international financial system together with the first oil crisis led to a joint increase in inflation and unemployment caused by declining demands, a phenomenon known as stagflation.

15 Between 1960 and 1973, the average level of unemployment was 0.8 per cent (Schmidt 1987, p. 140).

16 In the 'Varieties of Capitalism' literature (Hall and Soskice 2001; Thelen 2001), Germany is the most typical example of a 'coordinated market economy'. The competitive advantage of 'coordinated market economies' in the global economy is based on several factors: (1) a particular financial system that offers long-term support for companies allowing them to develop long-term strategies; (2) long-lasting work contracts and strong commitments of the employees to their employer; (3) industry-level wage bargaining; and (4) an education and training system that produces highly skilled workers.

17 The Varieties of Capitalism literature (Hall and Soskice 2001) views the German model as the ideal type of a coordinated market economy in which the different institutional frameworks, such as the financial infrastructure, the educational system and vocational training, and the state-led regulatory framework, constitute institutional complementarities that provide a highly stable environment for a prosperous economy.

18 All quotes are translated by the author.

19 In 1994, the DGB was the umbrella organisation for over sixteen unions and was mainly responsible for the representation of interest at the national level. DAG has previously been independent from the DGB and represented the interests of employees from various sectors.

20 Werner Schulz (Bündnis90/Die Grünen): 'the idea that the government plans to improve the conditions for self-employment is not wrong. The measure, however, is insufficient' (parliamentary minutes, 219. Sitzung, p. 18938).

21 Gregor Gysi (PDS/Linke Liste): 'your arguments cannot hide the fact that the government is trying to commercialise unemployment with negative effects for the unskilled labour force. This is an attempt to set up a business to organise unemployment and the unemployed, rather than leaving the responsibilities with

the public authorities' (parliamentary minutes, 219. Sitzung, 12. Wahlperiode 14.04.1994b, p. 18936).

22 The 'first' labour market is the common, competitive labour market. The so-called second labour market refers to jobs within (public) job-creation schemes.

23 The paper essentially outlined the future of European Social Democracy and aimed at reconciling traditional Social Democratic values such as equality, fairness and solidarity with a pragmatic economic policy. According to the 'Third Way', economic policy-making should not be ideologically grounded but should take into account globalisation and increasing competition between industrialised countries, which require new sets of policy solutions.

24 The previous 'Bündnis für Arbeit', which was established in 1995/1996 during the last years of the Kohl-government, failed because of the withdrawal of the employers' organisations from the alliance. The second 'Alliance for Jobs' was active only during the first legislative period of the Schröder government.

25 AQTIV is the abbreviation for A = 'Aktivierung' (activation), Q = 'Qualifizierung' (qualification), T = 'Trainieren' (training), I = 'Investieren' (investment), V = 'Vermitteln' (brokerage/improved placement).

26 The 'Hartz Commission' was established in 2001 and was chaired by Peter Hartz, a former Volkswagen manager. The correct name of the legislative acts was 'Gesetze für moderne Dienstleistung am Arbeitsmarkt'. From 2002, four different 'Hartz' reforms were implemented, all aimed at strengthening the principle of activation and at increasing labour market efficiency and flexibility.

27 Unemployment assistance was paid after a person lost his or her entitlement to unemployment benefits. Unlike unemployment benefits, which were paid through the unemployment insurance scheme, unemployment assistance was financed with tax money.

28 The government expected that an average decrease of one month of unemployment per person resulting from better job placement strategies and additional qualification schemes would save up to two billion DM/year (see parliamentary minutes, 2001b, p. 19516).

29 Ursula Engelen-Kefer (DGB): 'We completely agree that additional qualification schemes are needed. However, we think that they should not be financed through the contributory insurance schemes but through tax money', minutes 'Ausschuss für Arbeit und Soziales' (10.10.2001, p. 9).

30 Karl-Josef Laumann (CDU): 'In my opinion, these instruments will lead to an inflated bureaucracy in the job placement centre without really helping the unemployed' (parliamentary minutes, 2001b, p. 19515).

31 'The principle of the wage bargaining autonomy, which is ensured by the social state, must not be broken' (DGB, written statement for the 'Ausschuss für Arbeit und Sozialordnung', 10.10.2001.)

32 Irmgard Schwaetzer (FDP): 'Why doesn't the government acknowledge that for most employees a decrease in salary would be better than losing their job entirely?' (parliamentary minutes, 14. Wahlperiode, 190. Sitzung, 27.09.2001a, p. 18519).

33 The frictions between the two schemes were mainly caused by the different duties and rights that the beneficiaries had. People on unemployment assistance,

for example, were eligible to participate in training schemes, whereas those on social assistance had no rights to further vocational training.

34 During the debate on the JobAQTIV legislation, Karl-Josef Laumann, responsible for social issues within the CDU, accused the government of not being brave enough to propose the combination of the two social security schemes to the parliament (parliamentary minutes, 2001b, p. 19515).

35 Similar discussions and changes occurred in Ireland, where the government had to eliminate so-called welfare traps that worked as disincentives to accepting jobs.

36 Irmgard Schwaetzer (FDP): her actual words in German were 'Sie, Herr Riester, haben in der Arbeitsmarktpolitik versagt. Sie werden Ihre Ziele nicht erreichen. Deshalb kann ich Ihnen nur sagen: Wachen Sie auf! Geben Sie endlich den Schmusekurs mit den Gewerkschaften auf. Er hat katastrophale Folgen für die Arbeitslosen gehabt' (parliamentary minutes, 27.09.2001a, p. 18519).

37 Schröder actually told the electorate that he should not get re-elected if unemployment was not down to 3.5 million after his first term in office.

38 Although in the draft of the legislative proposal, one emphasis of the reform was to facilitate and reconcile family and work, particularly for women, the actual final measures related to this aspect of the reform boiled down to how the time spent on child care would be taken into account when assessing their right for insurance entitlements (i.e. unemployment insurance). The actual problems women were facing, particularly the lack of child care facilities, were not addressed in the legislation but at times mentioned during the parliamentary debate.

39 Spermann (2014) shows that since 2009, the percentage of the unemployed who classify as long-term unemployed has increased from 33 per cent to 36 per cent.

40 Employment in the service sector in Germany rose from roughly 60 per cent in 1995 to 70 per cent in 2000 (see World Bank Data 2017).

41 See http://www.oecd.org/employment/emp/.

# Chapter 7

# Ireland

The following case study focuses on Ireland and the way different coalition governments shaped labour market policies in an institutional environment characterised by low levels of political constraints. As opposed to the leftist coalition government in Germany, the way the left-wing rainbow coalition reformed labour market and social policies does not show traits of clientelistic policy-making in favour of labour market insiders. By and large, the reform caters towards different societal groups with a clear focus on improving the situation of labour market outsiders. The chapter first focuses on the Irish political economy and party landscape before carefully assessing two reform processes which took place under different coalition governments.

## 7.1 WELFARE SYSTEM AND LABOUR MARKET

Ireland is often neglected in cross-country comparative research, partly because the Irish party system has been characterised as being too distinct and not suitable for cross-country comparison. Another reason that has been brought forward is that economic development in Ireland was delayed; therefore, the comparison of Ireland with other Western European countries in the sphere of public policy-making seemed inappropriate.[1] However, the reasons justifying the special treatment of the Republic of Ireland in comparative party politics no longer apply. The Irish economy, welfare state and labour market have undergone significant changes over recent decades and the growing interdependence and integration of the Irish economy into the world economy means that Ireland is facing the same challenges as other Western European countries.

In Ireland, the institutional setting and the initial social security schemes were established under British rule and kept once the country gained independence in 1921. Using Esping-Andersen's typology once again, Ireland comes closest to the prototype of a liberal welfare state which guarantees means-tested benefits but does not offer comprehensive social insurance schemes. The originally limited welfare system was largely identical to that of the United Kingdom. However, traditional Catholic values had a strong influence on the further development of the welfare state once the Republic of Ireland gained independence, and some schemes, especially the unemployment scheme, differ significantly from those of other liberal welfare states.[2] Existing scholarship has thus compared the Irish welfare state to those of Southern European countries such as Italy or Spain (see Callan and Nolan 2000; Leibfried 1992), in which political parties holding on to Christian values had a significant impact in designing social security schemes.[3]

The origins of the welfare state system go back to the 'Poor Relief (Ireland) Act' of 1838, implemented by the British authorities who then ruled the country. The scheme was implemented in the hope of tackling the problem of destitute Irish immigrants in British cities (Burke 1999). The key goal of the policy was to keep people off the streets by offering them housing (so-called workhouses) (Maguire 1986). Further to the poor law, a very basic health care system was introduced in 1851. However, the Poor Relief Act did not establish a social security network; it was only in 1897, with the implementation of the 'Workmen's Compensation Act' that the British authorities started to protect the rights of workers. This law required employers to compensate their employees in case of occupational injuries. In this respect, Ireland is similar to Germany, where occupational injury insurance was one of the first social security schemes to be implemented.

In 1908, a means-tested old-age pension reform system was introduced (at the same time as it was introduced in Britain), and three years later, in 1911, the first unemployment benefit scheme was implemented. The British were the first to implement an unemployment insurance scheme based on flat-rate contributions by employees, employers and the state. Even though only limited numbers of workers were covered by this initial unemployment insurance, its introduction was a novelty because it marked a move away from the poor law and established the idea that an employee had a right to be relieved from poverty. Shortly before Irish independence, the scheme was extended to cover all manual workers with the exception of people working in agriculture and domestic service. However, as the Irish economy was dominated by the agrarian sector at the time and only a minority of the workforce was employed in the industrial sector, not many people benefited from the expansion of this policy. In fact, the influential Catholic Church actually opposed the proposed changes, arguing that the scheme would be too expensive and also stressing that the small number of wage earners in Ireland would not justify the extension of the scheme (Burke 1999, p. 22).

After Irish independence and during the inter-war years, the Fine Gael–led government made no effort to further expand social policies. The key reasons for this stagnation was that Irish economic performance did not allow for a further expansion of social security schemes, but also because the Catholic Church was a key player in the provision of welfare and care, and used its political influence and the dominance of Catholic/Christian values within society to shape policies. After the Second World War, the Irish welfare state system started to slowly catch up with the rest of Western Europe (Ó Riain and O'Connell 2000) and the importance of the Catholic Church as a key actor started to decrease when social policies provided by the state gradually started to become more acceptable and were actively promoted by political parties.[4]

In 1952, the unemployment scheme, implemented in 1933, was reformed and extended: in addition to the unemployment scheme, sickness insurance and some child care/family policies were included in the new legislative bill. The new unemployment insurance now also encompassed people employed in the agricultural sector, which was a significant improvement since a large number of people were still gainfully employed in the agricultural sector. However, due to the severe economic crisis during the 1950s and 1960s, the expansion of social policies disappeared from the political agenda.[5] It was mostly due to the parties in opposition (Fine Gael and Labour), who brought forward social insurance issues, that the means-tested pension system, introduced in 1908, was substantially reformed and expanded in 1961. With this reform, pension rights became universal for blue- and white-collar workers and, from the age of seventy, people were entitled to flat-rate benefits (up to a certain earnings ceiling). Nevertheless, owing to Ireland's opt-out of common social provisions when joining the European Economic Community in 1973, a major window of opportunity to redesign the social policy legacy was missed.

During the 1980s, the Commission on Social Welfare published a report which documented the need for fundamental reforms. Even though it was widely acknowledged that health care, education and other social policies did not meet modern standards, the severe economic crisis of the time impeded the government from taking action. Only during the 1990s were social policies adjusted, mostly in collaboration with the social partners, together with the various programmes for 'national recovery'. In the meantime, economic circumstances had changed, and the economic boom made it impossible for the government to ignore the pending reform of the welfare state system. Benefiting from the advantageous economic conditions, the Irish welfare state made a substantial leap forward during the 1990s, expanding some of the residual social programmes. Conroy (1999) even argues that the Irish welfare state skipped the intermediary phase of development and advanced from having residual social security schemes to a more comprehensive welfare state. In short, the delayed development of the Irish welfare state had its roots in the country's late industrialisation and dominant agricultural sector. Moreover, the Catholic Church, as a voluntary provider of welfare, was interested in maintaining its dominant position (Fanning 1999). Even though the Irish social security system shares many similarities with a liberal welfare state, the unemployment, sickness, maternity and occupational injury insurance schemes are not means-tested but earnings-related, unlike those usually found in liberal welfare states. As in Germany, it was the social partners together with the government who were the major players in the design and implementation of the reforms.

## 7.2 INSTITUTIONAL FRAMEWORK AND POLITICAL ACTORS

The Irish political institutions are based on the Westminster model and were established under the tutelage of the British monarchy long before the Republic of Ireland became independent in 1921. Even under the British regime, Ireland had its own government, but all relevant legislative action took place in the parliament of the United Kingdom. The pathway that eventually led to the formation of an independent Republic of Ireland had already been established in the mid-nineteenth century with the foundation of various separatist groups, but it was only at the beginning of the new century that paramilitary groups started to intensify the rebellion against the occupying forces. Violence against the British security forces, together with the political decision of the elected nationalist Sinn Féin parliamentarians to build their own parliament (the later Dáil) and to abstain from the meetings of the House of Commons, finally led to the negotiation of the Anglo-Irish treaty of 1921.[6] Together with its political institutions, the newly independent country also inherited a fully working and complete administration. The constitution of 1922 was replaced in 1937, but the Irish state essentially kept its original institutional design and – to a large degree – also held on to major public policies.

Unlike Germany, the Irish state has a strongly centralised and unitary structure – some scholars even argue that Ireland is the most centralised state in Western Europe (Bulsara and Kissane 2009, p. 180). There are no regional tiers of government and the power of local government is very weak. Recently, efforts have been made to decentralise the administration but no additional political power has been passed on to lower administrative levels.

Even though the institutional setting has its origin in the British Westminster model, which is Lijphart's model case of a majoritarian democracy, Irish political institutions show characteristics of both consensus and majoritarian democracies (Gallagher 1999a). The two characteristics of Irish political institutions that differ most from a majoritarian democracy are its electoral rules and the multi-party system. Whereas in the United Kingdom, the members of the lower house are elected by a first-past-the-post voting system, the members of the Dáil are elected by a particular type of proportional representation which allows for the representation of minority parties in the political process but still gives the largest party in the system (Fianna Fáil) preferential treatment (see Chubb 1992; Sinnott 1999). This proportional character of the electoral rules meant that Ireland developed a multi-party system. The absence of a clear separation of power between the government and the parliament, however, are clear features of the Westminster tradition. In a recent contribution, Bulsara and Kissane (2009) argue that Ireland has moved further away from the Westminster model over recent years and increasingly emphasises and uses the institutional features that typically belong to consensus democracies, such as referenda and corporate industrial relations. Another important difference from the Westminster model is the fact that the Irish people are usually governed by a coalition government rather than a single party government.

The Irish parliament (the Oireachtas) is bicameral. However, unlike in Germany where the upper house represents the Bundesländer, the upper house in Ireland (the Seanad) has very little power and is often characterised as a 'talking shop'. Whereas the lower chamber (the Dáil) is elected by the people, the members of the Seanad are appointed by the government or elected by vocational panels. As is usually the case in majoritarian parliamentary democracies, the government is the most important political actor, and in essence all legislative actions have their origins with the government. The head of government (Taoiseach) appoints the members of the cabinet from the parliament and can dismiss ministers. Even though the parliament has the power to appoint or dismiss a government, in practice national elections predetermine the constellation of the subsequent party government. Parliamentary committees, which are important institutions in the policy-making processes in Germany, have a very limited effect on legislative action (see Gallagher 1999a, p. 195 and Murphy 2006).

## Partisan Actors

Due to the relative homogeneity of Irish society, the party system is less fragmented than in Germany. However, in line with recent developments in other West European party systems, the number of parties in Ireland has increased over recent decades, with the formerly dominant Fianna Fáil losing its central position in the party system and the overall political process. Studies on the peculiarities and characteristics of the Irish party system argue that Irish parties are non-ideological and do not comply with the differences political parties exhibit on the traditional economic left-right dimensions usually applied to differentiate different party families (Carty 1981; Garvin 1974). However, influential party scholars, such as Laver and Hunt (1992) and Mair (1987), argue that the Irish party system is less of a special case than has been argued in the past, and recent scholarship has shown that even though the typical left-right dimension might not have been applicable during the time when Fianna Fáil dominated the party system, this conclusion is no longer appropriate, and Irish parties nowadays offer different policies on the economic left-right axis (e.g. Garry and Mansergh 1999; Gilland Lutz 2003). Still, the position of the two main parties, Fine Gael and Fianna Fáil, are often similar with regard to economic policy issues, which is why assessing the role of coalition partners in government is particularly important. The following overview intends to capture the particularities of the Irish party system but also to emphasise the existing similarities with other Western European party systems.

Despite the fact that the Irish Republic is a relatively young state, its party system is much older. The basis of the Irish party system was established before the country's withdrawal from the United Kingdom. From the late 1930s until the 1960s, Ireland had a 2½ party system similar to that of Germany during the same period. The system consisted of three traditional parties: Fianna Fáil, Fine Gael and the Labour Party, plus some smaller parties of minor importance who did not participate in government. Fianna Fáil and Fine Gael (formerly Cumann na nGaedheal) emerged out of Sinn Féin, the movement mobilising for an independent Irish state. Their main dividing line was their attitude towards the status of Ireland: whereas Fianna Fáil was pushing for full independence from the United Kingdom, Fine Gael accepted its dominion. It was the nationalist issue, rather than the more traditional left-right dimension, which used to be the dividing line between the two parties, and a recent study argues that this remains the case even today (Gilland Lutz 2003).[7] Even though the Labour Party is the oldest party of these three, it is also the smallest. The weak support for the Labour Party is particular to the Irish party system, and is all the more striking as the Irish working class is relatively large (see Laver and Hunt 1992). Among Western European countries, Ireland is most similar to Switzerland when it comes to electoral support for the Left. However, even in Switzerland, support for the Social Democrats was twice as high as it was in Ireland between the late 1960s and early 2000s.[8] Unlike in the two other countries included in this study, there is no Christian Democratic Party. The reason why no party has organised itself to defend Catholic values in politics is because these values have never been challenged in Ireland. Catholicism in Ireland was neither threatened by the Reformation nor by any attempts by the state to secularise its policies (see Laver 1992; Mair 1999, 1987). What further distinguishes the Irish party landscape from the German party system is the comparatively small success of the Green Party. Even though the Green Party was founded only a few years later than its counterpart in Germany, the electoral success at the national level is not very significant. For instance, in the 2002 national elections, the Green Party won 4 per cent of the votes, which is equal to six seats in the Dáil.[9]

During the roughly thirty years included in this analysis, the number of parties in Ireland has increased slightly. This trend is similar to that witnessed in Germany, where the past decades have also been characterised by increasing dynamism in the party system. The increasing competition has also had an effect on the composition of party governments. Between 1932 and 1989, Ireland was led by Fianna Fáil governments (for thirty-eight years) or by a coalition government between Fine Gael and Labour. In 1989, Fianna Fáil had to enter a coalition government for the first time with the Progressive Democrats, a party founded in 1985. This newly established party supports market and socially liberal positions (e.g. lower taxes, privatisation, supporting divorce and the availability of contraception) and thus offers a different set of policies than the ones offered by Fine Gael and Fianna Fáil, which – to a significant degree – share an economic policy portfolio. With the entry of the Progressive Democrats during the 1980s and of Democratic Left during the 1990s, the outcome of national elections (and the subsequent coalition governments) became less predictable. In 1989, the time of single-party governments came to an end, and various types of coalitions have been formed in the years since.

## Industrial Relations

The unitary nature of the state and the majoritarian governmental system makes it more difficult for extra-parliamentarian actors to gain access to the policy-making process, which is as a result more centralised. In their early days, trade unions operating in the Irish Republic were heavily supported by British trade unions seeking to increase their membership base and influence, and their structure was therefore similar to those in Britain (Hardiman 1988).[10] However, as with Irish political parties, the trade unions were also divided by the national question, and a unifying class-based ideology was late in developing. In addition to the dividing line imposed by divisive views about the role of Britain, the trade union system as a whole was very fragmented, with almost 100 different trade unions existing in the early 1960s.[11] On the employer side, there were (and still are) fewer organisations, but centralisation and coordination among them was weak until the 1980s. The importance of stronger cooperation became evident only when the government changed its economic policy and decided to open up the Irish economy. Hence, the relationship between peak interest organisations and the government has changed since 1987, with social partnership in Ireland becoming stronger as a result. Hardiman (2000) claims that the experience of recurring economic crises was an important factor to bring employers and trade unions, and also the government, together. Before business organisations, unions and the government got involved in the negotiations of the 1987 agreement, known as the 'Programme for National Recovery', there had been attempts at social partnership or the conduct of tripartite negotiations with varying degrees of success. During the 1970s, only the peak organisations were engaged in bilateral negotiations, but the demand for more government participation in wage-bargaining rounds grew within both employer organisations and unions alike.

In 1987, a minority Fianna Fáil government initiated a reanimation of the tripartite bargaining processes and corporatist macroeconomic policy-making with the aim to take into account a broader range of interests and actors in the policy-making process. The persistent and severe economic crisis of the 1990s also showed the necessity of finding an economic policy that would meet the approval and support of all relevant actors.[12] After the 'Programme for National Recovery', the issues covered by various follow-up programmes have increased over the years, and six new programmes have since been put forward.[13] The by now well-established social partnership in Ireland is comparable to the way in which macroeconomic and social policies are developed in the two other countries included in this study. An important difference, however, remains: the social pacts are limited to delineating the negotiated broader policy goals covering a period of roughly three years. The more concrete policy design remains in the hands of the respective governing coalition, and with weak parliamentary committees that also exclude interest organisations from voicing their concerns, the government still retains a considerable amount of control over the final policies.

## 7.3 ECONOMIC CONTEXT OF LABOUR MARKET POLICY-MAKING (FROM 1970s UNTIL THE MID-1990s)

Similar to other small economies, Ireland faces greater vulnerability to contextual changes in the world economy, and in order to prosper, such small economies should ideally embark on a so-called double movement that combines open markets with social protection (Polanyi 1954). However, unlike other small countries such as Switzerland, which opened its economy relatively early and benefited from a strong and quickly growing German market, Ireland tried to wall off the domestic market by relying on protectionist policies which held the Irish economy hostage for most of the twentieth century. The poor performance of the Irish economy was the result of politically motivated protectionist policies which were first implemented by Fianna Fáil, the party that gained office for the first time in 1932 and was in office during thirty-eight of the following fifty-seven years. During its first term in office, the party immediately started to implement a programme of industrial protectionism. Their comprehensive protectionist policies were ideologically motivated and aimed at protecting the Irish economy from the world economy in general, but mainly from the British economy. Being economically independent from Britain was seen as an important component of political independence and unity. This approach to independence made Ireland one of the most protected economies in the world. The implemented protectionist policies encompassed industry as well as the large agrarian sector (Mjøset 1992, p. 114). These comprehensive protectionist policies did much harm to both the Irish economy and society and the politically driven macroeconomic agenda forced hundreds of thousands of Irish citizens to leave their country and seek work abroad.

This is why, for many years, the Irish economy ran counter to the general trend in Germany and other European countries. Whereas Germany and Ireland both performed well economically in the aftermath of the Second World War, the Irish economy had to deal with massive problems during the 1950s and 1960s when the economy stagnated or even declined. The major economic difficulties during these years increased pressure on the government to drastically change its economic policies and gradually open the Irish economy to foreign investment and trade. It was due to this mounting pressure that in 1957, the Irish government started to radically change its economic policies and the economy slowly started to catch up with the rest of Europe. Consequently, and in contrast with most other countries, Ireland did surprisingly well during the 1970s (see figure 7.1). Despite the oil crisis, Irish economic growth was higher than the OECD average, and the country did not experience negative growth rates. The basis of this relative success goes back to the publication of the 'Programme for Economic Expansion' (a government White Paper), published in 1958 and which aimed at gradually giving up economic protection and moving towards export-oriented growth. Subsequently, the government changed its policy and started to lower taxes for business in order to attract foreign investment and the establishment of foreign companies in Ireland. This is why Ireland was not hit as hard as other countries during the recession in the 1970s.

The settlement of companies from the United States played a dominant role in Ireland's economic development during the 1960s and 1970s. Indeed,

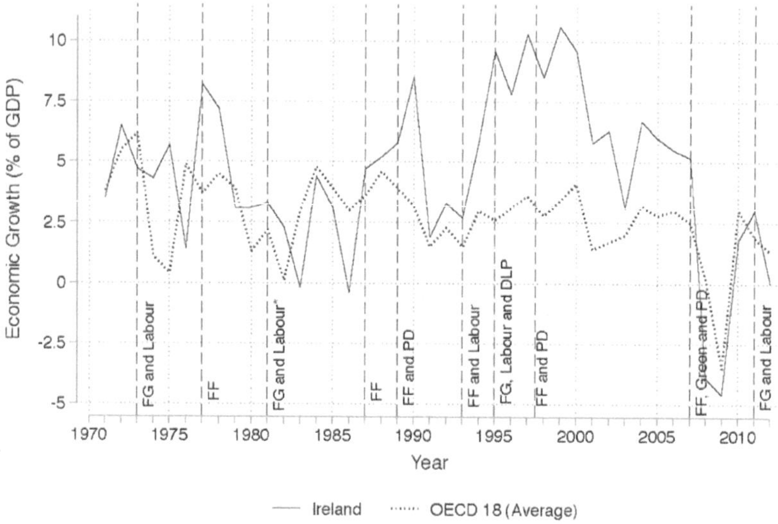


**Figure 7.1. Annual Economic Growth Rates in Ireland: 1970–2012**

most foreign investment came from U.S. companies. The Irish market was attractive not only due to the favourable tax system but also because the Irish economy offered well-educated employees, proximity to the common European market and the absence of language problems (e.g. Ó Riain 2004). In 1973, Ireland joined the European Economic Community (EEC) and therefore had to abolish trade barriers and protectionist measures within five years. The new economic policies worked well during the 1970s, but the 1980s was a politically and economically troubled decade. The decade was characterised by increasing unemployment (between 1980 and 1983 unemployment doubled) and frequent changes in government (between 1980 and 1989 Ireland saw five different governments). The recurrent economic downturn also led to a new wave of emigration by well-trained, highly skilled people (see Mjøset 1992, p.382). Despite considerable economic growth and increasing economic openness, the problems of the Irish labour market endured. The unemployment rate continued to increase until 1986/1987 and reached an all-time high of close to 17 per cent (see figure 7.2). The origins of this high figure lie in the dependence of the Irish workforce on the wellbeing of the UK economy. Although there was an attempt to make the domestic economy independent from the United Kingdom, the British labour market served for a long time as a 'safe haven' for – particularly unskilled – Irish workers (e.g. Walsh 2003). However, the demand for workers in the United Kingdom collapsed during the 1990s,

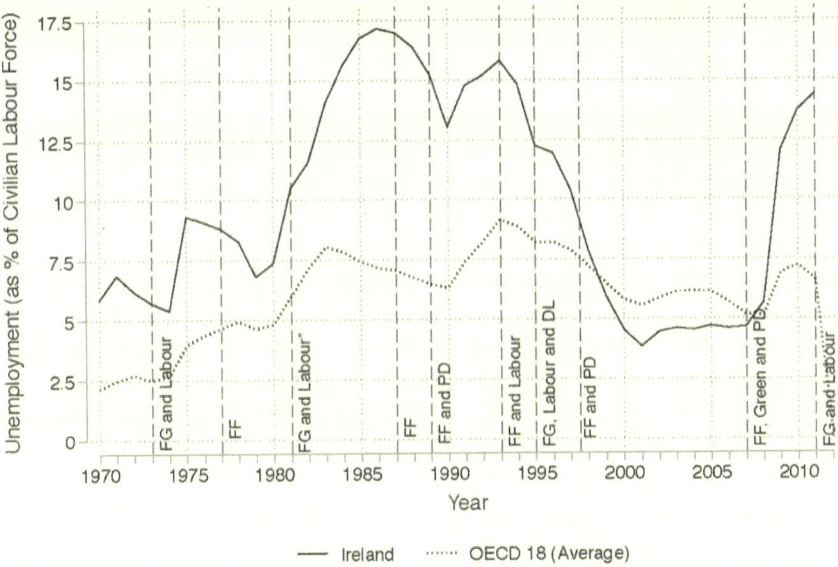


**Figure 7.2. Unemployment Rate in Ireland (as Percentage of Total Labour Force)**

with the results that Irish workers returned home, thus contributing to the increase in Irish unemployment. The economic downturn during the 1980s led to the launch of the 'Programme for National Recovery' in 1987. As with previous programmes, this initiative was supported by the government together with the social partners.

Ireland's economic fortunes started to change again during the past decade of the twentieth century. During this period, economic growth was almost ten percentage points higher than both the OECD average and the growth rate in Germany. Further, the level of unemployment started to decline slowly but continuously. The persistent growth of the Irish economy over the past three decades has also created thousands of new jobs in various sectors, with the service sector experiencing the biggest increase. For instance, employment in the service sector rose from 57.4 per cent to 63.9 per cent between 1991 and 2001 (see Smith 2005, p. 44). After another peak in the unemployment rate in 1993, unemployment rapidly decreased, falling below the OECD mean in 1999. The economic success and growing number of jobs has also attracted many foreign workers, an unseen phenomenon in Irish history, which had always previously been characterised by frequent waves of migration. The sectors benefiting most from the boom were the high-tech manufacturing industry, the financial-/insurance service industry and other private service industries.

Overall, the path to prosperity and growth was long, and despite the significant efforts consecutive governments made to improve economic performance, it was only during the 1990s that Ireland experienced a period of uninterrupted economic growth. In fact, between 1990 and 2002, the Irish economy boomed and until the country was hit hard by the financial crisis, Ireland showed some of the highest levels of economic growth among EU member states. The consequence of this boom period was a substantial transformation of the Irish economy and society. However, towards the end of the period included in this analysis, the massive economic growth had started to decline again. Even though the level of economic growth was still higher than in most other OECD countries, the recession at the beginning of 2000 sent a warning shot that the Irish economic development, which was heavily sponsored by foreign investment and companies loosely attached to the local economy, may be less sustainable than people were hoping for. The criticism (O'Hearn 2000, 2001) was confirmed by the forceful way Ireland was hit by the most recent financial crisis in 2008, from which the labour market and the economy have still not recovered.

## 7.4 ANALYSIS OF RECENT LABOUR MARKET REFORMS

Unlike in Germany, the Irish government is in the position to shape and introduce new legislation solely according to their partisan and coalition preferences and is only restricted by budgetary constraints. With majorities in both parliamentary chambers and a centralised government, policy-making is not complicated by institutional constraints, such as sub-national or regional entities with the ability to block legislative action. Extra-parliamentarian actors have little access to the legislative process, and parliamentary committees are relatively weak. Policy-making in Ireland is heavily inspired by the Westminster model, with the government as the most important actor in shaping and designing policy proposals. However, even though the role of the parliament as law-maker might be minor, the Dáil is still an important forum for the parties in government and opposition to express their opinion and signal policy preferences to the electorate. Even though the extra-parliamentarian actors have little access to the policy-making process, the peak interest organisations have a role in the regularly negotiated social partnership agreement between the government, trade unions and employers' organisations. These agreements establish goals for medium-term economic development and performance and to some extent set the stage for any reform project. In addition to wage agreements, the agreements covering a three-year period set the broader framework for the further development of the social welfare system. However, the exact design of the policies presented to the parliament is not discussed in this forum and remains at the discretion of the incumbent.

Unlike in Germany, where welfare state institutions and social security schemes are legislated in different legislative documents, most of the social policies which constitute the Irish social security system are summarised and set out in the Social Welfare Act. The Irish Social Welfare Act covers the main social insurance schemes, such as the pension scheme, unemployment benefit and unemployment assistance scheme, and health care, as well as child-care schemes. The act is subject to change on a yearly basis. Often, these changes are incremental and only concern contributory rates and benefits without substantially changing the policy instruments and schemes. If new schemes are implemented, their legislative set up is simply added to the existing act. Changes to the Social Welfare Act that have an influence on the budget are already announced in the Budget Speech at the beginning of the year and are also included in the Financial Bill. Both the Financial Act and the Social Welfare Act are presented by the respective ministers and followed by verbose discussions in parliament. The timing of these bills follows a regular, recurrent pattern. The Financial Bill is usually presented at the beginning of each calendar year and the discussions in parliament can last until May. The Welfare Bill is presented and discussed in late February or March and the final vote on this bill usually takes place in April. The parliamentary debates which follow the presentation of the annual budget to some extent anticipate the arguments dominating the debate which follows the presentation of the Social Welfare Bill. The following analyses hence draw on both, the parliamentary minutes of the Financial Bill and the Social Welfare Bill, because the arguments raised overlap to a great extent. In the Irish legislative process, the general debate on the key principles and proposals of the bill take place during the second reading. The third, committee, stage involves a detailed examination of each of the sections. The fourth and fifth stages usually consist of tidying up the decisions made at the committee stage and formally passing the bill. In effect, only the second and third stages offer the house any real opportunity to influence the content of a bill. The second-stage debates are thus the big events in the life of the Dáil, as it is here that the broad outlines of bills are argued over (Gallagher 1999b).

In common with Germany, the Irish social security scheme also distinguishes between unemployment insurance benefits (pay-related social insurance) and unemployment insurance assistance. Unlike in Germany however, where the administrative responsibilities for social assistance programmes often lies with the sub-national authorities, the unemployment assistance scheme in Ireland is administered entirely by the Department of Social and Family affairs. The payment-related contributions to the social insurance scheme cover both unemployment and pension benefits, with both benefits related to previous payments into the scheme. The overall structure of the insurance fund is comparable to the fund in Germany and is mainly financed by employers and employees.

**Table 7.1. Reforms in Ireland**

| *Year* | *Reform Title and Key Content* | *Party Government* |
|---|---|---|
| 1990 | Social Welfare Act: change of earning ceiling in pay-related social insurance schemes; implementation of carer's allowance scheme and lone parents' allowance. | Fianna Fáil and Progressive Democrats |
| 1991 | Programme for Economic and Social Progress (1990–1993): the programme was negotiated among the social partners and also includes measures for social protection in various areas, but also unemployment. | Fianna Fáil and Progressive Democrats |
| 1991 | Social Welfare Act: change of earnings ceiling in pay-related social insurance schemes, change of contribution scheme, new rates of benefits. Extension of social insurance benefits to part-time workers. | Fianna Fáil and Progressive Democrats |
| 1992 | Minor changes to the contributory schemes for payment-related social insurances. Introduction of a part-time job incentive scheme. | Fianna Fáil and Progressive Democrats |
| 1993 | Social Welfare Regulation (amendment that provides that a person who has lost at least one day of insurable employment in any week will be regarded as having suffered a substantial loss of employment). | Fianna Fáil and Labour Party |
| 1993 | Social Welfare Act: PRSI exemption schemes for employers, training for job seekers, changes in benefits and contributions. | Fianna Fáil and Labour Party |
| 1994 (February) | Programme for Competitiveness and Work (1994–1997): states that the social insurance system should be maintained. | Fianna Fáil and Labour Party |
| 1994 (March) | Social Welfare Act: regulation (provision that a person under age fifty-five who receives money in respect to redundancy in excess of a prescribed amount may be disqualified for receiving unemployment benefits for a period of up to nine weeks), implementation of survivors' pension, minor changes to the contributory scheme. | Fianna Fáil and Labour Party |

| Year | Reform Title and Key Content | Party Government |
|---|---|---|
| 1995 | Social Welfare Act: minor changes to the contributory scheme, extension of the contributory pension scheme for widows/widowers. | Fine Gael, Labour Party, Democratic Left (since December 1994) |
| 1996 | Social Welfare Act (Treatment Benefits): exempts people of age fifty-five or over who are signing for credited contributions in respect of proved unemployment from the requirement of having to have thirteen paid contributions in the relevant contribution year in order to qualify for benefits, changes to the contributory scheme, policy changes directed towards long-term unemployed (e.g. back-to-work allowance), and PRSI exemptions for low-paid workers. | Fine Gael, Labour Party, Democratic Left |
| 1997 | Partnership 2000 (1997–2000); includes active labour market policies for target groups and the further implementation of active labour market policies in general. New rules for seasonally unemployed people. | Fine Gael, Labour Party, Democratic Left |
| 1998 | Social Welfare Act: adjustment of the contributions and benefits, small changes of contributory ceilings. | Fianna Fáil and Progressive Democrats |
| 1999 | Social Welfare Act: adjustment of contributory rates and benefits, implementation of a PRSI carer's benefit scheme. | Fianna Fáil and Progressive Democrats |
| 2000 | Social Welfare Act: implementation of a new scheme for carers, adjustment of pension rates, improved pension rates for people with pre-1953 pensions, minimum rate of $100 for social welfare old age pensioners. | Fianna Fáil and Progressive Democrats |
| 2001 | Social Welfare Act: change of contributory ceilings, reduction of PRSI rates, change of social insurance contributions for self-employed. | Fianna Fáil and Progressive Democrats |

National elections held in 1989, 1992, 1997 and 2002.

Table 7.1 summarises the various changes to the unemployment scheme since the early 1990s.[14] A fair number of reforms were implemented by differently composed party governments. Social policy was designed predominantly by a coalition between Fianna Fáil and the Progressive Democrats or the Labour Party until the mid-1990s and again after 2000. In between, a centre-left coalition of Fine Gael, the Labour Party and Democratic Left was in government and thus was in charge of social policy. This centre-left coalition was unusual for Ireland because it was one of the most left-wing governments in recent Irish history. While Fine Gael is positioned only slightly more on the Left compared to the other major party, Fianna Fáil, the inclusion of Democratic Left, a truly left-wing party, pulled the coalition towards the left of the overall political spectrum. This study will therefore examine the main social policy reforms of this specific coalition, the Social Welfare Act of 1996. I have chosen for comparison the 2001 Welfare Act because this was the main social welfare reform implemented by the conservative coalition of Fianna Fáil and the Progressive Democrats. Apart from the 1991 Act, which was also implemented by a coalition between the Fianna Fáil and the Progressive Democrats, all the other social policy reforms under the leadership of the Fianna Fáil were designed together with the Labour Party. The coalitions between Fianna Fáil and the Labour Party are best characterised as a centre than as a right-wing government, while the coalition between Fianna Fáil and the Progressive Democrats can be clearly classified as centre-right.

## 7.5 FINANCIAL ACT AND SOCIAL WELFARE ACT 1996

In 1996, the Irish cabinet consisted of a three-party coalition between Fine Gael, Labour and Democratic Left. The three-party government came into power after the coalition government between Labour and Fianna Fáil collapsed in 1994. A first attempt to form a new government between Fianna Fáil and Labour failed late in that year, after which Labour initiated talks with the three main opposition parties, which led to the formation of a new government at the very end of the year. Democratic Left was represented by one minister only, Proinsias De Rossa, who was the party leader and served as Minister for Social Welfare.[15] The so-called rainbow coalition included parties with fairly divergent policy preferences, ideology and history. Still, due to a consensus-oriented decision-making process, the cabinet worked well together. Throughout its term in office, however, the cabinet faced criticism from the opposition parties which complained that crucial bills were heavily influenced by De Rossa, the minister from Democratic Left. The government was thus de facto more left-wing than would be suggested by its nominal allocation of ministries or by theories which assume that the influence of a coalition partner on policy output is proportional to the number of portfolios the party holds (Browne and Franklin 1973; Gamson 1961; Warwick 2006).

The 1996 bill was announced as one that would bring major changes to the existing welfare state legislation. The social policy reforms presented by the newly formed centre-left government primarily aimed at addressing the needs of the very poor, particularly those of the long-term unemployed, who represent the majority of the labour market 'outsiders' in the Irish context. De Rossa, on behalf of the cabinet, presented the Social Welfare Bill as the 'first integrated approach to address the most pressing social and economic problem, long-term unemployment' (parliamentary minutes, 12.03.1996). Even though the Irish economy was booming, long-term unemployment was still a major problem for the Irish economy. The government thus proposed programmes specifically designed to integrate those people into the labour market who had been excluded for many years. The Minister for Social Welfare, De Rossa, justified the measures proposed in the budget and the welfare act with the words that 'they are intended to give particular help to our unacceptably large number of people who are long-term unemployed because this group is not benefiting enough from the current dynamic growth in employment. . . . That group needs positive help and support and this budget provides it' (parliamentary minutes, 23.01.1996a). The Social Welfare Minister could count on support from other members of the coalition who also emphasised that the social needs of 'outsiders' should finally be addressed. Exponents from the Labour Party, for instance, stated that 'this is the first time the long-term unemployment problem has been the main focus of a budget. I am delighted to support the measures announced in the budget to tackle it'. The Junior Minister of State at the Department of the Environment, Liz McManus from the Democratic Left, also explicitly highlighted the failure of previous governments to design social policies to help the very poor. She mentioned that 'for decades, social and economic policy has failed to address the needs of two groups in society, those without work and those in low paid jobs'. (Both quotations are from the parliamentary minutes, 31.01.1996e.) These statements lend further support to the fact that the proposed policies had the agreement of more than just a single member of the coalition.

The welfare bill included important measures that considerably affected the generosity dimension of the existing social security schemes. First, the government proposed to increase the ceiling of the key social security scheme PRSI ('Payment-Related Social Insurance'). This ceiling defines the maximum amount of a person's income that is subject to social insurance payments.[16] An increase of this ceiling has redistributive effects because people with high incomes will pay a relatively greater contribution to the social insurance scheme. Second, and of particular benefit for people at the bottom of the income distribution, the government suggested that social insurance contributions would only have to be paid by people earning more than £80 per week, thus increasing the amount that was exempt from social insurance contributions by £30. Through this measure, workers with very low salaries would contribute less, thus increasing their net salary. Finally, and also affecting the generosity dimension, the government proposed to compensate any long-term unemployed who accepted a low-wage job by paying the difference between the salary and the benefits they had received while being unemployed. The aim of this measure was to create incentives for the long-term unemployed to escape the so-called welfare trap; that is, to take a job that pays less than the benefits, they would be entitled to through the social insurance scheme. This specific proposal essentially had an influence on both the generosity and the spending dimensions. On the one hand, it guaranteed that poor people would not be worse off by entering the labour market, while on the other hand, it should also lead to a decrease in social expenditure. This measure was similar to one of the policies by the German Conservative government in the 1994 'Beschäftigungsförderungsgesetz', described in the previous chapter. Of the three policy proposals, the first two clearly have greater redistributive effects than the third.

On the spending dimension, the proposals particularly aimed at incentivising labour market participation and the creation of new employment through subsidies of individuals and employers. In particular, the contributory rates to the social security schemes for employers were lowered in the hope that this measure would have a positive effect on job creation. Second, recruitment subsidies for employers creating jobs for the long-term unemployed were offered. The third proposal affecting the spending dimension was a back-to-work allowance that allowed the long-term unemployed who accepted a job to retain – in addition to their wage – a certain percentage of their previous social welfare payments. Lastly, community employment schemes were introduced to reintegrate the long-time unemployed into the (second) labour market. Table 7.2 summarises the most important reform issues included in the Social Welfare Bill/Financial Act 1996.

## Actor's Policy Preferences on the Generosity Dimension

Besides the actual level of social welfare benefits for the unemployed, a much-debated issue in Irish social welfare and labour market politics was the take-home pay, or the net income, of employees. The 'rainbow coalition' government was committed to securing and increasing the transfer of resources to the very poor while simultaneously increasing the net earnings of the low-income workforce. In order to increase the take-home pay of these groups, the government introduced a scheme in 1995 that exempted the first £50 of the

**Table 7.2. Key Policy Proposals Included in the 'Financial and Social Welfare Bill, 1996'**

| *Generosity Dimension* | *Spending Dimension* |
|---|---|
| Increase of minimum income subject to social insurance payment | Lowering of employers' contributions to the scheme (promoting enterprise) |
| Increase of PRSI ceiling | Recruitment subsidy to create jobs for long-term unemployed |
| Compensation for acceptance of low-income job | Community employment schemes |
| | Back-to-work allowance |

weekly income from contributions to the PRSI system. In 1996, this amount was increased to £80. The measure was mainly introduced to relieve employees with a low income from payment of the full rate of PRSI, which was set at 5.5 per cent of the weekly income. Even though workers from all income brackets benefited from the increase of the PRSI-free allowance, employees with the lowest pay clearly benefit the most.

The Minister for Enterprise and Employment (Richard Bruton, Fine Gael) stressed that the reform would also help to improve the incentive to accept a job: '[we] reinforced a strategic shift in the structure of employees' PRSI by introducing an allowance last year of £50, rising this year to £80 per week . . . . This will open new opportunities for the lower-paid [workers] and all areas of employment' (parliamentary minutes, 24.01.1996b). The conservative opposition, however, criticised the exclusive focus on the very poor while ignoring the needs of middle- and high-income workers. Fianna Fáil, the biggest party in the opposition, agreed that some low-income families would benefit from this measure and be slightly better off, but they demanded that the government should also take measures directed at middle-income families (see parliamentary minutes, 23.01.1996a). Members of the opposition parties also explicitly disapproved of the aim to increase the overall generosity and redistributive dimension of the social security net. In particular, they opposed the plan that employees with higher earnings would contribute relatively more to the PRSI system than before.

As with to the new PRSI allowance for low incomes, the opposition was also against the government's plan to increase the PRSI ceiling. The reasons for this related to the fact that changing the existing insurance system in this direction would shift the burden towards high-income groups, something that Fianna Fáil and the Progressive Democrats were strongly against. Initially, the Irish social insurance system was designed in such a way that contributions to the insurance fund only applied up to a certain income; employees whose income exceeded the threshold specified by the government did not have to pay contributions for the amount above the threshold.

Relative to their income, the contributions from people in higher income brackets were thus lower. In 1996, the government increased this ceiling by £800 (from £21,500 to £22,300). The plan to raise the ceiling basically coincided with demands from interest groups. The Irish National Organisation of the Unemployed (INOU), for instance, had even asked for the ceiling on PRSI payments to be abolished altogether because it disproportionately favoured high earners (see the *Irish Times*, 20 December 1995). Fianna Fáil argued that the combined effect of the two measures (PRSI allowance for low incomes plus an increase of the ceiling) would be negligible (see parliamentary minutes, 31.01.1996e, Martin Cullen). In contrast, the Progressive Democrats, who generally oppose payment-related social security systems altogether, opposed the government plans because they did not approve of the redistributive effects these changes would have. In addition, the party made the criticism that 'the Government has merely shifted the burden of PRSI from the lower paid to the top of the structure. . . . It has shifted the burden of taxation but has never considered reducing it' (Michael McDowell, parliamentary minutes, 23.01.1996a). Overall, the two measures can be viewed as a significant change in Irish social policy. For the first time, a government had designed a reform that exclusively focused on the needs of the very poor. Moreover, the redistributive effects of the reform were considerable because it had a positive impact on net incomes in the lowest bracket while simultaneously shifting the burden of social insurance contributions towards the higher income brackets. Poor people benefited from the reform because their take-home pay increased, while at the same time, their social security entitlements and the coverage of benefit schemes (e.g. the duration of benefits) remained unaltered by the 1996 Social Welfare Act.

The third measure, which affects the generosity dimension, was less contested because it also aimed at changing the incentive structure for the long-term unemployed. In a manner similar to the instruments implemented by the German government in 1994, the Irish government intended to promote part-time jobs. To increase the incentives to work part-time, the coalition proposed that the long-term unemployed who accepted part-time or occasional employment would continue to receive social benefits. Specifically, the government proposed to compensate workers for the difference between the income generated from part-time work and the amount of social security that they would have received if they had remained unemployed. The promotion of part-time jobs was further accompanied by a simplification of the unemployment assistance scheme. This simplification of the administrative procedures would ensure that the unemployed would be able to correctly assess which welfare benefits they would be entitled to while being employed part-time. Increasing the overall transparency of the various social insurance schemes was a key intention of the reform and would ensure that people seeking to be re-integrated into the labour market were guaranteed that they would not be worse off with a part-time job than they had been before. While this policy proposal did not increase the overall generosity of the social security system, it still included a compensatory mechanism benefiting the poor and long-term unemployed. With this specific reform proposal, the government aimed at changing the incentives to accept jobs that many unemployed people had so far declined. Indeed, due to the particular design of various social benefit schemes, people living on welfare benefits had had very little incentive to actively seek work, take a low-paid job, or engage in occasional and short-term employment. The eligibility to social assistance usually ceased as soon as a person entered a working relationship, no matter that the entry salary of a formerly unemployed person who accepted a part-time position or a job in the low-wage sector was often below the amount provided by social assistance. The reform was thus to address these financial disincentives. This particular part of the reform was also supported by the Conservative opposition parties. The Progressive Democrats acknowledged that the government was finally starting to fight the disincentives set by the welfare system: 'there is one message of hope, it [the government] is beginning to see that PRSI operates as a disincentive; it is a regressive tax on employment' (Michael McDowell, parliamentary minutes, 23.01.1996a). Fianna Fáil, the party which had significantly contributed to the design of the Irish welfare system, mainly emphasised the increasing number of part-time jobs available and their importance for the Irish economy. While the overall effort to fight a system creating the wrong incentives was welcomed, the opposition criticised the proposals of the 'rainbow coalition' for not going far enough, as the government had failed to evaluate the potentially negative effect of other welfare schemes and income supplements on the willingness of unemployed people to take on a part-time job.

A number of minor proposals which also affect the generosity dimension were the extension of the PRSI scheme and the promotion of part-time jobs, which went hand in hand with a simplification of the calculation of unemployment assistance. From 1996 onwards, people working within community employment schemes (job creation schemes) were entitled to full coverage by the various types of social insurance included in the PRSI scheme. Previously, these workers had been entitled to benefits for occupational injuries only, but now they had the possibility to contribute to the pension fund and also to get an occupational pension after retiring. The extension of the PRSI scheme to community workers was not extensively discussed in parliament and was generally well received. Nevertheless, it should be noted that, by implementing this change, the 'rainbow coalition' closed one of the last gaps left in the Irish welfare system once the self-employed had been included into the PRSI scheme.

## Actor's Policy Preferences on the Spending Dimension

The 1996 Social Welfare and Budgetary Bills also included policy proposals which considerably affected the spending dimension. Unlike in Germany, the changes implemented by the left-wing 'rainbow coalition' led to an increase in public expenditure and expanded spending for specific social welfare issues. This was possible because the Irish economy was booming and tax income had increased during the 1990s. In addition to the favourable economic situation, there was a consensus that long-term unemployment was a serious problem in the Irish society and economy which needed to be addressed. Despite the overall consensus, many measures proposed by the 'rainbow coalition' were opposed by the Conservative parties. In line with the overall priority to help the lower-paid and the long-term unemployed in society, the government attempted to create incentives for employers to hire long-term unemployed people by offering a subsidy of £80 per week for jobs filled by people who had been without work for at least three years. Another measure to raise incentives for employers to create additional jobs was to lower the employer contributions to the PRSI fund. Again, the measures were targeted at low-wage employees. For low-income jobs, the employer's PRSI contributions were reduced from 9 per cent to 8.5 per cent and the income threshold to which this reduced rate applied was increased by £1,000 (from £12,000 to £13,000 per annum). At the same time, the ceiling up to which employers had to pay PRSI contributions was increased by £1,000 up to £26,800. These changes altered the structure of employers' contribution to the PRSI. After the reform, employers had to pay proportionally more PRSI contributions for high-salary earners than for employees with low salaries, the goal being to increase the incentives for employers to create more jobs for the low-skilled workforce.

The Labour Party, which was part of the governing coalition, although welcoming the initiative to offer a subsidy of £80 to employers for hiring a long-term unemployed person, were concerned that this specific measure disproportionately favoured employers:

> we need to be extremely careful to ensure that proper guidelines are in place to safeguard against its [the implementation of the recruitment subsidy] resulting in the displacement of existing workers by long-term unemployed people – on the back of a subsidy such as this – with the potential of benefiting employers only. (Roisin Shortall, parliamentary minutes, 01.02.1996f)

Table 7.3. **Policy Proposals Affecting the Spending Dimension, 1996**

| | *Critical of Government Proposal* | *Supportive of Government Proposal* |
|---|---|---|
| **Long-Term Unemployed** | Progressive Democrats<br>Fianna Fáil | Fine Gael<br>Labour Party<br>Democratic Left |
| **Lower PRSI Contributions** | Fianna Fáil<br>Progressive Democrats | Fine Gael<br>Labour Party<br>Democratic Left |
| **Community Employment** | Progressive Democrats | Fine Gael<br>Labour Party<br>Democratic Left<br>Fianna Fáil |

This concern echoed the criticism from trade unions. The ICTU, which generally supported the new budget, was worried that the budget neglected the interests of PAYE workers, that is, employees with regular working relationships who contributed fully to the PRSI fund (see the *Irish Times*, 24 January 1996).[17] Still, other representatives from Labour acknowledged the need for such a scheme, particularly because

> hiring people who are long-term unemployed is not an attractive proposition to many employers . . . . The job subsidy in some sense recognises this and provides employers with a level of subsidy, a contribution towards the extra costs incurred when taking on a long-term unemployed person. (Pat Rabbitte, parliamentary minutes, Dáil Éireann, 25 January)

The reactions from the opposition towards these measures were mixed. Although the opposition generally welcomed PRSI reductions, the Progressive Democrats considered the measures taken by the government to be insufficient. Mairin Quill (Progressive Democrats) stated that 'the key to ensuring competitiveness is a reduction in costs for industry. In particular we must seek to reduce the cost of employing people. That means substantial cuts in personal taxation and PRSI both for employees and employers' (parliamentary minutes, 30.01.1996d). Further cuts of contributory rates, however, would have significantly undermined the social security scheme, particularly for people in the low-wage sector. Fianna Fáil exponents argued that 'the PRSI breaks given are insignificant. They have been written off as useless by all the industry federations' (David Andrews, parliamentary minutes, 08.02.1996g). The party thus seriously questioned whether the incentives the government was hoping for would really work.[18]

The employer organisations did not have a unified position and they disagreed about the proposed policy instruments and their impact. While the union representing people working in the service and industrial sectors (SIPTU) was sceptical about the implementation of the recruitment subsidy, the Small Firms Association welcomed this measure (see the *Irish Times*, 24 and 29 January 1996). SIPTU, which represents mainly low to middle-income PAYE workers, was particularly disappointed about the minimal tax concessions that their constituents received. The criticism voiced by SIPTU was echoed by representatives from Fianna Fáil whose main concern was the neglect of the interests of middle and high-income groups. Bertie Ahern, the leader of Fianna Fáil, criticised the reform for not including sufficient measures to alleviate the burden shared by the regularly employed workforce: 'The tax and PRSI concessions announced in the budget are minimal from the point of view of all but the lowest paid individual taxpayers' (parliamentary minutes, 23.01.1996a). In addition to their discontent about the size of tax cuts and other compensatory measures, trade unions were particularly sceptical about the implementation and strengthening of community employment schemes. While this new programme was welcomed by most parties, the trade unions were asked to take a more generous view of the opportunities this and other schemes were offering people in difficult circumstances (parliamentary minutes, 30.01.1996d). Trade unions were traditionally sceptical about community employment schemes as they were afraid that these schemes would undermine the competitive first labour market. Both major parties, Fianna Fáil (in opposition) and Fine Gael (in government), stressed the potentially crucial impact such schemes could have for people who had been unemployed for most of their lives.

In addition to the proposals discussed earlier, the social welfare bill provided a 3 per cent increase in the weekly benefits paid to people dependent on social welfare. This measure, however, simply followed and executed the recommendations by the Commission on Social Welfare made in the mid-1980s, which – among other things – had suggested that the weekly benefit rates should increase to an adequate level over the coming years.[19] Based on these suggestions, all governments had increased the benefits on an annual basis. This increase thus did not constitute a reform issue as such. The steady annual increases in social welfare payments did not go uncontested, however. Whereas the employer confederations opposed the 3 per cent increase, the INOU criticised the peak trade union organisation (ICTU) for not asking for more than a 3.5 per cent increase (see the *Irish Times*, 20 December 1995).

The INOU, which was established in 1987, was one of the first non-governmental organisations (NGOs) to participate in the discussions preceding the partnership agreements. However, due to the difficulties of mobilising unemployed people, the voice of the INOU was less prominently heard than that of the trade unions.

As table 7.3 shows, the conservative opposition would have preferred tax reductions and a substantial reform of the taxation system instead of the additional measures that the government proposed to help the very poor. Both Fianna Fáil and the Progressive Democrats stressed their disappointment with both the budget and the Social Welfare Bill as presented by the government. They expected the government to take advantage of the booming economy, which would have allowed the implementation of tax cuts. This disappointment was forcefully expressed in parliament, and the government was accused of having failed a large number of people, particularly the (upper) middle class.[20] Fianna Fáil and, more prominently, the Progressive Democrats, both of which supported tax cuts, also argued that major tax reductions, particularly for employers, would boost employment and also indirectly help the long-term unemployed.[21]

## Mediating Effects of Political Constraints

Policy-making processes in Ireland are not subject to institutional constraints. Even though Ireland also has a bicameral system, the Seanad has limited competencies in the legislative process and because the Taoiseach has the right to appoint eleven senators, the governing coalition always has the majority in the upper chamber. Moreover, the Seanad cannot block bills but only delay the final vote by a maximum of three months. In addition to a powerless upper chamber, the bills presented to the parliament usually undergo only small changes which do not alter the core intentions of the legislative proposal. The amendments proposed by the opposition parties are usually discussed during consultations at the committee stage and are mostly rejected.

As mentioned previously, Irish governments – together with the peak labour and employers' organisations – negotiate three-year macroeconomic programmes which set the lines for broader macroeconomic policies and, more importantly, lay the groundwork for the increase in industrial wages. Both the annual Social Welfare Bill and the Financial Bill need to be in line with the broader principles and lines that have been defined within the programme. However, the final design of the proposals and reforms is in the hands of the respective government. Interest organisations have only limited access to the policy-making process during the legislative process. Thus, interest groups exert only very limited direct pressure on the Financial Bill and the Social Welfare Bills, and the government can, by and large, design the policies in line with its programme. In the bill presented in 1996, we can clearly see the decisive impact of Democratic Left on the coalition's policy-making processes. This influence was particularly visible in the area of social policy. Even though Democratic Left only had one ministry, De Rossa and Democratic Left were 'running the show' (Mary Harney from the Progressive Democrats) and pulling the 'rainbow coalition' towards the Left with regard to the social policy. John O'Donoghue (Ceann Comhairle (speaker), Fianna Fáil) even suggested that

> in delivering the Budget Statement, the Minister for Finance, Deputy Quinn, showed all the sincerity of a hostage speaking at gun point. When the Minister for Social Welfare, Deputy De Rossa, demanded a political ransom from the Government, it decided to pay, and the Minister, Deputy Quinn, was sent out to read the terms of surrender. The Minister, Deputy De Rossa, is the real Taoiseach. (parliamentary minutes, 25.01.1996c)

Bertie Ahern (Fianna Fáil) also complained that 'economic policy has been hijacked by Labour and Democratic Left, a party with one percent of national support' (parliamentary minutes, 23.01.1996a). While the Irish government is relatively immune to direct external pressure and constraints, the 'rainbow government' was subject to internal constraints from Democratic Left. In his role as a member of the government and the only representative of the Democratic Left in government, his support was needed in order to sustain the further existence of the coalition. De Rossa though significantly shaped the social policy agenda and was also able to have an impact on the overall budget process.

## Discussion

With few political and institutional constraints and a marginalised Fine Gael within the 'rainbow coalition', the left-wing government was able to design the Social Welfare Bill in such a way that it addressed the needs of those societal groups that had generally been neglected, specifically the long-term unemployed and other groups not represented by trade unions and other interest organisations. This focus was not appreciated by the centre-right parties which made the accusation of the Labour Party that 'it has deserted the trade union movement again. The PAYE workers, the trade union members and the small entrepreneurs have been let down by this government' (Bertie Ahern, parliamentary minutes, 17.04.1996). The emphasis on the long-term unemployed and other labour market 'outsiders' was equally criticised by trade unions, which were critical about the creation of public employment schemes and the implementation of recruitment subsidies. This critical stance of the peak trade unions towards the budget and social welfare plans of the government did not go unnoticed by Labour MPs. However, while the exponents from the Labour Party did take this criticism seriously, they also agreed that the government had to discriminate in favour of the long-term unemployed (Jim Kemmy, parliamentary minutes, Dáil Éireann, 01.02.1996f).

Overall, table 7.4 shows that the majority of the policy changes proposed and implemented by the 'rainbow' coalition had a favourable or neutral impact on workers in the low-wage sector and on the long-term unemployed. The policy mix also indicates a shift from passive labour market policies towards policies that emphasise activation and re-integration of the long-term unemployed, a trend that can also be observed in Germany and other European labour markets. The policy proposals which benefit people in the low-wage sector are related to the changes made to the contributory schemes. Proposals that predominantly benefit the unemployed are the activation policies, such as the recruitment subsidies, the back-to-work allowance and the community employment schemes. Naturally, 'insiders',

**Table 7.4. Reform Issues and Direction of Changes 'Financial and Social Welfare Bill, 1996'**

| | | *Effect on* | |
|---|---|---|---|
| | *Reform Issues* | *'Insiders'* | *'Outsiders'* |
| **Generosity** | Increase of ceiling/contributory ceiling of core social security programmes (PRSI) | + | – |
| | Exemption of the first £80/ week income from payments to core social security programmes (PRSI) | + | – |
| | Compensation of long-term unemployed for taking low-wage or part-time jobs | – | + |
| | Compensation for part-time jobs | + | + |
| **Spending** | £80 recruitment subsidy for employers when hiring long-term unemployed | neutral | – |
| | Back-to-work allowance for long-term unemployed | (–) | + |
| | Implementation of community employment schemes | neutral | + |
| | Cut rate for employer's contribution to the PRSI schemes | neutral | neutral |

*Legend*: + implicates that the implemented measure had a positive effect for the group indicated; – implicates that the reform negatively affected 'insiders'/'outsiders'.

or workers with regular employment relations, also benefited from the change to the contributory schemes; however, the positive impact of this change for people on low income was more significant than for middle- and high-income earners.

The opposition mainly called for a serious tax reform and accused the government of putting forward a budget that hardly rewarded pensioners and tax payers, essentially labour market 'insiders' and those who contributed the social security schemes prior to retirement. Members of Fianna Fáil also claimed credit for the current economic prosperity and favourable labour market conditions which they attributed to their efforts in the previous legislative period (Michael J. Woods, Fianna Fáil, parliamentary minutes, Dáil Éireann, 23.01.1996a).[22] However, the policy-making dynamics and the changes in social policy brought in by the 1996 Social Welfare Bill illustrate that left-wing party governments are willing and able to implement policies that are beneficial to societal groups which are generally under-represented in political systems if the policy-making processes are not subject to political constraints and compensatory mechanisms. After many years of centre and centre-right governments, the parliamentary discourse and media coverage also demonstrate that the government's focus on poorly organised labour market 'outsiders' was perceived as unusual and as a clear neglect of the middle class or the franchised labour market 'insiders'. Such a shift in the government's attention was mainly possible because the coalition consisting of Fine Gael, Labour and Democratic Left did not have to find a compromise with the centre-right parties.

## 7.6 FINANCIAL ACT AND SOCIAL WELFARE ACT 2001

The second reform assessed here took place in 2001 and was implemented by a conservative/liberal coalition consisting of Fianna Fáil and the Progressive Democrats. The change in government took place in 1997 and for the first time in the history of Fianna Fáil, the party formed a pre-election agreement with the Progressive Democrats. Whereas Fianna Fáil won quite a number of additional seats in parliament (if not votes), the Progressive Democrats lost six seats and were represented with four members of parliament (Teachta Dála) only. Due to this low electoral support for the Progressive Democrats, the coalition could only be formed with the help and support of three independent members of parliament. Nominally, the Progressive Democrats were fairly weak, but just as for Democratic Left in the previous government, their influence on the policy agenda was quite strong. Mary Harney, the party leader, was appointed as deputy prime minister (Tanáiste) and was in charge of the important Ministry of Enterprise, Trade and Employment, which was essentially responsible for drafting significant parts of the labour market policy changes.

With regard to economic performance, the economy grew steadily between 1996 and 2000 but experienced a downturn in 2001 for the first time in several years. Still, the economic boom during the previous years had a very positive impact on the level of unemployment and state revenues. Unlike in 1996 when unemployment was still comparatively high (close to 12 per cent) and long-term unemployment was a serious problem in Irish society, in 2001, the Irish government found itself with a level of unemployment below 4 per cent (the lowest unemployment rate since 1964 when the level of unemployment was at 4.6 per cent), significantly below the average level of unemployment in other EU countries. While both economic growth and unemployment figures were very positive, inflation was increasing and had reached the alarmingly high level of 7 per cent in 2000. This was twice the Eurozone average, which led to complaints by the social partners that wage increases and the adjustment of benefits were being wiped out by high inflation. As with the previously assessed reform of 1996, the budget and the Social Welfare Act, presented at the end of 2000 and the beginning of 2001 respectively, were the last in the ongoing electoral cycle and were therefore particularly important.

The budget, as well as the Social Welfare Bill 2001, was heavily influenced by the positive economic situation and the prospect of a healthy economy and near-full employment. But although money spent on social welfare increased substantially, the increase was mainly used to adjust the rates and benefits to the increasing wages and to keep up with inflation. The rhetoric used by Dermot Ahern, the minister for social, community and family affairs, when presenting the Social Welfare Bill in 1999 and 2001 was strong and indicated that the Irish welfare system was going through an expansionary period.[23] However, in reality, the shifts and expansion of the Irish social welfare system were much less pronounced than in the bills proposed and implemented by the preceding left-wing government. The focus of the Social Welfare Bills presented by the Fianna Fáil-Progressive Democrat government essentially mirrored the different approaches of these governments towards social policies and their reform. Budgets and Social Welfare Bills by Fianna Fáil-Progressive Democrat coalitions did not include specific measures to target the unemployed and the still-existing problems in the labour market. The government also did not advance or implement any encompassing new programmes or policies. This was the case not only during the incumbency of the conservative government after 1997 but also during the period preceding the left-wing 'rainbow coalition' when unemployment was still high and the Irish economy was not performing well. The main focus of the Fianna Fáil-Progressive Democrat government was a reform of the Irish tax system with the aim of reducing income tax. This focus on tax reform did not come as a surprise since the call for lower taxes had already accompanied parliamentary debates during the previous legislation. More specifically, it was felt that the tax schemes applied to firms and companies should ideally also be applied to individuals, which would require the implementation of significant cuts in income tax. Mary Harney (Tánaiste, Progressive Democrats) described this plan in the following way:

> This government is committed to cutting tax rates . . . if low tax works for corporations, it works for the workers who work in those corporations. If the profits generated by workers are to be taxed at 10 percent or 12.5 percent, it is not fair that the worker should have to pay tax at more than 40 percent or 20 percent. (parliamentary minutes, 07.12.2000c)

Assessing the 2001 Budget and Social Welfare Bills, five major issues can be identified (see table 7.5). On the generosity dimension, the PRSI ceiling for employees increased, which means that the income threshold at which employees were required to contribute to the social insurance fund was increased. At the same time, the contributory rate (for employees) to the insurance fund was reduced by 0.5 per cent. Whereas the first measure mainly affected people in higher income brackets, the second measure was of benefit to all. Neither issue was contested, and there was very little discussion in parliament. On the expenditure dimension, the government increased the social welfare benefits in all categories of social spending (unemployment benefits and assistance, pension, etc.), which was a standard procedure to align the benefits to higher costs of living because of inflation. In addition, the ceiling for wages subject to PRSI contributions by employers was abolished. The overall characteristics of the social welfare programmes in place did not change and the government abstained from introducing new schemes. However, various changes included in the 2001 Financial Bill/Social Welfare Act indirectly affected the Irish labour market. The extension of child support, parental leave, and the increasing acceptance of carers' work in general aimed at making the labour market more attractive for women. The most significant

**Table 7.5. Key Policy Proposals Included in the 'Social Welfare Act, 2001'**

| *Generosity Dimension* | *Spending Dimension* |
|---|---|
| Increase of PRSI ceiling for employees | Increase of social welfare benefits (unemployment benefits and other) |
| Reduction of the main employee PRSI rate (4.5 per cent to 4 per cent) | Abolition of PRSI ceiling for employers |
| Tax cuts | Reduction of Social Insurance contributions for the self-employed (5 per cent to 3 per cent) |

changes that affected the income distribution of individual workers and the population as a whole were part of the Financial Bill, which included significant tax cuts. The issue of consecutive cuts in taxes also dominated the debates of the two bills in parliament. In contrast, the comparatively small changes more directly related to social policies and mentioned earlier did not play a major role in the parliamentary debate.

## Actor's Policy Preferences on the Generosity Dimension

The two issues that had an impact on the generosity dimension did not provoke much discussion or criticism in parliament. An increase in the PRSI ceiling relevant for the employees' contribution had been common-place over the previous years and was not considered to be an ideological issue. The increase of the ceiling went hand in hand with the further increase in wages and the good performance of the Irish economy. Similarly, the slight decrease in the level of employees' PRSI contributions was not prominently discussed either. The lowered contributions resulted in a slight increase in net income for employees, a fact that was generally welcomed. The relatively uncontested measures concerning the PRSI system stand in stark contrast to the criticism of changes affecting the general taxation system. In fact, most of the debate in parliament that was related to the generosity dimension of policies revolved around changes affecting the tax system. The centre-right government implemented tax cuts for the fourth consecutive time. Revamping the tax system by lowering taxation rates was one of the major policy projects of the Progressive Democrats, also featuring prominently in their electoral manifesto, and was taken on board by Fianna Fáil.

After several years of tax cuts, Mary Harney, the Tánaiste, proposed another 2 per cent cut for top rate taxes in the 2001 Financial Bill. The governments' policy of cutting taxes on a yearly basis was strongly criticised by the opposition, but also by parts of the trade union movement, particularly the union representing women, low-skilled and part-time workers in the service sector (SIPTU). The criticism of the governments' tax policy concentrated on the government's focus on the expansion of privileges for the wealthy while doing too little for those on low and middle incomes. CORI (Conference of Religious of Ireland) emphasised that 'the Government's approach to the poorest and most excluded in Irish society is not acceptable and is contrary to the aims and objectives of the Programme for Prosperity and Fairness . . . for this government to claim that social justice is at the heart of its action is not credible' (in the *Irish Times*, 13 March 2001). The organisation also stressed that the previous budgets had widened the gap between rich and poor in Ireland (in the *Irish Times*, 23 July 2001).[24] Derek McDowell from the Labour Party emphasised that 'a reduction in the upper rate of tax is of no benefit whatever to two-thirds of taxpayers and it is worth very little to the majority of the rest. . . . Reducing tax rates in itself favours the better off' (parliamentary minutes, 06.12.2000a). Fine Gael, who generally welcomed further tax breaks, also attacked the government for going in the wrong direction. Jim Mitchell mentioned in parliament that 'the Minister's policy of providing income tax reductions is correct but [the government] is going about it in the wrong direction for the following reasons. He has consistently given more to the rich than the poor' (parliamentary minutes, Dáil Éireann, 27 February 2001).

Against this criticism, the government contended that a substantial number of people were fully exempt from paying taxes. However, the growing number of workers exempt from tax payments essentially confirmed the worries of the volunteer associations that the boom in the Irish economy only partially benefited the unskilled and workers with low levels of education. The reductions in unemployment were mainly achieved by the expansion of part-time and low-wage jobs, which further polarised Irish society. The fact that a growing part of the Irish workforce was living on salaries too low to be taxed is confirmed by figures showing that Ireland had the second largest proportion of low-paid workers after the United States. Moreover, the continuing policy of tax cuts for companies and people in the top-income brackets almost provoked the collapse of the so far successful social partnerships. Interest groups representing the unemployed and groups in society that unequally benefited from the economic boom threatened to leave the agreement. In particular, the continuation of the 'Programme for Prosperity and Fairness', launched in November 1999, was in danger because the volunteer associations threatened to resign from this agreement due to the heavy emphasis on tax breaks by the government and the little investment in substantively improving Irish social policies and public services.

## Actor's Policy Preferences on the Spending Dimension

In 2001, the budget and the Social Welfare Bill offered an increase in social welfare payments for all categories of social security payments. This increase, however, was moderate even though nominal spending on welfare and social policies increased from £4.5 billion in 1997 to more than £6 billion in 2001. The increase in nominal spending was mainly caused by new programmes funded through welfare state policies, such as career allowances, increased family allowances and extended maternity leave programmes. These programmes were generally well received and also benefited less privileged groups in the labour market, particularly women. However, the traditional social security programmes did not benefit. Despite this increase in nominal spending, relative spending on social welfare decreased significantly during the Fianna Fáil/Progressive Democrat government, from 11.5 per cent of

GDP in 1997 to approx. 7 per cent in 2001. Furthermore, the programmes implemented by the government did nothing to help the large group of people who had not benefited from the economic boom, and the increase in their benefits (i.e. unemployment assistance) was considered insufficient to cover the general increase in the cost of living.

Along with the uneven cuts in income taxation discussed in the previous section, the minimal increase in benefits was another major reason for the near failure of the social partnership programme. The INOU, for instance, commented that 'the £8 a week raise in unemployment payments was the absolute minimum increase that could have been made without provoking a crisis in social partnership' (the *Irish Times*, 7 December 2000). Politicians from the Labour Party and Fine Gael supported the INOU's position:

> Given the rate of inflation projected for next year, the increase of £8 per week across a range of social welfare assistance and benefit payments is pathetic. . . . Social welfare spending has fallen year after year from 11.5 percent of GDP when the Government took office to around 7 percent this year. . . . It can clearly be seen where the real priorities of the Fianna Fáil Progressive Democrats Government lie. (parliamentary minutes, 07.12.2001d, Tommy Broughan, Labour Party)

Even the *Irish Times* adopted this position and commented on the insufficient increase in social benefits and the government's tax policy: 'This is a government which sees tax relief as returning to people what they have earned. Benefit payments, meanwhile, are regarded as State largesse to the needy, largesse which drives up Government expenditure' (28 November 2000).

The second proposal related to the spending dimension, the abolition of the PRSI ceiling for employers, was rather surprising as it did not correspond to the asserted and much promoted policy preferences of the government, which wanted to keep taxes on labour cheap in order to remain competitive on the world market. This change also faced criticism from opposition parties but was also met with considerable resistance from employers' organisations (see table 7.6). The abolition of the employers' ceiling essentially generated additional funds for the social insurance schemes, an increase exclusively financed by employers. However, without the ceiling, employers' contributions on high salaries rose, thus increasing labour costs. The major parties in opposition were divided with regard to this issue, with Labour supporting it and Fine Gael opposing the abolition of the PRSI ceiling for employers. The abolition of the ceiling corresponds to the expected policy preferences of a left-wing party, and Derek McDowell commented as follows on the measure:

> The Minister has my support in removing the ceiling for employers as there is a need to claw back the reduction in corporation tax in a fair and reasonable way. In most places of employment there are employees on salaries above and below

**Table 7.6. Policy Proposals Affecting the Spending Dimension**

| | *Critical of Government Proposal* | *Supportive of Government Proposal* |
|---|---|---|
| **Benefit Increase** | Labour Party<br>Fine Gael<br>Volunteer associations (CORI) | Fianna Fáil<br>Progressive Democrats |
| **Abolition of PRSI Ceiling** | IBEC<br>Fine Gael | Fianna Fáil<br>Progressive Democrats<br>Labour Party<br>ICTU |

> the ceiling. There would be relatively few places of employment, therefore, where the employer would be at a significant disadvantage. It is an equitable and reasonable move which I am happy to support. (parliamentary minutes, 28.02.2001c)

Fine Gael opposed the proposal. Several Fine Gael parliamentarians expressed concerns about the potentially reduced competitiveness of the Irish economy if the costs of labour to be paid by employers increased. They also feared that firms would create fewer jobs or fire people more readily: 'The proposal to abolish the employers' PRSI ceiling threatens competitiveness and employment, particularly high earning employment. We will reintroduce a ceiling' (Jim Michell, Fine Gael, parliamentary minutes, 27.02.2001b).

The employers' organisations in general welcomed the budget, but also warned the government that IBEC would seek to reverse the abolition of the PRSI ceiling in the future (see the *Irish Times*, 6 December 2001). In a manner similar to the concern expressed by members of Fine Gael, the employers' organisations feared a loss in competitiveness. In addition, they emphasised that the measure contradicted the general rationale of the previous budgets and other measures taken in this budget. The government defended itself against criticism by referring to the substantial reduction in business taxation and the reductions over previous years in the level of PRSI to be paid by employers. This, the government argued, should be taken into account while evaluating the overall measures implemented through the Social Welfare Bill 2001.

In general, the two bills together reinforced the rather orthodox economic policies of the Fianna Fáil/Progressive Democrats government and '[resulted] in an increasing polarisation between the super-rich and the very highly-paid on the one hand, and the poor and low middle-income earners, on the other hand' (Joe Higgins, Socialist Party, parliamentary minutes, 28.02.2001c). Because the next general elections were soon to be held, the budget was considered as an 'election budget with a Government that succumbed to the temptation to attempt to buy votes by large-scale tax cuts' (the *Irish Times*, 28 November 2000). The Bills, however, well represent the overall policy priorities of the Fianna Fáil-Progressive Democrat government. The set of policies that can be attributed to the redistributive dimension was dominated by changes affecting the taxation of income, with an emphasis on tax cuts that privileged those in higher-income brackets. The changes that altered the redistributive characteristic of genuine social policies (e.g. the contributory schemes) were limited to the standard increase in the employees' PRSI ceiling and a very limited decrease to the PRSI contributory rate for employees. Policy changes affecting the expenditure dimension included moderate increases to social insurance benefits and social welfare assistance. However, in most categories, these increases were just enough to compensate for the generally increasing costs of living and the persistently high level of inflation.

## Mediating Effects of Political Constraints

The governing coalition between Fianna Fáil and the Progressive Democrats faced good economic conditions which considerably reduced the pressure on social institutions and the demand for significant reforms. Whereas unemployment was still very high at the beginning of the Irish economic recovery in the early 1990s, which also marks the beginning of the successful social partnership agreements, the labour market was characterised by near-full employment in 2000/2001. It was during these years that the trade unions became more critical of the partnership agreements between the government, the employers' organisations and the trade unions. After years of wage restraints, which helped the Irish economy to successfully compete in the world market and attract a great deal of foreign investment, the trade unions expected that their constituencies to be significantly rewarded and finally receive more generous benefits. The government, however, refused to invest in more generous social insurance schemes but nevertheless managed to save the partnership agreement and the initiation of new negotiations by accommodating both the trade unions and the employers' organisations with a pay review, tax cuts and a minimal increase in benefits. Cutting taxes in general was the government's preferred method of maintaining industrial peace and securing the further support of employers and unions for their chosen economic policies.

With regard to the formal institutional setting, the situation did not change between 1996 and 2001, but the de facto political constraints that the two governments faced did change slight. In particular, the government of Fianna

Fáil and the Progressive Democrats had to accommodate organised interests to save the social partnership agreement, as the ICTU and other volunteer organisations implicitly threatened to leave the Programme for Prosperity and Fairness. The threat was credible because the balance of power between the actors negotiating the partnership programme had shifted. In the beginning of the partnership programmes, the three participating groups had similar interests and were heavily dependent on each other. In 2001, however, the balance of power had shifted towards organised labour. With near-full employment and even a possible shortage of labour, the unions had much greater bargaining power than in 1996 when unemployment was still high. While labour overall was in a more powerful position to negotiate favourable deals, there was significant disagreement about how their increasing importance and influence should be used and which segments of the workforce should benefit. The union representing workers in the low-paid service sector (SIPTU), which included many women, was particularly critical about the government agenda and the continuation of the partnership agreements. The ICTU, the peak organisation representing all trade unions, however, was mostly supportive of the partnership programmes and also of the governments' overall policy. During internal discussions between the various trade unions, the union representing the low-paid sector was not able to mobilise a majority of its members, and in the end, the different partners managed to successfully agree on a new partnership programme despite the internal differences among the trade unions.

## 7.7 DISCUSSION AND OUTLOOK

Despite these shifts in relative power and economic performance, the 2001 reform perfectly illustrates how social policy preferences and actual welfare state reforms differ for a conservative government which emphasises market mechanisms and small public budgets. The needs of labour market 'outsiders' and disenfranchised people in Irish society were not an issue that the government took seriously, or even took into account at all, when designing reforms that affected the functioning and performance of the labour market. The overall generosity of established social security institutions thus did not change very much and, if it did, it mostly helped the well-organised 'insiders' for reasons discussed in the previous paragraph. The increase in social spending that can be observed in 2001 was mostly due to standard adjustments of benefits which helped to offset inflation, although these adjustments barely covered the increasing cost of living in the booming country, a fact that was widely criticised by the trade unions and various volunteer organisations representing the less well-off.[25] The unions also made clear that the benefits offered to their members (mainly 'insiders') in this package were close to the minimum that they would accept. However, in a setting where institutional constraints are low, governments do not need to accommodate the 'insiders' let alone 'outsiders', and this liberal-conservative government did little to improve the situation of the latter.

Table 7.7 summarises the impacts of the different changes included in the 2001 Financial Act and Social Welfare Bill and gives a brief overview on how specific groups in the labour market benefited from these changes. As mentioned during the previous paragraphs, most budgets announced by the coalition focused on implementing tax cuts and the government did not present a clear social agenda at any point during its time in office. This is in line with the ideological profile and party programme of both parties in government, particularly the Progressive Democrats. While this government agenda did little to alter or strengthen social security institutions insuring people against labour market risks, the changes implemented, particularly the tax breaks, still had a clear bias towards 'insiders' and people with regular salaries as opposed to people employed in the low-wage sector and labour market 'outsiders'.

Due to the exceptional economic performance of Ireland during the 1990s and until 2008, the government was not forced to cut spending and the reform pressure on the spending dimension thus was not as pronounced as in other countries. This was also true during the early years of the new millennium

**Table 7.7. Reform Issues and Direction of Changes 'Social Welfare Act, 2001'**

| | | *Effect on* | |
|---|---|---|---|
| | *Reform issues* | *'Insiders'* | *'Outsiders'* |
| **Generosity** | Tax cuts for higher-income brackets | + | neutral |
| | Increase of PRSI ceiling | +/– | neutral |
| | Reduction of contribution rate (for regular employees) | + | neutral |
| **Spending** | Abolition of PRSI contributory ceiling for employers | neutral | neutral |
| | Reduction of social insurance contributions for the self-employed | neutral | neutral |
| | Minimal increase of social welfare benefits (adjustment to annual inflation) | + | – |

*Legend*: + implicates that the implemented measure had a positive effect for the group indicated; – implicates that the reform negatively affected 'insiders'/'outsiders'.

when Europe, including Ireland, experienced a downturn in the economy. Nonetheless, the examined reform processes illustrate the proposed mechanisms very well. The 1996 Social Welfare Bill in particular exemplifies the impact that ideologically different party governments have on the design of social policy reforms and the reactions of the parties in opposition. Whereas the 'rainbow coalition' government aimed at generating a more inclusive society by strengthening the redistributive effects of the welfare state system, the opposition called for tax cuts and a reduction of national debt. However, the left-leaning government did not care and did not have to care since the opposition had no leverage or possibility of blocking the government's plans. If the left-wing government had faced institutional constraints, it would have likely had to accommodate the conservative opposition and cut spending, or at least could not have increased spending for specific groups by as much as it did. The strong focus on the needs of 'outsiders' (the long-term unemployed, mainly) would not have been possible in an institutional context where constraints are high.

The second Social Welfare Bill/Budget analysed in this chapter exemplifies how different the focus of an unconstrained liberal-conservative government was. The focus of the governing coalition between Fianna Fáil and the Progressive Democrats was mainly on cutting taxes with the aim to maintain the competitiveness of the Irish economy in the world market and to attract foreign investment and companies. Not only the significant tax cuts were for firms and corporations but the government also lowered taxes on income for most societal groups. In fact, the government actively narrowed the tax base to the extent that at the end of the coalition's time in office, 50 per cent of employees were exempt from paying income-related taxes. The significant decrease in income-related taxes, such as the tax on capital income which was halved (from 40 per cent to 20 per cent), was accompanied by a shift in the overall tax base from reliable tax sources (e.g. VAT and income-related taxes) towards taxes that are sensitive to economic cycles (e.g. corporate taxes and stamp duties) (Honohan 2009).[26] While the government actively re-shaped and reformed the Irish tax system, the importance it ascribed to labour market policies was limited and the impact of the labour market-specific measures implemented by the government for 'outsiders' were marginal. The government's non-actions, particularly related to the minimal adjustment of public spending for social and labour market programmes, however, had a significant and negative indirect effect on labour market 'outsiders' because of the 'low-tax and low-spend' economy, which was pursued over a period of nearly ten years. In fact, in 2001, public spending in Ireland was at 29 per cent, which was almost as low as in the United States (28.4 per cent).[27] This development adversely affected general social and public services, such as the provision of health care. The deterioration of these services affected 'outsiders' more than 'insiders' since this group of people did not have the necessary means to resort to the private sector. This purposeful underinvestment in public services was regularly criticised in the media and also in parliament.[28] The negative impact of this policy agenda was particularly felt by the long-term unemployed and the still relatively large number of people (25 per cent) living on less than half the average income of an Irish worker.

In the years that followed the reforms assessed in this study, the Irish economy continued to experience significant levels of growth and outperformed fellow EU states until the financial crisis hit the Irish banking system and the domestic economy with all its force in 2008. The foundations of the collapse of the Irish banking system and the subsequent severe public finance crisis were essentially laid during the incumbency of the coalition between Fianna Fáil and the Progressive Democrats, during which the government turned its back on regulating banking practices and actively contributed to the emergence of a housing and construction bubble, which burst after the Irish banking system went bust.[29] The emergency interventions and rescue packages the government had to resort to in order to prevent the implosion of the Irish banking sector subsequently led to a severe public finance crisis. The overall bank support package which saved the Irish banks from collapsing was one of the biggest rescue packages seen in the EU, with a size that equalled 33 per cent of the Irish GDP (Chari and Bernhagen 2011; Honohan 2009). These enormous rescue packages to save the banking sector forced the government to implement a series of emergency budgets including severe cuts in a number of public services and entitlements (e.g. child benefits, health services and social welfare programmes) and the implementation of various measures to increase revenues (i.e. a new income levy, a VAT increase and other types of taxes). Despite the harsh budgetary cuts and the intention to establish new channels of revenue, the Irish government had to sign a bailout package of over €67.5 billion from the stabilisation fund jointly put together by the International Monetary Fund (IMF) and the EU at the end of 2010.[30]

The collapse of the Irish economy did not come as a complete surprise as there had already been warnings regarding sustainability of the Irish growth model and the booming construction industry as early as 2002. The political elites, however, and the government in particular, ignored the signs and further fuelled the housing and property boom.[31] One particular development that was criticised was the enormous growth in the construction sector and the frenzied building activity which led to an inflation of house prices from 1996 onwards. The media and politicians alike called for action against this development as it was generally expected that the property boom and the policies which triggered this boom could have undesirable consequences. However, the government continued to deregulate the financial market and set incentives to battle the economic downturn and the looming recession, which in turn led to a further overheating of the property market. The financial and macroeconomic policy decisions (through cheap credit, low interest rates and low taxes) this government took during its incumbency thus significantly contributed to the development of the Irish construction boom and housing bubble, which in 2008 led to the severe crisis of the domestic banking system and the subsequent fiscal, economic and employment crises.

The crisis obviously had a significant impact on the Irish labour market. Unemployment, both long-term and short-term, increased significantly, reaching a peak of 14 per cent in 2011, with the majority of the jobs being lost in the construction sector, followed by the banking sector. The fact that most jobs were lost in the construction sector meant that unemployment among men rose significantly more than among women. Unemployment would have increased even more had not many Irish citizens and migrants from EU countries (mostly from Central and Eastern Europe) left the country. The various retrenchment programmes, and particularly the agreement negotiated between the government and the public sector unions, led to an increasing division among labour market 'insiders', that is between those with jobs that were relatively protected from the crisis, particularly employees with long-standing public sector jobs and those employees in the private sector whose jobs were increasingly precarious and were therefore in danger of losing their 'insider' status. An additional divide opened within the public sector, with newly hired workers having to accept lower wages and fixed-term positions. This division goes back to the so-called Croke Park agreement which was negotiated during the last months of the Fianna Fáil–Green Party coalition government. The aim of the agreement, negotiated between the government, the public sector union (ICTU), the police and the military forces, was to significantly reduce the costs of public services and the number of people working in the public sector. The people employed in the sector were subject to various levies and a hiring freeze, which, together with early retirement schemes, were to reduce the number of employees and increase the overall efficiency of the public sector. This public sector agreement was novel in the Irish history of social partnership as it specifically targeted the public sector and did not seek to involve private industry. This led to a twofold increase in dualisation: on the one hand, the gap between employees in the public sector and the private economy increased, and on the other hand, a gap opened between newly hired public sector workers whose social security plans and salaries were lower and the old-time public sector workers who were able to retain their privileged status to a certain degree.[32]

Despite the Irish economy's turbulent recent history, assessing the development of net income inequality over the past twenty-five years, we can see that inequality decreased steadily, with the exception of the spikes

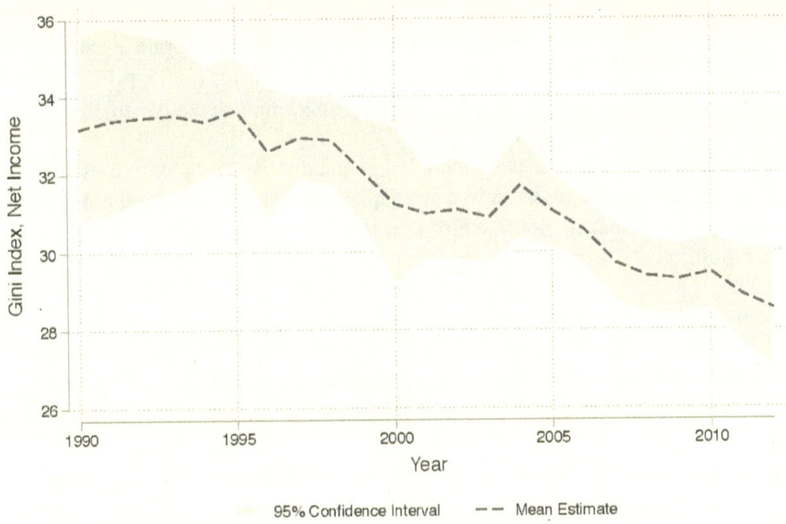


**Figure 7.3. Net Income Inequality in Ireland (1990–2012)**

in 2004 and 2010 (see figure 7.3). The reason why inequality in Ireland has not increased again to date is related to concrete policy changes which affected the design of income tax. The coalition government consisting of Fine Gael and Labour which followed the conservative Fianna Fáil/Progressive Democrats coalition implemented a more progressive tax system and broadened the tax basis again.[33] In addition, while both the top and bottom income percentiles lost out after the crisis, the salaries of people in the top income bracket decreased significantly more than incomes in the low-wage sector (Callan et al. 2013). Overall, the level of inequality in Ireland and Germany has converged over the past twenty-five years, with Germany experiencing an increase in inequality and Ireland a significant decrease.[34]

## NOTES

1 Mair (1999, p. 128) writes that 'comparative research has tended to overlook the Irish case. . . . It has long been believed that the patterns and structures of mass politics, which are evident elsewhere in Europe, have little relevance to the Irish case'. Doyle and Hogan (2008) and Cousins (1997) also point out that Ireland is often ignored in comparative studies of policy change and welfare state development.

2 In Esping-Andersen's (1990) seminal work on the various 'worlds of welfare', the United Kingdom is the main prototype of a residual/liberal welfare state.

Liberal welfare states are mainly characterised by providing means-tested benefits and universal services based on public services or insurance schemes. In a recent contribution to the welfare state literature, Cousins (2005, p.125) describes the United Kingdom as 'the main (if not only) representative of the "liberal" world or the Anglo "family of nations" in Europe'.

3 Even though Ireland is usually included in quantitative comparative studies, there is little comparative research of a more qualitative nature on social policy change and its determinants. Some claim that this has to do with Ireland's peripheral location, others ascribe it to the late development of a welfare 'state' (Cousins 1997).

4 More than in many other European states, social welfare in Ireland was provided mainly by the family and the Catholic Church. The Christian principle of subsidiarity, which sees the family as the basic unit of social provision, was deeply embedded in the political elite and inhibited the further development of state-led social security (Conroy 1999). The critical attitude of the Catholic Church towards the role of the state in general and in welfare provision more specifically started to only significantly change during the 1960s, when the Church was increasingly concerned by the poor state of society and increased its support for more adequate welfare provision (Maguire 1986, p. 250).

5 During the 1960s, approx. 600,000 people emigrated from the country, mainly young men and women in their early twenties. The late 1960s marked the end of a long wave of mass migration due to which the overall population of the Irish Republic was reduced to less than three million people.

6 For a brief overview of the founding years of the Republic of Ireland and the struggles of the young republic after 1922, see, for example, Coakley (1999).

7 For a more detailed discussion on the cleavage structure in Irish politics and the evolution of the party system, see Mair (1987, 1992) and Coakley (2002).

8 The average support for left-wing parties between the late 1960s and 2002 was about 12 per cent in Ireland (figure based on the electoral support for Labour (and the Green Party) in national elections. Switzerland, which figures second after Ireland, still has an average support for left-wing parties of about 27 per cent (between 1967 and 2003, the figure is based on the support in national elections for the Social Democrats and the Green Party).

9 After the 2007 national elections, however, the Green Party entered a coalition government with Fianna Fáil (without substantially increasing its electoral support).

10 In 1912, the Irish Trade Union Congress (the forerunner organisation of the later Irish Congress of Trade Unions – ICTU) also funded the Irish Labour Party with the intention to exert more influence on politics (Hardiman 1988).

11 This number significantly decreased. In 2016, there were forty-eight individual trade unions affiliated with the ICTU, the umbrella organisation.

12 The successful reanimation of social partnership in Ireland and the various programmes initiated over the past years have received plenty of attention from scholars of industrial relations (see work by Baccaro and Lim 2007; Hardiman 2002, 2005b; House and McGrath 2004). Interestingly, the scholarly interest in the development of more comprehensive social policies, which were to some extent also part of these programmes, is much smaller.

13 1990–1993: 'Programme for Economic and Social Progress' (PESP), 1994–1996: 'Programme for Competitiveness and Work' (PCW), 1997–2000: 'Partnership 2000', 2000–2003: 'Programme for Prosperity and Fairness' (PPF), 2003–2005: 'Sustaining Progress', 2006–2015: 'Towards 2016'.

14 The sources are http//www.irishstatutebook.ie (data base of Irish legislative acts) and http//www.ilo.org/dyn/natlex/natlex_browse.home (the database of the ILO on Social Security legislation).

15 Democratic Left existed only for a short period during the 1990s (1992 until 1999). It emerged out of the Workers' Party (in 1992) and merged with Labour in 1999.

16 In Ireland, social insurance contributions apply only to a fixed amount of the annual salary. A person who earns more than the amount to which the ceiling applies does not have to pay social insurance contributions on the income exceeding the determined ceiling.

17 PAYE is the abbreviation for 'pay as you earn' and includes workers who contribute to a social insurance scheme, such as pension, and unemployment insurance through regular contributions.

18 Martin Cullen, member of Fianna Fáil, took a similar position, arguing that 'employers, large and small, have told me that they will not base their decision to recruit somebody on the basis of an £80 per week subsidy but on purely competitive criteria, which result in real jobs' (parliamentary minutes, 31.01.1996e).

19 The Commission on Social Welfare was established in 1983 and presented its report in 1986. The main task of the commission was to revise the Irish social security system and to establish new guidelines for its future development. The following principles were to guide the further development of the Irish welfare system: adequacy, redistribution, comprehensiveness, consistency and simplicity.

20 Liam Aylward from Fianna Fáil: 'there were great expectations about this budget. The economy was doing so well that substantive cuts for taxpayers were expected, but unfortunately, that did not happen . . . the Minister for Finance made much of his concessions to the low paid and unemployed. . . . In reality he failed a large number of people' (parliamentary minutes, 08.02.1996g).

21 So, for example, Mairin Quill, Progressive Democrats: 'the key to ensuring competitiveness is a reduction in costs for industry. In particular we must seek to reduce the cost of employing people. That means substantial cuts in personal taxation and PRSI both for employees and employers' (parliamentary minutes, 30.01.1996d).

22 The economic environment during the mid-1990s was indeed favourable, and by the end of 1996, Irish unemployment had fallen to its lowest level since 1992. This positive development can mainly be attributed to economic growth and labour market policies, such as job creation schemes, which helped the unemployed to return to work.

23 In 1999, Ahern promised in his speech presenting the Social Welfare Bill, 'a radical shift in the way we look at social welfare. In the past, social welfare started out from an assumption that the State should try to prevent abject poverty and should try to alleviate grinding disadvantage. The State, it was felt, should not allow people to be pushed over the edge. However, in the past that was felt to be enough. Nobody felt that social welfare could be a positive force,

could register that we value older people, we value what carers contribute' (parliamentary minutes, 24.02.1999). In 2001, he opened the second reading of the bill by claiming that 'we have turned around our social welfare system from one that simply compensates people for economic failure to one that helps people to help themselves' (Dermot Ahern, Fianna Fáil, parliamentary minutes, 21.02.2001a).

24 The organisation was a member of the group of community and voluntary actors participating in the negotiations of the national partnership agreements including the Programme for Prosperity and Fairness covering the years between 2000 and 2003.

25 The 'Conference of Religious in Ireland' (CORI) repeatedly stated that 'the governments' commitment to social justice is simply not credible' (*Irish Times*, 13 March 2001) and that if the government were to meet the commitments made in the Programme for Prosperity and Fairness, benefits would have to be increased by a significantly greater amount (*Irish Times*, 23 October 2000).

26 Many of these decisions were made by Charlie McCreevy, who served as Ireland's minister of finance between 1997 and 2004 and showed a strong ideological commitment to reducing taxation. According to Hardiman (2005a), McCreevy exercised ministerial discretion in decision-making in a greater degree than most of his ministerial colleagues, despite the fact that government decisions are the collective responsibility of the cabinet. He thus had a significant role in shaping the Irish tax system and budget during a crucial period in Irish history.

27 As a comparison, public spending in other EU countries was at 46.6 per cent in France, and over 50 per cent in Denmark and Sweden.

28 The Economic and Social Research Institute (ESRI), for example, called for more investment in social services and infrastructure rather than further tax cuts (see *The Irish Times*, 13 November 2000).

29 One of the key reasons that the Irish property market was so overheated and the construction sector so inflated was the decision of the government to battle the recession looming in 2001 by lowering interest rates, which made mortgages affordable for many people and led to a veritable property boom and to a surge in property-related lending by banks from less than 40 per cent (before 2002) to more than 60 per cent after 2005 (Chari and Bernhagen 2011).

30 For more in-depth scholarship about the Irish economic and political crisis, see – among others – Clarke and Hardiman (2012), Honohan (2009, 2010), Donovan and Murphy (2013) and Hardiman (2012).

31 The *Economist* had already warned in March 2002 that the current development of the property market may have undesirable consequences and mentioned Ireland as the world leader in house price inflation since 1996. Other organisations, such as the ESRI, repeatedly warned about the high level of inflation, which was eroding the competitiveness of the Irish economy. During the discussion of the 2001 budget, John Bruton of Fine Gael also accused the government of fuelling the emerging housing bubble with the measures planned within the budget presented to the parliament (Dáil Éireann 13.12.2000b).

32 However, it is important to note that the agreement between the government and the public sector union (ICTU) also involved significant pension levies and a salary freeze that affected employees who were already in the system.

33 While Ireland used to be a low-income-tax country before the crisis, this has significantly changed in the aftermath and the income tax burden measured as a share of GNP can now be compared to the tax burden in the United Kingdom and Germany.

34 The jury is still out when it comes to a final evaluation of the impact the recent crisis has had on inequality in Ireland. While the figures plotted here indicate that up to 2014 inequality in Irish society decreased, there are other studies which conclude that the middle class in Ireland has been squeezed and is now more economically vulnerable than ever. Indeed, economic vulnerability has significantly increased and is not only affecting the poor but has also spread to other social classes, the so-called middle-class squeeze (Whelan and Maître 2014). This development can, though caused by different factors, also be observed in Germany.

## *Chapter 8*

# Discussion and Conclusion

During the past decade, the pressure to reform the social security schemes of mature welfare states has been constantly increasing. International economic interdependence and structural changes have affected party governments and their room to manoeuvre in Western democracies. The mutual and uncontested understanding among researchers in comparative welfare state research that government partisanship has a significant impact on the development and reform of welfare states was challenged by the aforementioned phenomena. This study evolved from the fundamental question as to whether party politics and political competition still manifest themselves in divergent social policy solutions implemented by party governments with differing ideological backgrounds. The study examined this question by particularly focusing on the impact of party governments on two segments of labour market participants and two dimensions of social and labour market policy-making. The core research question on which this book is based is fundamental because electoral competition between political parties is largely based on the competition between different policy solutions and policy proposals. Policy proposals and reforms that have an impact on social security schemes and the organisation of labour markets have increased in saliency during recent years and large segments of society have high expectations regarding social security schemes and services. Therefore, we would expect that parties still aim at distinguishing themselves from their competitors for office.

This study was guided by the question regarding the manner in which ideologically different party governments affect the redistributive generosity of core welfare state programmes and other dimensions of welfare state policy-making and how different groups in society, mainly labour market 'insiders' and labour market 'outsiders', are affected by the respective governments. The room to manoeuvre and the policy-making capacities of party governments are conditioned by the level of political and institutional constraints that are present in a country. The study thus contributes to the existing literature in two ways: first, unlike the majority of scholars interested in the impact of party governments on welfare state policy-making, it focused on more than just the expenditure dimension while examining the impact of party governments on changes to the welfare state in open economies. Second, the theoretical framework acknowledges that the policy-making capacity of party governments is significantly mediated by institutional and political constraints. Indeed, these constraints do not affect leftist and conservative governments in the same way.

This chapter first summarises and discusses the main findings in the light of the theory presented in the introduction. The second section qualifies and critically scrutinises the empirical evidence and offers alternative approaches that help to interpret the findings. The third and final section discusses the implications for future research on theoretical, empirical and methodological grounds.

## 8.1 CONTEXTUALISATION OF THE RESULTS

The underlying framework of this study suggested that party governments exploit the multi-dimensionality of social and labour market policies based on their policy preferences and conditioned by the level of political constraints. The policy dimensions at the centre of this study were redistributive generosity and spending. The results of the analyses confirm that left-wing party governments, in situations where they face high levels of political constraints, do indeed increase the redistributive generosity towards labour market 'insiders', but not towards 'outsiders'. This was confirmed by the country case studies included in the second part of the empirical analyses, which further illuminate the relationship between the level of political constraints, government partisanship and whether welfare state reforms tend to take a clientelistic form. The country studies mainly focus on one field of social policy-making: the reform of labour market policies. The changes implemented by varying party governments have been analysed along the lines of their impact on the redistributive generosity dimension of the programme and on whether the reform was implemented with the aim of reducing spending on the programme, the two dimensions proposed in the theoretical part. In addition, the reforms were evaluated as to whether the impact of the legislative changes was the same for all labour market participants or whether specific groups, in particular labour market 'insiders' and labour market 'outsiders', enjoyed preferential treatment.

Investigating the multi-dimensionality of welfare state changes and reforms has been a key response to the *New Politics* literature and scholarship promoting the declining importance of party politics in policy-making. While this study focuses on two relatively broad dimensions, redistributive generosity and spending, other work has identified alternative dimensions of policies that party governments can change in order to reform social policies without significantly altering the costs of a given policy, and while still addressing some of the more pressing issues welfare states face. In a study which focuses on the reform of pension schemes in continental European welfare states, Häusermann (2010a) assesses the design and the characteristics of the implemented reforms according to four different reform dimensions: *insurance, capitalisation, targeting, and recalibration*, as these dimensions become salient in times of fiscal constraints and austerity. Similar to the underlying argument presented in this book, reform of an existing policy can produce winners and losers along those four dimensions, leading to political conflicts. These lines of conflict are likely to result in new divisions between different segments of the workforce, and between employees and employers. Conflicts along the *insurance* dimension involve questions related to the level of benefits, and more generally, conflicts over cost control. The second dimension of conflicts is related to the *capitalisation* of the policy in question, in particular the underlying financing mechanisms. The *targeting* dimension refers to issues that are related to the key societal groups the policy change is targeted at, either in terms of eligibility or in terms of expenditure cuts. The final dimension, *recalibration*, also deals with questions of eligibility, more specifically with the adaption of the existing system to new demands, especially the demand to increase gender equality and react to increasing female labour participation and the decreasing importance of the male breadwinner or the rise of the single-income household model.

Not all of these dimensions are of equal importance for the reform processes assessed in this book. While the question of *capitalisation* was not central to the reforms assessed in this study, some of the reforms did affect aspects related to the *insurance*, *targeting* or *recalibration* dimension. Related to labour market reforms, the reforms affecting the *insurance* dimension are likely to generate or increase conflicts between labour market 'insiders' covered by unemployment insurance schemes and labour market 'outsiders' who lack (full) coverage. The *targeting* dimension is equally important to labour market issues and also includes questions related to eligibility. In Häusermann's work, eligibility mainly refers to the pension scheme, while in the field of labour market policies, the 'eligibility' conflict can be related to the unemployment insurance scheme but can also have a broader meaning, for example, whether a person is eligible to participate in a training programme. Again, the lines of conflict that are likely to open predominantly run between 'insiders' and 'outsiders' but can also open up between different age groups (i.e. between the active workforce and pensioners).

The suggested dimensions of reform and the resulting conflict lines could be used to meaningfully analyse reform processes and political struggles in the field of labour market policy-making. The following paragraph offers an illustrating example but by no means exhausts the possibilities this approach offers. The 'Financial and Social Welfare Bill' implemented by the Irish 'rainbow coalition' in 1996 partly focused on measures to bring people back to work because long-term unemployment was one of the most pressing problems during the mid-1990s. The measures proposed and implemented by the government mostly affected the *targeting* dimension as they were directed at specific societal groups. The discussions in parliament and the statements by unions showed that these measures, which mostly benefited labour market outsiders, did not meet the approval of all actors who had a stake in labour market policies. Trade unions in particular took a critical stand towards these measures and would have preferred the government to opt for tax relief for PAYE workers (*The Irish Times*, 30.11.1995). The INOU therefore criticised the trade unions for not doing enough for the unemployed (*The Irish Times*, 20.12.1995). This shows that the expected lines of conflict within a particular dimension in labour market policy-making show similarities with other fields of social policy-making (such as old-age pension politics). Due to the low level of political constraints in Ireland, the pressure by trade unions had only a limited effect on government policy-making.

The approach discussed earlier offers an analytical lens to examine a broad range of social policy reform. However, with the increasing pressure on labour markets and an increase in policy instruments used to render labour markets and employment relations more flexible, research on the varieties of labour market reforms and their economic and societal implications has increased as well. Recently, labour market policies in general, and the use of active labour market policies in particular, has received a lot of attention from scholars of public policy and comparative politics (e.g. Anderson 2009; Bonoli 2008; Dingeldey 2007; Rueda 2006). While most work examining labour market policies has made a distinction between passive and active labour market policies, recent contributions have particularly highlighted the relationship between employment protection and partisanship on the one hand and the use of specific combinations of active labour market policies and party government on the other. Within the framework of this study, the differentiation between different 'ideal types' of active labour market policies is particularly relevant. The four ideal types that Bonoli (2010) suggests are the following: reinforcement of incentives to work, providing employment assistance, offering schemes to keep people occupied, and investment in human capital. Table 8.1 provides a description of these ideal types and indicates how different policy instruments fall into the four categories.

**Table 8.1. Active Labour Market Policies (Ideal Types)**

| | *Ideal Type* | *Policy Objective(s)* | *Policy Instruments* |
|---|---|---|---|
| 1 | Incentive reinforcement | Strengthen positive and negative work incentives for people on benefits | - Tax credits work benefits<br>- Time limits on recipiency<br>- Benefit reductions<br>- Benefit conditionality<br>- Sanctions |
| 2 | Employment assistance | Remove obstacle to employment and facilitate (re-)entry into the labour market | - Placement services<br>- Job subsidies<br>- Counselling<br>- Job search programmes |
| 3 | Occupation | Keep jobless people occupied; limit human capital depletion during unemployment | - Job creation schemes in the public sector<br>- Non-employment-related training programmes |
| 4 | Human capital investment | Improve the chances of findings employment by 'upskilling' jobless people | - Basic education<br>- Vocational training |

Source: Adapted from Bonoli (2010, p. 11).

The proposed typology helps to systematise the study of (active) labour market policies and offers a framework to compare and contrast the policies implemented across different countries and over time. The policy measures of the third and fourth category are 'classical' active labour market policies which aim at helping people to acquire the right skill set to compete in the labour market or aim at keeping people in an employment relationship (through job-creation schemes, etc.). The measures included in the first and second category include a mix of traditional, passive labour market policies related to the comprehensiveness and eligibility dimension of existing unemployment schemes (i.e. the reduction of benefits and limitation of recipient's eligibility) and new services, such as a stronger emphasis on placement and counselling services. Measures that belong to the first category, such as the focus on increasing the pressure on the unemployed to return to work by reducing benefits or implementing stricter time limits for recipients of benefits, reduce the rights of labour market 'insiders'. Based on the argument proposed at the beginning, leftist governments should refrain from implementing such measures, especially in a context where they are exposed to high levels of political constraints.

Table 8.2 offers a classification of the policy issues proposed within the four reform processes according to Bonoli's typology. The first two rows include the reforms implemented by conservative governments, rows three and four show the results for the reforms implemented by left-wing governments. Sometimes, the 'ideal types' proposed by Bonoli do not exactly fit

**Table 8.2. Categorisation of Reform Issues Based on Bonoli's Ideal Types of ALMP**

| *Reform* | *Incentive Reinforcement* | *Employment Assistance* | *Occupation* | *Human Capital Investment* |
|---|---|---|---|---|
| *Beschäftigungsförderungsgesetz 1994* (Germany) | 2 | 4 | – | – |
| *Financial and Social Welfare Bill 2001* (Ireland) | 5 | – | – | – |
| *Job-AQTIV 2001* (Germany) | 1 | 3 | 1 | 3 |
| *Financial and Social Welfare Bill 1996* (Ireland) | 2 | 6 | 1 | – |

*Reading example:* The conservative government in Germany (1994) implemented two measures with the aim to reinforce the incentive to work and four measures which offer assistance to the unemployed. The first three reforms have been implemented by conservative party governments.

the implemented measures, or rather, the measure follows two policy goals which belong to two different categories. In such cases, the policy measure was counted twice. By classifying the reform issues identified and analysed in the case study chapters, we can clearly see that the portfolio of reforms implemented by conservative governments differs from the reforms implemented by social democratic/left-wing governments. The emphasis on reform issues that aim at keeping people employed or offer them additional training are mostly used by left-wing governments.[1]

This is in line with findings by Huo, Nelson and Stephens (2008), which show that Social Democratic governments implement 'employment-friendly' labour market policies. In addition, it was mainly left-wing governments that made use of typical active labour market policies, such as the implementation of training programmes and the creation of public employment schemes. At first sight, this evidence contradicts Rueda's argument that leftist party governments have only a slight interest in active labour market policies (because ALMP have the potential to bring more people into the labour market and therefore may undermine the privileged position of labour market insiders). However, a closer examination of the results makes it evident that the ALMP implemented by the German left-wing government always included a part that positively affected labour market insiders and actually helped them to keep their jobs or their status (none of the measures affected the employment security of insiders).[2] The empirical evidence further supports Rueda (2006, p. 390), who argues that Social Democratic governments are more likely to produce pro-'insider' policies when they are subject to a greater amount of pro-'insider' pressure from unions. The fact that ALMP measures were mostly linked to policies directed at labour market 'insiders' and had a potentially negative impact on labour market 'outsiders' is a hint in this direction.[3]

This section does not exhaust the possibilities offered by these approaches, especially the rich theoretical framework proposed by Häusermann based on four different lines of conflict, which help to examine and identify different reform coalitions, beneficiaries and losers of distinct reform strategies. The section mainly confirms that the evidence presented in this study resonate well with related literature on welfare state reforms and could be interpreted from different angles and that these different explanations are not necessarily mutually exclusive but are meant to amend the interpretation and discussion of the results in the empirical chapters.

## 8.2 MAIN FINDINGS AND IMPLICATIONS

This section critically evaluates the empirical results in the light of the theoretical framework presented in chapter 3. It discusses whether the relatively rigid theoretical framework which yielded a set of clear hypotheses was helpful to assess the impact of party governments on the two dimensions of social policy-making. More important, this section also discusses whether the propositions made regarding the impact of party governments on different groups of labour market participants can be validated using the empirical evidence at hand.

This book analysed how party governments influence reform outcomes of social and labour market policies in times of fiscal austerity and economic interdependence. The theoretical framework proposed at the beginning of the book suggests that party governments alter their strategy to reform welfare state policies depending on the level of political constraints. As a reminder, the theory suggested that this mediating mechanism between party governments and political constraints should lead to the following two implications: first, we should see an increase in generosity of core welfare state programmes such as unemployment benefit schemes and pensions under governments dominated by left-wing parties. Second, we should also find that left-wing governments, on average, aim at implementing smaller retrenchment packages in a context where they experience low levels of political constraint.

The results of the quantitative analyses show that leftist governments that need the consent of a strong conservative opposition in parliament and are in addition held accountable by organised labour unions outside parliament choose a clientelistic way of reforming social policies. A successful reform strategy for left-wing party governments includes the accommodation of the opposition, on the one hand, through higher cuts in social spending and, on the other hand, through the protection of the core workforce through an increase in or the maintenance of the generosity of core welfare state programmes.

The results further show that the degree of clientelistic policy-making used by parties in government has increased and became more prominent only since 1990. The study thus partially confirms that the politics of retrenchment and welfare state cuts show different facets and qualities than the politics of welfare state development. This result resonates well with the early 'New Politics' literature. The quantitative analyses, however, also yield the conclusion that party politics still matter, in particular for dimensions of policy-making which are not entirely subject to greater macroeconomic constraints, such as general and social spending.

The way party politics and party governments influence public policies, however, has changed. This conclusion is particularly applicable for left-wing party governments. In this respect, the findings resonate with contributions by Beramendi and Cusack (2009) and Beramendi and Rueda (2007), who indicate that leftist party governments are not necessarily successful in creating egalitarian policy outcomes, especially in the presence of corporatist arrangements. In addition, the analysis corroborates the findings of Jensen and Mortensen (2013, p. 161), who conclude that the Left and the Right still entertain distinct policy agendas. This finding is important because it refutes claims that party competition over substantive policy issues has ceased to structure political discourses in advanced industrialised democracies, and it also refutes the claims of earlier literature that welfare states are converging.

Based on the results of the quantitative analysis, a first tentative conclusion of this study is that policies designed by Social Democratic governments in settings with high institutional and political constraints may lead to an increasing gap between labour market 'insiders' and 'outsiders'. This mechanism between constraints and party government does not hold for conservative or right-wing parties in office. These results add to the research by Korpi (1989) and Korpi and Palme (1998), who observe that the middle class, which mostly consists of the core workforce, is the social group that is most privileged by the redistributive efforts of the state. This finding has been characterised as the 'paradox of redistribution'. Further, the results of the quantitative analysis confirmed the findings of other scholars of comparative welfare state research that party governments have lost their room to manoeuvre on the expenditure dimension. Unlike during the formative years of welfare state policies, it is no longer possible to differentiate between leftist and conservative positions on the expenditure dimension, at least on statistical grounds. Shifting the scholarly attention towards other dimensions of social policy-making is therefore of the utmost importance. This shift will also help to advance our knowledge regarding the ability of party governments to shape policies in times of scarce resources. Recent scholarly work has made significant contributions which take into account alternative dimensions of social policy-making which go beyond spending measures. These studies also confirm that party politics still plays a significant role. The conclusions that can be drawn about the impact of party governments on the redistributive generosity, however, pertain only to the effects that government policy has on labour market 'insiders'. Based on these results alone, it is not possible to see how ideologically different party governments affect labour market 'outsiders' and whether and under what circumstances party governments implement policies that are beneficial to the so-called losers of globalisation.

The findings of the quantitative section also show that the way the different policy agendas of the government parties come into play is mediated by political constraints or the way policy responsibility is attributed in the system. The constraining effects of political institutions have a considerable influence on the policy-making capabilities of left-wing party governments. While the literature on institutions and the implications of institutional constraints on public policies and political actors has an important place within the wider comparative welfare state research, the institutionalist literature has traditionally turned a blind eye on how the effect of institutions differs for partisan actors from different ideological backgrounds. Recently, interest in how political constraints influence policy-making processes has been critically reassessed, which in turn has led to more finely grained and nuanced propositions about the relationship between political constraints and political actors (Ansell and Lindvall 2013; Avdagic 2013; Gingrich and Häusermann 2015; Iversen and Soskice 2006b). The results presented in this study contribute to this development and confirm the importance of institutional settings for policy-making, particularly in contexts where the room to manoeuvre is narrowed by scarce financial resources.

The second part of the empirical analysis, which is based on case studies from two different countries, followed a two-fold aim: first, the case studies should further substantiate the results of the quantitative analysis by examining their underlying mechanisms, and second, they assess whether ideologically different party governments focus on different reform dimensions and whether reforms by different types of party governments differently affect labour market 'outsiders'. The analysis of labour market and unemployment insurance reform processes in Germany and Ireland respectively showed that institutional constraints enable organised interests to capture the dynamics of politics and influence the design of the policy reform in favour of their constituents. It also showed that Social Democratic party governments are particularly responsive to organised interests, in particular organisations which represent the core workforce. Again, higher levels of political constraints lead to more compensation for 'insiders' and preclude more egalitarian and inclusive policy-making which would be beneficial to 'outsiders'.

The two case study chapters illustrate the mechanisms observed in the quantitative section on the policy-making level by examining specific reform processes in two countries that differ with respect to their levels of political constraints. The policy changes assessed in the Irish context took place in an environment with low levels of political constraints, enabling party governments to make use of the full range of the room to manoeuvre they have. This proved to be particularly important for left-wing party governments. In contrast to the Irish case, the reform processes in the German context are subject to high levels of political constraints, which significantly limit the room to manoeuvre for both party governments and lead to the observed clientelistic policy outcomes which spare specific groups from being hit too hard by these reforms.

How the political constraints and the institutional setting interfere with a party government's preferences and policy agenda has been demonstrated in the German case studies. Neither type of government was able to implement policies that fully reflect the coalition's preferences as both party governments were obliged to accommodate the opposition parties to some extent. In addition, the coalition between the Social Democrats and the Green Party had to consider the interests of the trade unions. Even though the government was under severe pressure to cut spending, no cuts in unemployment insurance benefits were suggested at this point. Also, knowing that the trade unions would oppose the abolition of the unemployment benefit scheme and its merger with the social assistance scheme, the government refrained from including this cost-saving measure in this proposal. Still, the 'Job-AQTIV' law is an important landmark in German labour market policy-making and already included many aspects of the subsequent series of reforms known as 'Hartz reforms' (see e.g. Berthold and von Berchem 2003; Fleckenstein 2006; Leschke, Schmid and Griga 2006).[4] The Job-AQTIV legislation was a first and significant shift away from a passive system of guaranteeing income security and a commitment to maintaining standards of living towards a more active labour market policy which aimed at activating the unemployed and increasing the flexibility of the rigid German labour market.

Though the Hartz legislations also included cuts in benefits for the core workforce and reduced the duration in which unemployment benefit is paid, the majority of the measures designed to open up the labour market and decrease the shadow economy had a negative effect on unskilled labour. This view is also supported by Martin and Thelen (2007, p. 34), who conclude that the Hartz reforms deepened the divide between labour market 'insiders' and 'outsiders'. In this sense, the legislation passed as the Hartz reforms, which are seen as atypical of reforms undertaken by a Social Democratic government, is still representative of the theoretical framework presented in chapter 3.

The series of legislative changes which was initiated with the Job-AQTIV law not only had serious and long-lasting implications for the organisation of the labour market in Germany but also proved to be bringing significant changes to the German party landscape. The German party system, which was characterised by a great deal of stability, experienced the emergence of new competitors in the years after the liberalisation of the labour market started to take effect. While the unification of East and West Germany can be identified as a first source of destabilisation of the German party system (Debus 2009), the policy agenda of the red-green coalition had significant negative repercussions on the electoral performance of the Social Democrats in the following general elections. Many agree that a key reason for their declining credibility and popularity was the liberalisation of the German labour market, which is still very unpopular with traditionally left-wing voters. The disappointment of some part of the Social Democratic electorate led to growing support for the more leftist 'Die Linke'.[5]

Despite the fact that the Social Democrats managed to push through a number of traditional leftist policies while governing in the Grand Coalition with Christian Democrats, for example, the implementation of the minimum wage in 2015 and the expansion of family and child care policies, the party is still suffering from an all-time low in electoral support. In addition to the long-term effects of the unpopular 'Agenda2010' policies implemented by the Schröder government, the party started to lose votes to a new populist competitor in the German party landscape, the 'Alternative für Deutschland' (AfD). Originally established as an anti-EU party, the party now attracts votes from people who are critical of the political establishment and call for a different policy agenda, particularly in relation to the field of migration and integration. It remains to be seen whether the Social Democrats can increase their appeal again among voters who used to be supportive of their agenda at a time when politics is increasingly dominated by calls for austerity and issues related to cultural openness and integration rather than questions related to inequality of opportunity and redistributive justice.[6]

As in Germany, Irish political parties entered government with very distinct policy aims which differed significantly across party lines. In contrast to the German example, Irish party governments were able to translate their policy preferences without significantly changing them during the legislative term. The limited institutional and political constraints enabled the parties in power to transform their visions and ideas about society into concrete policies while in office. The left-wing 'rainbow' coalition government managed to implement a policy agenda that predominantly focused on labour market 'outsiders' and aimed at improving their situation in the labour market. Long-term unemployment has been a persistent problem of the Irish economy, with many families affected by a lack of work over several generations. On the spending side, the reform packages implemented by the 'rainbow coalition' addressing this deficit of the Irish labour market ranged from subsidies for employers who offer jobs to the long-term unemployed to measures incentivising the long-term unemployed to accept job offers. With regard to the generosity dimension, the government took measures to compensate any long-term unemployed who accept part-time jobs and also implemented a rule that the first £80 of the weekly wage is not subject to any social security contributions. Both measures increase the take-home pay for people in the low-wage sector and make it more likely for the long-term unemployed to transition from a life on social assistance to being integrated into the labour market and gainful employment.

During the legislative period between 1994 and 1997, the Social Welfare Minister from the Democratic Left was able to implement encompassing social policy reforms that led to an increase in overall redistributive generosity. While the JobAQTIV reform in Germany and the content of the social welfare bill of 1996 in Ireland partly aimed at similar outcomes, mainly to activate and integrate the long-term unemployed into the first labour market, they were not equally successful in doing so. Indeed, the Irish government, whose agenda on labour market and social policy-making was dominated by a Minister for Social Affairs from the Democratic Left, was able to successfully translate its ideological preferences and promote policies designed to help the long-term unemployed and low-skilled workers. It could – by and large – do this without making concessions to the skilled workforce represented by organised interests, mainly trade unions. The reforms implemented between 1994 and 1997 particularly helped the very poor in society by increasing the redistributive effort of the state. The calls for a comprehensive reform of the tax system and for lower taxes in particular, coming from opposition parties, were not taken on board and remained unheard. In a similar vein, the complaints and requests from exponents of trade unions and employers' organisations did not alter the government agenda. The key concern of trade unions and employers' organisations was that government was not doing enough for employees who were already integrated in the labour market, and that regular employees would not benefit enough from the booming economy. They either expected the government to significantly cut taxes or to increase core social insurance benefits. Had this left-wing government faced political constraints by the conservative parties in opposition, the government would have had to partly accommodate their demands by implementing changes in the tax system or by increasing social security benefits for 'insiders', mainly skilled workers.

While the 'rainbow' government focused on labour market 'outsiders', the subsequent coalition between Fianna Fáil and the Progressive Democrats advanced an agenda that focused primarily on tax cuts. This policy agenda stands in stark contrast to the changes implemented between 1994 and 1997. Though only a minor partner in the coalition, the Progressive Democrats played a pivotal role in shaping both the Social Welfare and the Financial Bills. In accordance with the party's preferences, overall welfare state effort decreased and the government did not attempt to address the increasing wage inequality and the low-paid sector. In order not to endanger the trilateral agreements, the government decided to grant minimal adjustments to the benefits of labour market 'insiders'. Overall, the relative absence of political constraints enabled party governments to pursue their policy agenda without having to compensate partisan opposition and crucial interest groups along the way. This has implications for policy outcomes. In such a low-constraint environment, left-wing party governments have the opportunity to take into account the needs of the whole working-age population and design policy packages accordingly. Ideally, this would lead to a narrowing of the gap between labour market 'insiders' and 'outsiders'. Conservative party governments, however, have the ability to contribute to an increase in the heterogeneity of the labour market. Based on their partisan ideology, their agenda is likely to be dominated by policies which focus on minimising spending while at the same time lowering taxes and increasing labour market flexibility. In this respect, the agenda on macroeconomic and labour market policy by the coalition between Fianna Fàil and the Progressive Democrats serves as a perfect example of a series of policy changes that follow a logic that is driven by the aim of boosting employment through changing the incentive structure for employers. In addition to this business-friendly approach, the Conservative Irish government had an 'insider' focus in the way tax laws and contribution rules were reformed.

The analysis of the reform processes within these two countries clearly shows that the discussions in parliament continue to be characterised by diverging party preferences and struggles over issues related to redistributive generosity and spending. In this respect, politics and political processes over welfare state issues seem to be the same as they were during the formative years of welfare states. However, when we focus on the outcomes of the political struggles over reform agendas and policy design, we can see that the effects of policy changes are different nowadays than they were in the past. Pushed to the extreme, my argument yields the somewhat counter-intuitive result that left-wing parties together with trade unions increase rather than decrease inequality in society, at least when compared to the expectations that generally exist when people think of left-wing governments. Overall, the impact of Conservative party governments on redistributive equality is certainly worse, and several empirical studies show that stretches of Conservative rule have a statistically significant negative effect on inequality and also lead to an increase in poverty (see e.g. Bradley et al. 2003; Brady and Leicht 2008; Mahler, Jesuit and Roscoe 1999; Wright 2000).[7]

This result is counterintuitive in the sense that left-wing parties tend to focus on the wellbeing of the poor in public debates and also claim to help the disadvantaged in society. However, where organised interests have access to the policy-making process, Social Democratic or left-wing governments, under pressure to reform and retrench social policies, will try to accommodate the demands of trade unions on dimensions other than spending. I do not claim that the intentions of these party members to help the very poor or the 'outsiders' in modern societies are not genuine. However, the traditionally strong ties with organised interests, mainly trade unions, are an obstacle to the translation of the party's 'true' preferences. During the formative years of welfare states, the close ties between trade unions and Social Democratic party governments led to an outcome that was beneficial to most people regardless of their employment status. However, this has changed dramatically due to the developments discussed in the introductory chapters. The mechanisms of social policy-making therefore have not changed but the outcome of these processes has due to the continuing strong link between party governments and organised interests. This is particularly true for Social Democrats and leftist parties.

To some extent, trade unions, which publicly denounce social inequality, may help to reinforce rather than relieve the problem. When groups (implicitly) compete for scarce social policy resources, trade unions, which by definition are interest groups, primarily defend the interests of their members. These members, who provide the funding for the unions, are 'insiders' rather than 'outsiders'. It therefore follows that trade unions first defend the interests of 'insiders', while the interests of 'outsiders' are secondary. In times of fiscal austerity, most resources available for social policy tend to be spent on issues that are of concern to 'insiders'. This is particularly true when it comes to the reform of core social policies, such as the unemployment insurance scheme, active labour market policies and pensions. This mechanism is especially apparent in political settings where interest groups have many access points to the policy-making process. To some extent, this explains why countries with a higher level of political constraints, which were connected with more egalitarian policies during the formative years and the golden age of welfare states, have not been able to cope well with the adverse effects of globalisation. However, this conclusion needs further empirical examination and research.

The results of the study also indicate that labour markets in post-industrial democracies have become more segmented and that the so-called dualisation of labour markets is increasing further. The most important features of labour markets in post-industrial economies are the prevalence of a larger number of part-time and fixed-term employees (contractors), and an increasing number of people in precarious working relationships. Depending on the national context and the general structure of the labour market, people in atypical employment (part-time, contractors) face the risk of social exclusion or are systematically disadvantaged in the labour market. The risk of suffering from atypical employment, however, is not equally distributed across people in society. Often, women, elderly workers, and people with little education are groups that are most vulnerable in this regard. Divided labour markets have become a characteristic of the most recent wave of globalisation (e.g. Blanchard 2006; Goldthorpe 1984; Lindbeck and Snower 2001; Rueda 2006), and the fear of losing employment regularly ranks high in public opinion polls (Kenworthy and McCall 2008; Scheve and Slaughter 2006). This makes labour market policies a salient issue for party governments of any ideological background. In order to address the challenges related to increasing social inequality and societal risks for particular groups in society, party governments are under pressure to reform not only social security schemes but also labour market institutions. The aspects that governments emphasise while designing and implementing these reforms, however, differ greatly in scope and range. This study contributes to the dualisation literature with regard to the political factors that influence dualisation and the role political parties and also trade unions have to play. Future research should further examine the political factors that drive labour market dualisation and how this unhealthy development can be stopped or how the consequences of atypical work for society can be alleviated.

In connection with that, the role of organised interests needs to be reconsidered. The important role trade unions play in some countries because of their organisational strength and ability to gain access to political processes, e.g. in Germany, was generally perceived favourably with regard to equality in society. In practice, however, a large group of 'outsiders' exists in these countries, and studies show that the performance of these governments with respect to reducing inequality has not been impressive during recent decades. This book offers a partial explanation for this empirical phenomenon. The strong linkage between left-wing parties and trade unions and the influence of the latter in some political systems pulls social policy towards the concerns of the middle class and away from those who need help most. The participation of groups and citizens in policy-making is certainly useful and a central aspect of democratic politics. However, political systems with many access points but no important direct democratic instruments do not necessarily yield normatively desirable outcomes in the distributive struggle over scarce resources. The results based on the case studies suggest that a useful alternative could be to delegate more power to citizens. If 'outsiders' can exert the same political pressure as 'insiders' (by means of participation in referenda or popular initiatives), then this should bring about change as governments will be forced to design policies that also benefit the very poor. However, the implementation of direct democratic instruments is certainly no guarantee of more egalitarian politics/policies because bringing an issue to the public sphere is costly and not all groups have enough resources available to successfully launch a public initiative or a referendum. In addition, depending on the country context, labour market 'outsiders' (low-skilled people in low-wage jobs) are often immigrants who do not have the right to vote and would need organised interests or political parties to adopt their concerns.

One of the reasons why political scientists are interested in whether party politics has an impact on the outcome of public policies is because this impact is expected by the electorate. For most people, this is the reason why they vote and make a decision for or against a particular party in government. Knowing that a change in government will have no effect on the kind of policies implemented may lead to a declining interest in politics and to a further decrease in political participation, which eventually has a negative effect on the well-functioning of democracies. This may also lead to the emergence of extremist groups. However, the empirical results of the study imply that political competition and party politics still matter, although in a slightly different way than that usually expected. Structural changes to the economy and increasing internationalisation have altered the configuration of the labour market. Therefore, the demands made by the workforce have also changed. The manner in which party governments are able to address and meet these demands is influenced by the political constraints present in a country and the degree to which extra-parliamentarian actors have access to the policy-making process. The influence of external actors, mainly trade unions, is not new; what has changed is the fact that Social Democratic governments in political systems where constraints are high will not necessarily pursue (or are not able to pursue) and translate the policies most in line with their partisan preferences.

The definition of additional criteria was also necessary because the change from the quantitative to the qualitative framework also included a change in the level of analysis.[8] Whereas in the quantitative framework the empirical evidence was based on aggregated macro-level data, the case studies focused on processes that eventually drive these macro-level outcomes. Ideally, the concepts on which the macro-level analysis is based represent the sum or the total of the underlying reform processes. However, we cannot be completely sure whether this is the case because these aggregate concepts are often influenced by a number of developments and constraints that are beyond the influence of politics and party governments. Furthermore, they may not even take place on the country level. This is obviously not the case if the case studies focus on the same level of analysis and the explanatory concepts are measured in exactly the same way for the aggregate analysis as well as the analysis that focuses on processes on a different level. In comparative welfare state research, however, this is often not the case. This is to a great extent related to the kind of data most research relies on, something I will elaborate on further in the concluding paragraphs.

## 8.3 CONCLUDING REMARKS

The evidence found in this study has implications for comparative welfare state research, theoretically as well as empirically or methodologically. Theoretically, comparative welfare state research should strengthen its focus on the way that party politics is mediated by constraints. In addition, the systematic inclusion of different dimensions of social policy change proved to be a helpful strategy when evaluating how party governments influence the development of social policies and how (and if) they are able to transform their distinct ideological preferences into social policies. Empirically, research should move away from highly aggregated data to capture welfare state change in times of austerity and fiscal constraints.

The joint impact of political constraints and party governments should be investigated further. In particular, the linkage between different trade unions, representing different sectors, and Social Democratic parties in government in post-industrial societies should be more closely analysed. Rueda's 'insider' – 'outsider' approach (2005, 2007) is a helpful start to examine potential new cleavages and political preferences of different sectoral groups and industries. However, Rueda's framework is based only on a rough differentiation between 'insiders' and 'outsiders', and it would be beneficial to integrate the role of politics and trade unions more explicitly in the theoretical framework and tie it more closely to recent developments and research on class-based voting and newly developed or revised class schemas (see e.g. Oesch 2006a, b). Even though union membership is decreasing, the ties between unions and Social Democratic parties are still strong. A recent study has shown that an overwhelming majority of Social Democratic members of parliament are also members of a trade union, either of the peak organisation or a union representing a particular economic sector. In contrast with the numbers of unionised workers, which has been constantly decreasing during recent years, the ratio of members of parliament who represent both their party and the interests of a trade union has been increasing. Comparative welfare state research should take this phenomenon into account when examining welfare state change and theorising the political processes associated with it.

Theories aimed at investigating the impact of partisanship on social policy-making in post-industrial societies should also take into account the multi-dimensionality of social policies and policy-making in general and how party politics can have diverging impacts on the multiple dimensions. To break the tradition of focusing on spending (or retrenchment) is important in order to further develop theories of welfare state change and to reintegrate assumptions concerning political and partisan preferences. The interest in how different groups in society are affected by differing party governments is likely to grow in the future. The same goes for the patterns pertaining to how labour markets are changing and which political economies are more likely to have large shares of labour market 'outsiders'. Empirical analyses focusing on these questions and developments should also take into account the priorities party governments give to the reform of tax systems. Even though tax reforms were not explicitly part of the empirical analysis and not a policy field that has been examined in the case studies, when analysing the reform processes, it became clear that tax reforms and tax issues are an underlying topic in most of the reform processes. The discussions in parliament related to the implementation of the Financial and Social Welfare Bill 2001 in Ireland were actually dominated by issues related to the overall tax system and income taxes in particular. The tax issue was less prominent in Germany but references to potential tax reforms or the necessity of reforming taxes occurred during most debates. To systematically analyse changes in the tax scheme and examine the impact of these changes on various groups in society would complement the analysis and possibly provide further insight into the way in which different social groups are privileged under one government or another. Comparative research on tax reforms and their impact on individuals, firms and societal inequality are challenging and complex, mostly because tax regimes differ greatly across countries (e.g. in some federal states, taxes vary greatly across the sub-national units and it is hard to disentangle the effects). One possibility would be to focus on tax reforms that predominantly affect taxes connected to the labour market, such as taxes on labour, business and companies, and combine the evidence with evidence gained from the analysis of social policy and labour market reforms.

A shift in theories aimed at explaining changes in contemporary welfare states and the impact of these changes on various groups in society should ideally also include a shift in the data generated to document this shift. Comparative research on welfare state change either is generally based on quantitative studies that rely on highly aggregated data or consists of case studies that focus on reform processes within a small number of countries. The first research strategy is based on indirect operationalisations of reform processes and mainly captures overall policy outcomes, such as those relating to social spending. Case study work on the other hand has proven to be very important for the adaptation of theoretical approaches and their testing. Case study work is better able to capture policy shifts, critical junctures and policy punctuations, and scholars are able to more directly observe and document policy changes. Nonetheless, insight based on case studies is usually limited to certain countries, a particular period or policy field. The potential to generalise based on insights gained through case studies is therefore limited. To address these problems, more appropriate data should be generated which captures the changes in the design of policies and that will provide a more appropriate picture of the incremental changes going on in mature welfare states.

Empirically, comparative welfare state research should start building up a tradition that is not based on highly aggregated (spending) data. The use of aggregated data, especially of social and public spending data, has been widely criticised within the literature, but only a few people have tried to establish alternative measures. The focus on aggregated spending measures might have been appropriate to explain welfare state growth and the factors that influenced it. However, it is difficult to address questions related to the impact of party politics on welfare state retrenchment, the persistence of social policies in certain domains and the development of new social policies by relying on aggregate macroeconomic indicators. One possibility to get a better picture of how social policies are changing is to generate data that are based on reform processes. Ideally, these data would include both successful and failed reform efforts per country for various social policy fields and for various dimensions (or issues) of social policy-making. A collection of coded reform processes (successful and failed processes) across various policy fields has the potential to provide insight into a variety of research questions related to social policy-making in mature welfare states and other areas of comparative politics. On the one hand, and related to comparative welfare state research, data based on coded reform processes (failed and successful) could provide insight into the circumstances in which party governments are able to successfully reform social policies and whether changes in one dimension are systematically related to changes on other dimensions in a particular institutional setting and in a particular actor constellation. On the other hand, it would also be possible to compare whether systematic differences in reform efforts exist across policy fields. More specifically, do we find a different set of policy issues and reform dimensions emphasised in social policy fields where the 'insider'-'outsider' cleavage is not as apparent as in labour market policy. Related to the impact of party governments and differing coalition agreements, using the data base, it would then be possible to examine how the content of reform proposals may change between different types of governments. For instance, scholarship should assess whether the reform packages by oversized coalition governments significantly differ in their scope and dimensionality from reform packages proposed by minority governments. Related to this question, the impact of close elections on the design and the implementation of policies should be evaluated as well. Recent research shows that governments in which the prime minister's party obtains only a small margin of victory over the main opposition party will implement unpopular reforms, such as fiscal consolidation packages, at the very beginning of the legislative cycle (Hübscher and Sattler 2017). It is very likely that such a pattern is also the case in other policy fields, particularly labour market and pension politics.

Overall, comparative welfare state research would significantly benefit from more sophisticated quantitative data on policy changes, both in terms of reform content, that is, on the different steps of the reform process, information on the substantive reform issues and the actors involved. First, and unlike the highly aggregated data on policy output that is often used to examine social policy, data on the legislative actions of parliaments would provide a *direct* measure of social policy-making and social policy changes. Such data could be used as an alternative to indirect concepts (e.g. social spending) that are influenced by many other variables unrelated to the theory of interest.[9] Second, the data would not only be useful for quantitative analyses but would also provide additional information for qualitative research. They could also help to guide case study research by presenting a full list of reforms, which would be useful for a proper selection of cases. This strategy is also an attempt to link comparative welfare state reforms to neighbouring and related field of research such as the comparative research on legislative processes and policy-making. Some examples are the quantification of legislative action by coding policy agendas of party governments (see e.g. Baumgartner and Jones 1991, 1993; Bräuninger, Debus and Wüst 2005; John 2006; Jones and Baumgartner 2005) and the use of roll-call data to examine legislative output and policy-making (see e.g. Hug and Schulz 2007; Hix, Noury and Roland 2005; Ringe 2005; for the use of roll-call data within the European context).[10]

The explicit analysis of both successful and failed reform efforts is important for a number of reasons. Usually, the analysis of reform processes focuses on reforms that were approved and implemented at the end of the process. However, the analysis of 'negative' cases (failed reform processes or blocked attempts to reform a particular social policy) provides a more complete picture of the circumstances under which party governments are successful in building a 'reform coalition' because it allows us to draw conclusions when pivotal actors deny their support. The unit of analysis therefore should be a reform effort and not simply a successful reform. Levy (2007) and Mahoney and Goertz (2004) emphasise that the analysis of 'negative' cases can yield important information on the further development of theory. The potential problem of analyses that only select 'positive' cases, namely selection-bias and incorrect inference, has been discussed, for example, by Geddes (2003) and Collier and Mahoney (1996). The extended analysis would show whether the 'reform coalitions' are the same across policy fields and, more importantly, over time. This encompassing analysis would also show how similar the policy positions of parties and other pivotal actors need to be in order to find a common ground and to pass a reform bill.[11]

To approach fundamental research questions such as the impact of politics on policy design and policy changes using a different database that more directly captures policy change is a promising way to analyse various topics in comparative politics and could be a strategy to move away from highly aggregated data on policy outputs and policy outcomes. This research strategy would also bring comparative welfare state research closer to related strands of research, which – in my view – would further advance the field. All too often researchers rely on the same data and the same research strategies, neglecting the fact that political science and the analysis of public policies has advanced in related fields. To combine different approaches could be a fruitful and innovative way to extend our knowledge about policy-making processes in mature welfare states, party competition and the relationship between party governments and their assumed constituencies.

## NOTES

1 It is important to note that the number of reforms and the number of reform issues are too small to draw definite conclusions. In order to do that, further reforms should be analysed.

2 One example is the implementation of the job-rotation scheme, which gave 'insiders' the possibility to increase their skills by participating in further vocational training and 'outsiders' the possibility to gain on-the-job experience during the absence of the regular employee.

3 The reason why unions are able to pressure the government has to do with the political and institutional constraints, which also originate in the coordinated nature of the German economy.

4 The better known and more influential 'Hartz reforms' further promoted instruments such as the 'self-employment' scheme (known as 'Ich-AG'), tightened and further enforced the 'capability to work' definition and put more emphasis on personnel service agencies (temporary job agencies), to name but a few. Already discussed during the preparation phase of the Job-AQTIV legislation – but only implemented in the course of Hartz IV – was the merger of unemployment assistance and social assistance into a single means-tested scheme (see Konle-Seidl, Eichhorst and Grienberger-Zingerle (2007) for an overview over the changes implemented by Hartz I-IV).

5 In the 2005 general elections, the leftist party 'Die Linke' won 8.8 per cent of the national vote which allowed them for the first time to enter the Bundestag. In 2009, the party confirmed its success and increased its vote share to 12.2 per cent. The SPD at the same time went down from 38.5 per cent in 2002 to 34.2 per cent in 2005, then to an all-time low of 23.0 per cent in 2009.

6 The 2017 German elections, however, just showed that an electoral platform emphasising traditional social democratic values, such as social justice and fairness, does not win elections. The Social Democrats won 20.5 per cent of the votes, which marks the lowest level of electoral support for the party since 1949.

7 However, Scheve and Stasavage (2009) and Wallerstein (1999), for example, could not find a statistically significant relationship between right-wing party rule and an increase in (earnings) inequality.

8 In this study, the reform processes that take place on the meso-level were mostly chosen according to the reform content and the party government in charge of the process. This strategy leaves room to pick cases that fit particularly well, which should – in the end – be a representative example of government performance in certain policy field during the whole legislative period. To focus on the reform of unemployment insurance schemes and labour market policies was a hard test of the theoretical assumptions, and the results show that the lines of reasoning comply with the two dimensions set previous to the examination of the cases.

9 Data on social spending are influenced by factors that are not (or only to a limited extent) in control of parties in government, such as random economic shocks, and other, often unobservable, variables.

10 Research on policy agenda is influenced by the seminal work on agenda setting in the U.S. context by Baumgartner and Jones (1991, 1993) and Jones and Baumgartner (2005). Following the original research on the United States, European scholars are currently engaged in the 'comparative agendas project' (see e.g. Baumgartner, Green-Pedersen and Jones 2006; Bräuninger, Debus and Wüst 2017; John 2006; Sieberer 2006; Walgrave, Varone and Dumont 2006). This strand of research is influenced by scholarly interest in the agenda-setting capacity of party governments, issues of salience and public opinion. The agenda-setting literature is issue centred rather than actor centred and focuses on the dynamics of issue changes, issue attention and saliency. Legislative output and policy-making is also at the centre of the study of roll-call votes. Research based on the analysis of roll-call votes also has its origins in the United States. Recent developments in the field is the analysis of roll-call votes of the European parliament and the extension of the method to Western European countries, see e.g. Ringe (2005), Hix, Noury and Roland (2005, 2006) and Hug and Schulz (2007). The analysis of roll-call votes gives insights into the voting behaviour of members of parliament, party cohesion and coalition building in different subject areas of parliamentary work.

11 For some policy fields and some countries, a collection of successful reform processes exists, for example, Häusermann's (2007) collection of pension reforms in France, Germany and Switzerland. However, comparative data on a larger set of reforms across various social policy fields are not available, to the best of my knowledge.

# Bibliography


Abou-Chadi, Tarik and Ellen M. Immergut. 2014. 'Public Opinion, Institutions and Welfare State Change'. Paper prepared for presentation at the 110th Annual Meeting of the American Political Science Association, Washington, DC.

Achen, Christopher H. 2000. 'Why Lagged Dependent Variables Can Suppress the Explanatory Power of Other Independent Variables'. *The Society for Political Methodology, Working Papers*. http//polmeth.wustl.edu/workingpapers.php

Alber, Jens. 1986. Germany. In *Growth to Limits: Western European Welfare States since World War II*, ed. Peter Flora. Vol. II, Gruyter, pp. 3–154.

Alber, Jens. 1987. *Vom Armenhaus zum Wohlfahrtsstaat. Analysen zur Entwicklung der Sozialversicherung in Westeuropa*. European Social Science Studies. Campus.

Alesina, Alberto. 1987. 'Macroeconomic Policy in a Two-Party System as a Repeated Game'. *The Quarterly Journal of Economics* 102(3):651–678.

Alexiadou, Despina. 2013. 'In Search of Successful Reform: The Politics of Opposition and Consensus in OECD Parliamentary Democracies'. *West European Politics* 36(4):704–725.

Allan, James P. and Lyle Scruggs. 2004. 'Political Partisanship and Welfare State Reform in Advanced Industrial Societies'. *American Journal of Political Science* 48(3):496–512.

Alt, James. 1985. 'Political Parties, World Demand and Unemployment: Domestic and International Sources of Economic Activity'. *American Political Science Review* 79:539–556.

Amable, Bruno, Donatella Gatti and Jan Schumacher. 2006. 'Welfare-State Retrenchment: The Partisan Effect Revisited'. *Oxford Review of Economic Policy* 22(3):426–444.

Anderson, Christopher J. 2009. 'The Private Consequences of Public Policies: Active Labor Market Policies and Social Ties in Europe'. *European Political Science Review* 1(3):341–373.

Andersson, Staffan, Torbjörn Bergmann and Svante Ersson. 2012. The European Representative Democracy Data Archive. Main sponsor: Riksbankens Jubileumsfond (In 2007 0149:1-E). www.erdda.se

Ansell, Ben and Johannes Lindvall. 2013. 'The Political Origins of Primary Education Systems: Ideology, Insititutions, and Interdenominational Conflict in an Era of Nation-Building'. *American Political Science Review* 107(3):505–522.

Armingeon, Klaus and Kai Guthmann. 2014. 'Democracy in Crisis? The Declining Support for National Democracy in European Countries, 2007–2011'. *European Journal of Political Research* 53:423–442.

Armingeon, Klaus, Kai Guthmann and David Weisstanner. 2016. 'Choosing the Path of Austerity: A Neo-Functionalist Explanation of Welfare-Policy Choices in Periods of Fiscal Consolidation'. *West European Politics* 39(4):628–647.

Armingeon, Klaus and Lisa Schädel. 2015. 'Social Inequality in Political Participation: The Dark Sides of Individualisation'. *West European Politics* 38(1):1–27.

Armingeon, Klaus and Nathalie Giger. 2008. 'Conditional Punishement: A Comparative Analysis of the Electoral Consequences of Welfare State Retrenchment in OECD Nations, 1980–2003'. *West European Politics* 31(3):558–580.

Armingeon, Klaus, Romana Careja, David Weisstanner, Sarah Engler, Panajotis Potolidis and Marléne Gerber. 2012. 'Comparative Political Data Set III (35 OECD Countries)'. Berne: University of Berne.

Ausschuss für Arbeit und Soziales. 10.10.2001. 'Beschlussempfehlung und Bericht des "Ausschuss für Arbeit und Soziales", 103. Sitzung, October 10th 2001'. Published online. http//dip.bundestag.de/

Aust, Andreas, Frank Bönker and Hellmut Wollmann. 2002. 'Welfare State Reform in Germany from 1982 to the Present'. Report for the 2002 WRAMSOC Conference. September 2002. Project: Welfare Reform and Management of Societal Change (Framework Programme 5).

Avdagic, Sabina. 2013. 'Partisanship, Political Constraints, and Employment Protection Reforms in an Era of Austerity'. *European Political Science Review* 5(3):431–455.

Baccaro, Lucio and Sang-Hoon Lim. 2007. 'Social Pacts as Coalitions of the Weak and Moderate: Ireland, Italy and South Korea in Comparative Perspective'. *European Journal of Industrial Relations* 13(1):27–46.

Baggesen Klitgaard, Michael. 2007. 'Why Are They Doing It? Social Democracy and Market-Oriented Welfare State Reforms'. *West European Politics* 30(1):172–194.

Bartels, Larry M. 2005. 'Homer Gets a Tax Cut: Inequality and Public Policy in the American Mind'. *Perspectives on Politics* 3(1):15–31.

Baumgartner, Frank R. and Bryan D. Jones. 1991. 'Agenda Dynamics and Policy Subsystems'. *Journal of Politics* 53(4):1044–1074.

Baumgartner, Frank R. and Bryan D. Jones. 1993. *Agendas and Instability in American Politics*. Chicago, IL: University of Chicago Press.

Baumgartner, Frank R., Christoffer Green-Pedersen and Bryan D. Jones. 2006. 'Comparative Studies of Policy Agendas'. *Journal of European Public Policy* 13(7):959–974.

Beck, Nathaniel and Jonathan N. Katz. 1995. 'What to Do (and Not to Do) with Time-Series Cross-Section Data'. *American Political Science Review* 89(3):634–647.

Beck, Nathaniel and Jonathan N. Katz. 1996. 'Nuisance vs. Substance: Specifying and Estimating Time-Series-Cross-Section Models'. *Political Analysis* 6(1):1–36.

Beck, Nathaniel and Jonathan N. Katz. 2004. 'Time-Series-Cross-Section Issues: Dynamics 2004'. *The Society for Political Methodology, Working Papers.*

Becker, Rolf and Thomas Saalfeld. 2004. The Life and Times of Bills. In *Patterns of Parliamentary Behavior: Passage of Legislation across Western Europe*, eds. Herbert Döring and Mark Hallerberg. Aldershot: Ashgate, pp. 57–90.

Bélanger, Éric and Bonnie M. Meguid. 2008. 'Issue Salience, Issue Ownership, and Issue-Based Vote Choice'. *Electoral Studies* 27:477–491.

Bennett, Andrew and Colin Elman. 2006. 'Qualitative Research: Recent Developments in Case Study Methods'. *Annual Review of Political Science* 9:455–476.

Beramendi, Pablo and David Rueda. 2007. 'Social Democracy Constrained: Indirect Taxation in Industrialized Democracies'. *British Journal of Political Science* 37(4):619–641.

Beramendi, Pablo and Thomas Cusack. 2009. 'Diverse Disparities: The Politics and Economics of Wage, Market, and Disposable Income Inequalities'. *Political Research Quarterly* 62(2):257–275.

Berthold, Norbert and Sascha von Berchem. 2003. 'Job-AQTIV, Hartz, Agenda 2010 – Aufbruch zu neuen Ufern oder viel Lärm um Nichts?' Wirtschaftswissenschaftliche Beiträge des Lehrstuhls für Volkswirtschaftslehre, Wirtschaftsordnung und Sozialpolitik, Julius-Maximilians-Universität Würzburg (Nr. 66).

Birchfield, Vicki and Markus M. L. Crepaz. 1998. 'The Impact of Constitutional Structures and Collective and Competitive Veto Points on Income Inequality in Industrialized Democracies'. *European Journal of Political Research* 34(2):175–200.

Blais, André, Donald Blake and Stephane Dion. 1993. 'Do Parties Make a Difference? Parties and the Size of Government in Liberal Democracies'. *American Journal of Political Science* 37:40–62.

Blanchard, Olivier. 2006. 'European Unemployment: The Evolution of Facts and Ideas'. *Economic Policy* 45:5–59.

Blekesaune, Morten. 2007. 'Economic Conditions and Public Attitudes to Welfare Policies'. *European Sociological Review* 23(3):393–403.

Bleses, Peter and Martin Seeleib-Kaiser. 2004. *The Dual Transformation of the German Welfare State*. New Perspective in German Studies. Palgrave Macmillan.

Blondel, Jean. 1968. 'Party Systems and Patterns of Government in Western Democracies'. *Canadian Journal of Political Science* 1(2):180–203.

Boeri, Tito, Axel Börsch-Supan, Guido Tabellini, Karl Ove Moene and Ben Lockwood. 2001. 'Would You Like to Shrink the Welfare State? A Survey of European Citizens'. *Economic Policy* 16(32):9–50.

Boix, Carles. 1998. *Political Parties, Growth and Equality – Conservative and Social Democratic Economic Strategies in the World Economy*. Cambridge Studies in Comparative Politics. Cambridge: Cambridge University Press.

Bonoli, Giuliano. 2001. Political Institutions, Veto Points, and the Process of Welfare State Adaption. In *The New Politics of the Welfare State*, ed. Paul Pierson. Oxford University Press, pp. 238–264.

Bonoli, Giuliano. 2003. 'Two Worlds of Pension Reform in Western Europe'. *Comparative Politics* 35(4):399–416.

Bonoli, Giuliano. 2008. 'The Political Economy of Activation. Explaining Cross-National Variation in Active Labor Market Policy'. *Working Paper IDHEAP* (1):1–21.

Bonoli, Giuliano. 2010. 'The Political Economy of Active Labour Market Policy'. *Working Papers on the Reconciliation of Work and Welfare in Europe (REC-WP)* (01/2010):1–29.

Bortolotti, Bernardo and Domenico Siniscalco. 2004. *The Challenges of Privatization: An International Analysis*. Oxford: Oxford University Press.

Box-Steffensmeier, Janet M. and Bradford S. Jones. 2004. *Event History Modeling – A Guide for Social Scientists*. Cambridge: Cambridge University Press.

Bradley, David, Evelyne Huber, Stephanie Moller, François Nielsen and John D. Stephens. 2003. 'Distribution and Redistribution in Postindustrial Democracies'. *World Politics* 55(2):193–228.

Brady, David, Evelyne Huber and John D. Stephens. 2016. 'Comparative Welfare States Data Set 2014'. Downloadable data set (updated to 2014). http//www.lisdatacenter.org/resources/other-databases/

Brady, David and Kevin T. Leicht. 2008. 'Party to Inequality: Right Party Power and Income Inequality in Affluent Western Democracies'. *Research in Social Stratification and Mobility* 26(1):77–106.

Bräuninger, Thomas, Marc Debus and Fabian Wüst. 2017. 'Government, Opposition, and Legislative Activity'. *Political Science Research and Methods* 5(3):529–554.

Brooks, Clem and Jeff Manza. 2007. *Why Welfare States Persist: The Importance of Public Opinion in Democracies*. Studies in Communication, Media, and Public Opinion. Chicago, IL: University of Chicago Press.

Browne, Eric C. and Mark N. Franklin. 1973. 'Aspects of Coalition Payoffs in European Parliamentary Democracies'. *American Political Science Review* 67(2):453–469.

Brunner, Martin and Marc Debus. 2008. 'Between Programmatic Interests and Party Politics: The German Bundesrat in the Legislative Process'. *German Politics* 17(3):232–251.

Budge, Ian and D. J. Farlie. 1983. *Explaining and Predicting Elections*. Allen and Unwin.

Bulsara, Hament and Bill Kissane. 2009. 'Arend Lijphart and the Transformation of Irish Democracy'. *West European Politics* 32(1):172–195.

Burgoon, Brian. 2001. 'Globalization and Welfare Compensation: Disentangling the Ties That Bind'. *International Organization* 55(3):509–551.

Burke, Helen. 1999. Foundation Stones of Irish Social Policy 1831–1951. In *Irish Social Policy in Context*, eds. Gabriel Kiely, Anne O'Donnell, Patricia Kennedy and Suzanne Quin. University College Dublin Press, pp. 11–32.

Caliendo, Marco, Alexander Kritikos, Viktor Steiner and Frank Wiessner. 2007. 'Existenzgründungen: Unterm Strich ein Erfolg'. *IAB Kurzbericht* (10).

Callan, Tim and Brian Nolan. 2000. Taxation and Social Welfare. In *Bust to Boom? The Irish Experience of Growth and Inequality*, eds. Brian Nolan, Philip J. O'Connell and Christopher T. Whelan. IPA Institute of Public Administration, chapter 10, pp. 179–203.

Callan, Tim, Brian Nolan, Claire Keane, Michael Savage and John R. Walsh. 2013. 'The Great Recession, Austerity and Inequality: Evidence from Ireland'. *Intereconomics* 6:335–339.

Cameron, David R. 1978. 'The Expansion of the Public Economy: A Comparative Analysis'. *American Political Science Review* 72(4):1243–1261.

Carter, David B. and Curtis S. Signorino. 2010. 'Back to the Future: Modeling Time Dependence in Binary Data'. *Political Analysis* 18:271–292.

Carty, R. Kenneth. 1981. *Party and Parish Pump: Electoral Politics in Ireland.* Wilfried Laurier Press.

Castles, Francis. 1982. *The Impact of Parties on Public Expenditure*. SAGE Publications.

Castles, Francis G. 2002. 'Developing New Measures of Welfare State Change and Reform'. *European Journal of Political Research* 41:613–641.

Castles, Francis G. 2005. 'Social Expenditure in the 1990s: Data and Determinants'. *Policy & Politics* 33(3):411–430.

Castles, Francis G. and Herbert Obinger. 2007. 'Social Expenditure and the Politics of Redistribution'. *Journal of European Social Policy* 17(3):206–222.

Chari, Raj S. and Hilary McMahon. 2003. 'Reconsidering the Patterns of Organised Interests in Irish Policy Making'. *Irish Political Studies* 18(1):27–50.

Chari, Raj S. and Patrick Bernhagen. 2011. 'Financial and Economic Crisis Explaining the Sunset over the Celtic Tiger'. *Irish Political Studies* 26(4):473–488.

Chubb, Basil. 1992. *The Government and Politics of Ireland.* 3rd ed. London: Longman.

Clarke, Blánaid and Niamh Hardiman. 2012. Crisis in the Irish Banking System. In *Banking Systems in the Crisis: The Faces of Liberal Capitalism*, ed. Sue Konzelmann. Routledge.

Clasen, Jochen and Nico A. Siegel. 2007. *Investigating Welfare State Change: The 'Dependent Variable Problem' in Comparative Analysis*. Edward Elgar.

Coakley, John. 1999. The Foundations of Statehood. In *Politics in the Republic of Ireland*, eds. John Coakley and Michael Gallagher. Routledge, pp. 1–31.

Coakley, John. 2002. 'Religion, National Identity and Political Change in Modern Ireland'. *Irish Political Studies* 17(1):4–28.

Collier, David and James Mahoney. 1996. 'Insights and Pitfalls: Selection Bias in Qualitative Research'. *World Politics* 49(1):56–91.

Connolly, Eileen and Eunan O'Halpin. 1999. The Government and the Governmental System. In *Politics in the Republic of Ireland*, eds. John Coakley and Michael Gallagher. Routledge, chapter 10, pp. 249–270.

Conroy, Pauline. 1999. From the Fifties to the Nineties: Social Policy Comes Out of the Shadow. In *Irish Social Policy in Context*, eds. Gabriel Kiely, Anne O'Donnell, Patricia Kennedy and Suzanne Quin. University College Dublin Press, pp. 33–50.

Cousins, Mel. 1997. 'Ireland's Place in the Worlds of Welfare Capitalism'. *Journal of European Social Policy* 7(3):223–235.

Cousins, Mel. 2005. *European Welfare States*. SAGE Publications.

Cusack, Thomas R. 1999. 'Partisan Politics and Fiscal Policy'. *Comparative Political Studies* 32(4):464–486.

Cusack, Thomas, Torben Iversen and Philipp Rehm. 2006. 'Risks at Work: The Demand and Supply Sides of Government Redistribution'. *Oxford Review of Economic Policy* 22(3):365–389.

Dáil Éireann. 1996a. 'Dáil Éireann, Volume 460, 23 January 1996 (Financial Resolutions, 1996, Financial Statement, Budget 1996)'. Electronic Database. https://www.oireachtas.ie/en/debates/debate/dail/1996-01-23/12/

Dáil Éireann. 1996b. 'Dáil Éireann, Volume 460, 24 January 1996 (Financial Resolutions, 1996, General)'. Electronic Database. https://www.oireachtas.ie/en/debates/debate/dail/1996-01-24/14/

Dáil Éireann. 1996c. 'Dáil Éireann, Volume 460, 25 January 1996 (Financial Resolutions, 1996, General)'. Electronic Database. https://www.oireachtas.ie/en/debates/debate/dail/1996-01-25/5/

Dáil Éireann. 1996d. 'Dáil Éireann, Volume 460, 30 January 1996 (Financial Resolutions, 1996, General)'. Electronic Database. https://www.oireachtas.ie/en/debates/debate/dail/1996-01-30/12/

Dáil Éireann. 1996e. 'Dáil Éireann, Volume 460, 31 January 1996 (Financial Resolutions, 1996)'. Electronic Database. https://www.oireachtas.ie/en/debates/debate/dail/1996-01-31/10

Dáil Éireann. 1996f. 'Dáil Éireann, Volume 460, 1 February 1996 (Financial Resolutions, 1996, General)'. Electronic Database. https://www.oireachtas.ie/en/debates/debate/dail/1996-02-01/3/

Dáil Éireann. 1996g. 'Dáil Éireann, Volume 461, 8 February 1996 (Financial Resolutions, 1996, General)'. Electronic Database. https://www.oireachtas.ie/en/debates/debate/dail/1996-02-08/8/

Dáil Éireann. 1999. 'Dáil Éireann, Volume 501, 24 February 1999 (Social Welfare Bill, 1999: Second Stage)'. Electronic Database. https://www.oireachtas.ie/en/debates/debate/dail/1999-02-24/11/

Dáil Éireann. 2000a. 'Dáil Éireann, Volume 527, 6 December 2000 (Financial Resolution, 2001, Budget Statement)'. Electronic Database. https://www.oireachtas.ie/en/debates/debate/dail/2000-12-06/19/

Dáil Éireann. 2000b. 'Dáil Éireann, Volume 528, 13 December 2000 (Financial Resolutions, 2001, General)'. Electronic Database. https://www.oireachtas.ie/en/debates/debate/dail/2000-12-13/5/

Dáil Éireann. 2000c. 'Dáil Éireann, Volume 527, 7 December 2000 (Financial Resolution No. 4: General)'. Electronic Database. https://www.oireachtas.ie/en/debates/debate/dail/2000-12-07/24/

Dáil Éireann. 2001a. 'Dáil Éireann, Volume 531, 21 February 2001 (Social Welfare Bill, 2001: Second Stage)'. Electronic Database. https://www.oireachtas.ie/en/debates/debate/dail/2001-02-21/6/

Dáil Éireann. 2001b. 'Dáil Éireann, Volume 531, 27 February 2001 (Financial Bill, 2001: Second Stage)'. Electronic Database. https://www.oireachtas.ie/en/debates/debate/dail/2001-02-27/25/

Dáil Éireann. 2001c. 'Dáil Éireann, Volume 531, 28 February 2001 (Financial Bill, Second Stage)'. Electronic Database https://www.oireachtas.ie/en/debates/debate/dail/2001-02-28/8/

Davidsson, Johan and Marek Naczyk. 2009. 'The Ins and Outs of Dualisation: A Literature Review'. *Working Papers on the Reconciliation of Work and Welfare in Europe* (02/09):1–45.

Debus, Marc. 2009. 'Analysing Party Politics in Germany with New Approaches for Estimating Policy Preferences of Political Actors'. *German Politics* 18(3):281–300.

Deutscher Bundestag. 1994a. 'Beschlussempfehlung und Bericht des Ausschusses für Arbeit und Sozialordnung (11. Ausschuss)'. http//dipbt.bundestag.de/doc/btd/14/066/1406628.pdf

Deutscher Bundestag. 1994b. 'Plenarprotokoll des Deutschen Bundestages, 12. Wahlperiode, 219. Sitzung (14. April 1994)'. http//dipbt.bundestag.de/doc/btp/12/12219.pdf

Deutscher Bundestag. 2001a. 'Plenarprotokoll des Deutschen Bundestages, 14. Wahlperiode, 190. Sitzung (27. September 2001)'. http//dip21.bundestag.de/dip21/btp/14/14190.pdf

Deutscher Bundestag. 2001b. 'Plenarprotokoll des Deutschen Bundestages, 14. Wahlperiode, 199. Sitzung (9. November 2001)'. http//dip21.bundestag.de/dip21/btp/14/14199.pdf

Devries, Pete, Jaime Guajardo, Daniel Leigh and Andrea Pescatori. 2011. 'A New Action-Based Dataset of Fiscal Consolidation'. *IMF Working Paper* (11/128):1–91.

Dingeldey, Irene. 2007. 'Between Workfare and Enablement – The Different Paths to Transformation of the Welfare State: A Comparative Analysis of Activating Labour Market Policies'. *European Journal of Political Research* 46(6):823–851.

Donovan, Donal and Antoin E. Murphy. 2013. *The Fall of the Celtic Tiger – Ireland and the Euro Debt*. Oxford University Press.

Downs, Anthony. 1957. 'An Economic Theory of Political Action in a Democracy'. *Journal of Political Economy* 65(2):135–150.

Doyle, David and John Hogan. 2008. 'Macroeconomic Policy Change: Ireland in Comparative Perspective'. *Irish Political Studies* 23(1):77–97.

Dreher, Axel. 2006. 'KOF Index of Globalization'. http//globalization.kof.ethz.ch/

Dreher, Axel, Jan-Egbert Sturm and Heinrich W. Ursprung. 2006. 'The Impact of Globalization on the Composition of Government Expenditures: Evidence from Panel Data'. *CESifo Working Paper* (1755):1–40.

Ebbinghaus, Bernhard. 2006. *Reforming Early Retirement in Europe, Japan and the USA*. Oxford University Press.

Ebbinghaus, Bernhard and Werner Eichhorst. 2006. 'Employment Regulations and Labor Market Policy in Germany, 1991–2005'. *IZA Discussion Paper* (2505):1–62.

Engbom, Niklas, Enrica Detragiache and Faezeh Raei. 2015. 'The German Labor Market Reforms and Post-Unemployment Earnings'. *IMF Working Paper* (WP/15/162):1–25.

Erikson, Robert S., Michael B. MacKuen and James A. Stimson. 2002. *The Macro Polity*. Cambridge: Cambridge University Press.

Esping-Andersen, Gøsta. 1985. *Politics against Markets: The Social Democratic Road to Power*. Princeton University Press.

Esping-Andersen, Gøsta. 1990. *The Three Worlds of Welfare Capitalism*. Cambridge University Press.

Fanning, Bryan. 1999. The Mixed Economy of Welfare. In *Irish Social Policy in Context*, eds. Gabriel Kiely, Anne O'Donnell, Patricia Kennedy and Suzanne Quin. University College Dublin Press, pp. 51–69.

Finseraas, Henning. 2009. 'Income Inequality and Demand for Redistribution: A Multilevel Analysis of European Public Opinion'. *Scandinavian Political Studies* 32(1):94–119.

Fitzenberger, Bernd, Karsten Kohn and Qingwei Wang. 2006. 'The Erosion of Union Membership in Germany: Determinants, Densities, Decompositions'. *IZA Discussion Paper* (2193):1–39.

Fleckenstein, Timo. 2006. 'Europeanisation of German Labour Market Policy? The European Employment Strategy Scrutinised'. *German Politics* 15(3):284–301.

Fredriksen, Kaja Bonesmo. 2012. 'Income Inequality in the European Union'. *OECD Economics Department Working Papers* (29):1–25.

Gallagher, Michael. 1999a. The Changing Constitution. In *Politics in the Republic of Ireland*, eds. John Coakley and Michael Gallagher. Routledge, Chapter 3, pp. 71–98.

Gallagher, Michael. 1999b. Parliament. In *Politics in the Republic of Ireland*, eds. John Coakley and Michael Gallagher. Routledge, Chapter 7, pp. 177–105.

Gallagher, Michael, Michael Laver and Peter Mair, eds. 1992. *Representative Government in Western Europe*. McGraw Hill.

Gamson, William A. 1961. 'A Theory of Coalition Formation'. *American Sociological Review* 26:373–382.

Garrett, Geoffrey. 1993. 'The Politics of Structural Change: Swedish Social Democracy and Thatcherism in Comparative Perspective'. *Comparative Political Studies* 25:521–547.

Garrett, Geoffrey. 1998. *Partisan Politics in the Global Economy*. Cambridge University Press.

Garry, John and Lucy Mansergh. 1999. Party Manifestos. In *How Ireland Voted, 1997*, eds. Michael Marsh and Paul Mitchell. Studies in Irish Politics. Westview Press, pp. 82–106.

Garvin, Tom. 1974. 'Political Cleavages, Party Politics and Urbanisation in Ireland: The Case of the Periphery-Dominated Centre'. *European Journal of Political Research* 2:307–327.

Geddes, Barbara. 2003. *Paradigms and Sand Castles – Theory Building and Research Design in Comparative Politics*. University of Michigan Press.

Giger, Nathalie and Moira Nelson. 2011. 'The Electoral Consequences of Welfare State Retrenchment: Blame Avoidance or Credit Claiming in the Era of Permanent Austerity'. *European Journal of Political Research* 50(1):1–23.

Gilland Lutz, Karin. 2003. 'Irish Party Competition in the New Millennium: Change, or Plus Ca Change?'. *Irish Political Studies* 18(2):40–59.

Gingrich, Jane and Silja Häusermann. 2015. 'The Decline of the Working-Class Vote, the Reconfiguration of the Welfare Support Coalition and Consequences for the Welfare State'. *Journal of European Social Policy* 25(1):50–75.

Goldthorpe, John H. 1984. The End of Convergence: Corporatist and Dualist Tendencies in Modern Western Societies. In *Order and Conflict in Contemporary Capitalism*, ed. John H. Goldthorpe. Clarendon Press, Oxford, pp. 315–343.

Green-Pedersen, Christoffer. 2001a. 'Minority Governments and Party Politics: The Political and Institutional Background to the "Danish Miracle"'. *Journal of Public Policy* 21(1):53–70.

Green-Pedersen, Christoffer. 2001b. 'Welfare-State Retrenchment in Denmark and the Netherlands, 1982–1998 – The Role of Party Competition and Party Consensus'. *Comparative Political Studies* 34(9):963–985.

Green-Pedersen, Christoffer. 2002. *The Politics of Justification – Party Competition and Welfare State Retrenchment in Denmark and the Netherlands from 1982–1998*. Amsterdam: Amsterdam University Press.

Green-Pedersen, Christoffer. 2004. 'The Dependent Variable Problem within the Study of Welfare State Retrenchment: Defining the Problem and Looking for Solutions'. *Journal of Comparative Policy Analysis* 6(1):3–14.

Green-Pedersen, Christoffer, Kees van Kersbergen and Anton Hemerijck. 2001. 'Neo-liberalism, the 'Third Way' of What? Recent Social Democratic Welfare Policies in Denmark and the Netherlands'. *Journal of European Public Policy* 8(2):307–325.

Green-Pedersen, Christoffer and Markus Haverland. 2002. 'The New Politics and Scholarship of the Welfare State'. *Journal of European Social Policy* 12(1):43–51.

Groh-Samberg, Olaf. 2015. 'No Way Out: Dimensionen und Trends der Verfestigung der Armut in Deutschland'. *Sozialer Fortschritt* 63(12):307–314.

Hall, Peter A. and David Soskice. 2001. An Introduction to Varieties of Capitalism. In *Varieties of Capitalism – The Institutional Foundations of Comparative Advantage*, eds. Peter A. Hall and David Soskice. Oxford University Press, pp. 1–70.

Hardiman, Niamh. 1988. *Pay, Politics, and Economic Performance in Ireland 1970–1987*. Clarendon Press, Oxford.

Hardiman, Niamh. 2000. Social Partnership, Wage Bargaining, and Growth. In *Bust to Boom? The Irish Experience of Growth and Inequality*, eds. Brian Nolan, Philip J. O'Connell and Christopher T. Whelan. Dublin: IPA Institute of Public Administration, Chapter 15, pp. 286–309.

Hardiman, Niamh. 2002. 'From Conflict to Co-ordination: Economic Governance and Political Innovation in Ireland'. *West European Politics* 25(4):1–24.

Hardiman, Niamh. 2005a. 'Partnership and Politics: How Embedded Is Social Partnership?' *Geary Discussion Paper Series* (WP 2005/08):1–38.

Hardiman, Niamh. 2005b. 'Politics and Markets in the Irish "Celtic Tiger"'. *The Political Quarterly* 76(1):37–47.

Hardiman, Niamh. 2006. 'Politics and Social Partnership: Flexible Network Governance'. *The Economic and Social Review* 37(3):343–374.

Hardiman, Niamh, ed. 2012. *Irish Governance in Crisis*. Manchester University Press.

Hassel, Anke. 1999. 'The Erosion of the German System of Industrial Relations'. *British Journal of Industrial Relations* 37(3):483–505.

Häusermann, Silja. 2006. 'Changing Coalitions in Social Policy Reforms: The Politics of New Social Needs and Demands'. *Journal of European Social Policy* 16(1):5–21.

Häusermann, Silja. 2007. 'Modernization in Hard Times: Post-Industrial Pension Politics in France, Germany and Switzerland'. Thesis presented to the Faculty of Philosophy at the University of Zurich, Switzerland.

Häusermann, Silja. 2010a. *The Politics of Welfare State Reform in Continental Europe: Modernization in Hard Times*. Cambridge University Press.

Häusermann, Silja. 2010b. 'Solidarity with Whom? Why Organized Labour Is Losing Ground in Continental Pension Politics'. *European Journal of Political Research* 49(2):223–256.

Häusermann, Silja, Georg Picot and Dominik Geering. 2013. 'Rethinking Party Politics and the Welfare State – Recent Advances in the Literature'. *British Journal of Political Science* 43(1):221–240.

Heller, William B. 2001. 'Making Policy Stick: Why the Government Gets What It Wants in Multiparty Systems'. *American Journal of Political Science* 45(4):780–798.

Henisz, Witold Jerezy. 2006. 'The Political Constraint Index (POLCON) Dataset, Codebook'. Electronic Database. http//www-management.wharton.upenn.edu/henisz/

Hibbs, Douglas A. 1977. 'Political Parties and Macroeconomic Policy'. *American Political Science Review* 71(4):1467–1487.

Hicks, Alexander and Christopher Zorn. 2005. 'Economic Globalization, the Macro Economy, and Reversals of Welfare: Expansion in Affluent Democracies, 1978–94'. *International Organization* 59:631–662.

Hicks, Alexander M. and Duane H. Swank. 1992. 'Politics, Institutions, and Welfare State Spending in Industrialized Democracies, 1960–82'. *American Political Science Review* 86(3):658–674.

Hicks, Timothy. 2016. 'Acting Right? Privatization, Encompassing Interests, and the Left'. *Political Science Research and Methods* 4(2):427–448.

Hix, Simon, Abdul Noury and Gérard Roland. 2005. 'Power to the Parties: Cohesion and Competition in the European Parliament, 1979–2001'. *British Journal of Political Science* 35(2):209–234.

Hix, Simon, Abdul Noury and Gérard Roland. 2006. 'Dimensions of Politics in the European Parliament'. *American Journal of Political Science* 50(2):494–511.

Hoffmann, Nick. 2010. 'Political Institutions and Policy Outcomes: The Political Constraints Approach of Henisz'. *CESifo DICE Report* 8(2):53–59.

Honohan, Patrick. 2009. 'Policy Paper: Resolving Ireland's Banking Crisis'. *The Economic and Social Review* 40(2):207–231.

Honohan, Patrick. 2010. 'The Irish Banking Crisis: Regulatory and Financial Stability Policy 2003–2008'. Report to the Minister for Finance by the Governor of the Central Bank.

House, J. D. and Kyla McGrath. 2004. 'Innovative Governance and Development in the New Ireland: Social Partnership and the Integrated Approach'. *Governance: An International Journal of Policy and Administration* 17(1):29–58.

Huber, Evelyne, Charles C. Ragin and John D. Stephens. 1993. 'Social Democracy, Christian Democracy, Constitutional Structure, and the Welfare State'. *American Journal of Sociology* 99(3):711–749.

Huber, Evelyne and John D. Stephens. 1998. 'Internationalization and the Social Democractic Model: Crisis and Future Prospects'. *Comparative Political Studies* 31(3):353–397.

Huber, Evelyne and John D. Stephens. 2001. *Development and Crisis of the Welfare State – Parties and Policies in Global Markets*. Chicago, IL: University of Chicago Press.

Hübscher, Evelyne. 2016. 'The Political Economy of Fiscal Consolidation Revisited'. *Journal of Public Policy* 36(4):573–601.

Hübscher, Evelyne. 2017. 'Party Governments, Clientelistic Reforms and Varying Levels of Political Constraints'. *Comparative European Politics* 15(6):848–871.

Hübscher, Evelyne and Thomas Sattler. 2018. 'The Fiscal Policy Trap: Deficits, Austerity, and Popularity' Unpublished Manuscript.

Hübscher, Evelyne and Thomas Sattler. 2017. 'Fiscal Consolidation under Electoral Risk'. *European Journal of Political Research* 56(1):151–168.

Hug, Simon and Tobias Schulz. 2007. 'Left-Right Positions of Political Parties in Switzerland'. *Party Politics* 13(3):305–330.

Huo, Jingjing. 2009. *Third Way Reforms – Social Democracy after the Golden Age*. Cambridge University Press.

Huo, Jingjing, Moira Nelson and John D. Stephens. 2008. 'Decommodification and Activation in Social Democratic Policy: Resolving the Paradox'. *Journal of European Social Policy* 18(1):5–20.

Immergut, Ellen M. 1990. 'Institutions, Veto Points, and Policy Results: A Comparative Analysis of Health Care'. *Journal of Public Policy* 10(4):391–416.

Immergut, Ellen M., Karen M. Anderson and Isabelle Schulze, eds. 2007. *The Handbook of West European Pension Politics*. Oxford University Press.

Iversen, Torben and Anne Wren. 1998. 'Equality, Employment, and Budgetary Restraint – The Trilemma of the Service Economy'. *World Politics* 50(4):507–546.

Iversen, Torben and David Soskice. 2006a. 'Electoral Institutions and the Politics of Coalitions: Why Some Democracies Redistribute More than Others'. *American Political Science Review* 100(2):165–181.

Iversen, Torben and David Soskice. 2006b. 'New Macroeconomy and Political Science'. *Annual Review of Political Science* 9:425–453.

Iversen, Torben and Thomas Cusack. 2000. 'The Causes of Welfare State Expansion: Deindustrialization or Globalization?' *World Politics* 52:313–349.

Jacoby, Wade and Martin Behrens. 2016. '"Breaking Up Is Hard to Do': German Trade Unions within the Social Democratic Party'. *Comparative European Politics* 14(3):273–297.

Jensen, Carsten. 2007. 'Fixed or Variable Needs? Public Support and Welfare State Reforms'. *Government and Opposition* 42(2):139–157.

Jensen, Carsten and Peter B. Mortensen. 2014. 'Government Responses to Fiscal Austerity: The Effect of Institutional Fragmentation and Partisanship'. *Comparative Political Studies* 47(2):143–170.

Jensen, Christian B., Sven-Oliver Proksch and Jonathan B. Slapin. 2013. 'Parliamentary Questions, Oversight and National Opposition Status in European Parliament'. *Legislative Studies Quarterly* 38(2):259–282.

John, Peter. 2006. 'The Policy Agendas Project: A Review'. *Journal of European Public Policy* 13(7):975–986.

Jones, Bryan D. and Frank R. Baumgartner. 2005. *The Politics of Attention: How Government Prioritizes Problems*. Chicago, IL: Chicago University Press.

Kalleberg, Arne L. 2000. 'Nonstandard Employment Relations: Part-Time, Temporary and Contract Work'. *Annual Review of Sociology* 26:341–365.

Katz, Richard S. and Peter Mair. 2009. 'The Cartel Party Thesis: A Restatement'. *Perspectives on Politics* 7(4):753–766.

Katzenstein, Peter J. 1987. *Politics and Policy in West Germany: The Growth of a Semisovereign State*. Philadelphia, PA: Temple University Press.

Keefer, Philip and David Stasavage. 2003. 'The Limits of Delegation: Veto Players, Central Bank Independence and the Credibility of Monetary Policy'. *American Political Science Review* 97(3):407–423.

Keele, Luke and Nathan J. Kelly. 2006. 'Dynamic Models for Dynamic Theories: The Ins and Outs of Lagged Dependent Variables'. *Political Analysis* 14(2):186–205.

Kenworthy, Lane. 2009. 'Research Note: The Effect of Public Opinion on Social Policy Generosity'. *Socio-Economic Review* 7(4):727–740.

Kenworthy, Lane and Leslie McCall. 2008. 'Inequality, Public Opinion, and Redistribution'. *Socio-Economic Review* 6(1):35–68.

Kim, HeeMin and Richard C. Fording. 1998. 'Voter Ideology in Western Democracies, 1946–1989'. *European Journal of Political Research* 33:73–97.

Kim, HeeMin and Richard C. Fording. 2002. 'Government Partisanship in Western Democracies, 1945–1998'. *European Journal of Political Research* 41(2):187–206.

Kitschelt, Herbert. 2001. Partisan Competition and Welfare State Retrenchment – When Do Politicians Choose Unpopular Policies? In *The New Politics of the Welfare State*, ed. Paul Pierson. Oxford University Press, pp. 265–302.

Kitschelt, Herbert and Wolfgang Streeck. 2003. 'From Stability to Stagnation: Germany at the Beginning of the Twenty-First Century'. *West European Politics* 26(4):1–34.

Kittel, Bernhard and Herbert Obinger. 2003. 'Political Parties, Institutions, and the Dynamics of Social Expenditure in Times of Austerity'. *Journal of European Public Policy* 10(1):20–45.

Klingemann, Hans-Dieter, Andrea Volkens, Judith Bara and Ian Budge. 2006. *Mapping Policy Preferences II: Estimates for Parties, Electors, and Governments in Central and Eastern Europe, European Union and OECD 1990–2003*. Oxford: Oxford University Press.

König, Pascal D. and Georg Wenzelburger. 2014. 'Toward a Theory of Political Strategy in Policy Analysis'. *Politics & Policy* 42(3):400–430.

Konle-Seidl, Regina, Werner Eichhorst and Maria Grienberger-Zingerle. 2007. 'Activation Policies in Germany: From Status Protection to Basic Income Support'. *IAB Discussion Paper* (6):1–76.

Korpi, Walter. 1978. *The Working Class in Welfare Capitalism: Work, Unions, and Politics in Sweden*. Routledge.

Korpi, Walter. 1989. 'Power, Politics, and State Autonomy in the Development of Social Citizenship: Social Rights during Sickness in Eigtheen OECD Countries since 1930'. *American Sociological Review* 54(3):309–329.

Korpi, Walter and Joakim Palme. 1998. 'The Paradox of Redistribution and Strategies of Equality: Welfare State Institutions, Inequality, and Poverty in the Western Countries'. *American Sociological Review* 63(5):661–687.

Korpi, Walter and Joakim Palme. 2003. 'New Politics and Class Politics in the Context of Austerity and Globalization: Welfare State Regress in 18 Countries, 1975–95'. *American Political Science Review* 97(3):425–446.

Kwon, Hyeok Yong and Jonas Pontusson. 2005. 'The Rise and Fall of Government Partisanship: Dynamics of Social Spending in OECD Countries, 1962–2000'. Unpublished Manuscript.

Kwon, Hyeok Yong and Jonas Pontusson. 2010. 'Globalization, Labour Power and Partisan Politics Revisited'. *Socio-Economic Review* 8(2):251–281.

Lane, Philip R. and Gian Maria Milesi-Ferretti. 2007. 'The External Wealth of Nations Mark II: Revised and Extended Estimates of Foreign Assets and Liabilities, 1970–2004'. *Journal of International Economics* 73:223–250.

Larsen, Christian Albrekt. 2006. *The Institutional Logic of Welfare State Attitudes: How Welfare Regimes Influence Public Support*. Hampshire: Ashgate.

Larsen, Christian Albrekt. 2008. 'The Institutional Logic of Welfare State Attitudes: How Welfare Regimes Influence Public Support'. *Comparative Political Studies* 41(2):145–168.

Launov, Andrey and Klaus Wälde. 2013. 'Estimating Incentive and Welfare Effects of Nonstationary Unemployment Benefits'. *International Economic Review* 54(4):1159–1198.

Laver, Michael. 1992. Are Irish Parties Peculiar? In *The Development of Industrial Society in Ireland*, eds. John H. Goldthorpe and Christopher T. Whelan. Proceedings of the British Academy, Oxford University Press, pp. 359–382.

Laver, Michael and W. Ben Hunt. 1992. *Policy and Party Competition*. Routledge.

Leibfried, Stephan. 1992. Towards a European Welfare State? On Integrating Poverty Regimes into the European Community. In *Social Policy in a Changing Europe*, eds. Zsuzsa Ferge and Jon Eivind Kolberg. Campus Frankfurt/New York pp. 245–280.

Leschke, Janine, Günther Schmid and Dorit Griga. 2006. 'On the Marriage of Flexibility and Security: Lessons from the Hartz-reforms in Germany'. *WZB Discussion Paper* (108):1–22.

Levy, Jack S. 2007. 'Qualitative Methods and Cross-Method Dialogue in Political Science'. *Comparative Political Studies* 40(2):196–214.

Levy, Jonah D. 1999. 'Vice into Virtue? Progressive Politics and Welfare Reform in Continental Europe'. *Politics & Society* 27(2):239–273.

Lewis, Jane and Ilona Oster. 1994. 'Gender and the Evolution of European Social Policies'. *Zes-Arbeitspapier* (4/94):1–63.

Lindbeck, Assar and Dennis J. Snower. 1988. *The Insider-Outsider Theory of Employment and Unemployment*. MIT Press.

Lindbeck, Assar and Dennis J. Snower. 2001. 'Insiders versus Outsiders'. *The Journal of Economic Perspectives* 15(1):165–188.

Maguire, Maria. 1986. Ireland. In *Growth to Limits: Western European Welfare States since World War II*, ed. Peter Flora. Vol. 2, Gruyter, pp. 243–383.

Mahler, Vincent A., David K. Jesuit and Douglas D. Roscoe. 1999. 'Exploring the Impact of Trade and Investment on Income Inequality – A Cross-National Sectoral Analysis of the Developed Countries'. *Comparative Political Studies* 32(3):363–395.

Mahoney, James and Gary Goertz. 2004. 'The Possibility Principle: Choosing Negative Cases in Comparative Research'. *American Political Science Review* 98(4):653–669.

Mair, Peter. 1987. *The Changing Irish Party System – Organisation, Ideology and Electoral Competition*. European Party System Series. London: Frances Pinter.

Mair, Peter. 1992. Explaining the Absence of Class Politics in Ireland. In *The Development of Industrial Society in Ireland*, eds. John H. Goldthorpe and Christopher T. Whelan. Proceedings of the British Academy, Oxford University Press, pp. 383–410.

Mair, Peter. 1995. 'Political Parties, Popular Legitimacy and Public Privilege'. *West European Politics* 18(3):40–57.

Mair, Peter. 1999. Party Competition and the Changing Party System. In *Politics in the Republic of Ireland*, eds. John Coakley and Michael Gallagher. Routledge, Chapter 5, pp. 127–151.

Mair, Peter. 2000. 'The Limited Impact of Europe on National Party Systems'. *West European Politics* 23(4):27–51.

Mair, Peter. 2006. 'Ruling the Void? The Hollowing of Western Democracies'. *New Left Review* 42:25–51.

Mair, Peter. 2008. 'The Challenge to Party Government'. *West European Politics* 31(1):211–234.

Manin, Bernard. 1997. *The Principles of Representative Government*. Cambridge University Press.

Manow, Philip. 1997. 'Social Insurance and the German Political Economy'. *MPIfG Discussion Paper* (97/2):1–48.

Manow, Philip. 2015. 'Workers, Farmers and Catholicism: A History of Political Class Coalitions and the South-European Welfare State Regime'. *Journal of European Social Policy* 25(1):32–49.

Manow, Philip and Eric Seils. 2000a. Adjusting Badly: The German Welfare State, Structural Change, and the Open Economy. In *Welfare and Work in the open Economy Volume II: Diverse Responses to Common Challenges in Twelve Countries*, eds. Vivien A. Schmidt and Fritz W. Scharpf. Oxford University Press, Chapter 6, pp. 264–307.

Manow, Philip and Eric Seils. 2000b. 'The Employment Crisis of the German Welfare State'. *West European Politics* 23(2):137–160.

Manow, Philip and Kees van Kersbergen. 2008. Religion and the Western Welfare State – The Theoretical Context. In *Religion, Class Coalitions and Welfare State Regimes*, eds. Kees van Kersbergen and Philip Manow. New York: Cambridge University Press pp. 4–37.

Manow, Philip and Simone Burkhart. 2007. 'Legislative Self-Restraint under Divided Government in Germany, 1976–2002'. *Legislative Studies Quarterly* 32(2):167–191.

Mares, Isabela. 1997. 'Is Unemployment Insurable? Employers and the Development of Unemployment Insurance'. *Journal of Public Policy* 17(3):299–327.

Mares, Isabela. 2000. 'Strategic Alliances and Social Policy Reform: Unemployment Insurance in Comparative Perspective'. *Politics & Society* 28(2):223–244.

Martin, Cathie Jo and Kathleen Thelen. 2007. 'The State and Coordinated Capitalism: Contributions of the Public Sector to Social Solidarity in Postindustrial Societies'. *World Politics* 60(1):1–36.

Martin, Lanny W. and Georg Vanberg. 2004. 'Policing the Bargain: Coalition Government and Parliamentary Scrutiny'. *American Journal of Political Science* 48(1):13–27.

Matthews, J. Scott and Lynda Erickson. 2008. 'Welfare State Structures and the Structure of Welfare State Support: Attitudes Towards Social Spending in Canada, 1993–2000'. *European Journal of Political Research* 47(3):411–435.

Mierau, Jochen O., Richard Jong-A-Pin and Jakob de Haan. 2007. 'Do Political Variables Affect Fiscal Policy Adjustment Decisions? New Empirical Evidence'. *Public Choice* 133:297–319.

Mishra, Ramesh. 1999. *Globalization and the Welfare State*. Edward Elgar.

Mjøset, Lars. 1992. *The Irish Economy in a Comparative Institutional Perspective*. Dublin: National Economic and Social Council.

Morgan, Kimberly J. 2013. 'Path Shifting of the Welfare State – Electoral Competition and the Expansion of Work-Family Policies in Western Europe'. *World Politics* 65(1):73–115.

Murphy, Mary C. 2006. 'Reform of Dáil Éireann: The Dynamics of Parliamentary Change'. *Parliamentary Affairs* 59(3):437–453.

Nanou, Kyriaki and Han Dorussen. 2013. 'European Integration and Electoral Democracy: How the European Union Constrains Party Competition in the Member States'. *European Journal of Political Research* 52:71–93.

Nordhaus, William D. 1975. 'The Political Business Cycle'. *The Review of Economic Studies* 42(2):169–190.

OECD. 2017. 'OECD Main Economic Indicators'. www.oecd.org/std/mei

Oesch, Daniel. 2006a. 'Coming to Grips with a Changing Class Structure: An Analysis of Employment Stratification in Britain, Germany, Sweden and Switzerland'. *International Sociology* 21(2):263–288.

Oesch, Daniel. 2006b. *Redrawing the Class Map – Stratification and Institutions in Britain, Germany, Sweden and Switzerland*. Palgrave Macmillan.

Oesch, Daniel. 2008. 'The Changing Shape of Class Voting – An Individual-Level Analysis of Party Support in Britain, Germany and Switzerland'. *European Societies* 10(3):329–355.

Offe, Claus. 1984. Some Contradictions of the Modern Welfare State. In: *Contradictions of the Welfare State*, ed. Claus Offe. Hutchinson pp. 147–161.

O'Hearn, Denis. 2000. 'Globalization, 'New Tigers', and the End of the Developmental State? The Case of the Celtic Tiger'. *Politics & Society* 28(1):67–92.

O'Hearn, Denis. 2001. *The Atlantic Economy: Britain, the US and Ireland*. University of Manchester Press.

Ó Riain, Seán. 2004. 'State, Competition and Industrial Change in Ireland 1991–1999'. *The Economic and Social Review* 35(1):27–53.

Ó Riain, Seán and Philip J. O'Connell. 2000. The Role of the State in Growth and Welfare. In *Bust to Boom? The Irish Experience of Growth and Inequality*, eds. Brian Nolan, Philip J. O'Connell and Christopher T. Whelan. Dublin: IPA Institute of Public Administration, Chapter 16, pp. 310–339.

Palier, Bruno. 2005. Ambiguous Agreement, Cumulative Change: French Social Policy in the 1990s. In *Beyond Continuity: Institutional Change in Advanced Political Economies*, eds. Wolfgang Streeck and Kathleen Thelen. Oxford University Press.

Petrocik, John R. 1996. 'Issue Ownership in Presidential Elections, with a 1980 Case Study'. *American Journal of Political Science* 40(3):825–850.

Pierson, Paul. 1994. *Dismantling the Welfare State? Reagan, Thatcher, and the Politics of Retrenchment*. Cambridge Studies in Comparative Politics. Cambridge: Cambridge University Press.

Pierson, Paul. 1996. 'The New Politics of the Welfare State'. *World Politics* 48(2):143–179.

Pierson, Paul. 1998. 'Irresistible Forces, Immovable Objects: Post-industrial Welfare States Confront Permanent Austerity'. *Journal of European Public Policy* 5(4):539–560.

Pierson, Paul. 2001. Coping with Permanent Austerity – Welfare State Restructuring in Affluent Democracies. In *The New Politics of the Welfare State*, ed. Paul Pierson. Oxford University Press, pp. 410–456.

Plümper, Thomas and Vera E. Troeger. 2007. 'Efficient Estimation of Time-Invariant and Rarely Changing Variables in Finite Sample and Panel Analyses with Unit Fixed Effects'. *Political Analysis* 15(2):124–139.

Plümper, Thomas, Vera E. Troeger and Philip Manow. 2005. 'Panel Data Analysis in Comparative Politics: Linking Method to Theory'. *European Journal of Political Research* 44(2):327–354.

Polanyi, Karl. 1954. *The Great Transformation*. Beacon Press.

Pollak, Reinhard. 2010. 'Kaum Bewegung, viel Ungleichheit: Eine Studie zu sozialem Auf- und Abstieg in Deutschland'. *Schriften zu Wirtschaft und Soziales* (5):1–67.

Pollak, Reinhard. 2012. 'Soziale Mobilität in Deutschland – Eine Expertise im Auftrag der Vodafone Stiftung Deutschland'. https://www.vodafone-stiftung.de/vodafone_stiftung_publikationen.html

Pontusson, Jonas and David Rueda. 2010. 'The Politics of Inequality: Voter Mobilization and Left Parties in Advanced Industrial States'. *Comparative Political Studies* 43(6): 675–705.

Przeworski, Adam, Susan C. Stokes and Bernard Manin. 1999. *Democracy, Accountability, and Representation*. Cambridge Studies in the Theory of Democracy. Cambridge: Cambridge University Press.

Rehm, Philipp. 2005. 'Citizen Support for the Welfare State: Determinants of Preferences for Income Redistribution'. *WZB Discussion Paper* SP II 2005(02):1–39.

Rehm, Philipp. 2009. 'Risks and Redistribution – An Individual-Level Analysis'. *Comparative Political Studies* 42(7):855–881.

Rehm, Philipp. 2011. 'Social Policy by Popular Demand'. *World Politics* 63(2):271–299.

Reidegeld, Eckhard. 2000. Der Krieg als Entwicklungsbedingung staatlicher Sozialpolitik. In *Abschied vom Staat – Rückkehr zum Staat?*, ed. Rüdiger Voigt. Institut für Staatswissenschaften – Universität der Bundeswehr München, pp. 327–351.

Ringe, Nils. 2005. 'Policy Preference Formation in Legislative Politics: Structures, Actors, and Focal Points'. *American Journal of Political Science* 49(4):731–745.

Roche, William K. 2007. 'Social Partnership in Ireland and New Social Pacts'. *Industrial Relations* 46(3):395–425.

Rodrik, Dani. 1997. 'Sense and Nonsense in the Globalization Debate'. *Foreign Policy* (107):19–37.

Rodrik, Dani. 1998. 'Why Do More Open Economies Have Bigger Governments?' *Journal of Political Economy* 106(5):997–1032.

Ross, Fiona. 1997. 'Cutting Public Expenditures in Advanced Industrial Democracies: The Importance of Avoiding Blame'. *Governance: An International Journal of Policy and Administration* 10(2):175–200.

Ross, Fiona. 2000a. '"Beyond Left and Right": The New Partisan Politics of Welfare'. *Governance* 13(2):155–183.

Ross, Fiona. 2000b. 'Framing Welfare Reform in Affluent Societies: Rendering Restructuring More Palatable?' *Journal of Public Policy* 20(2):169–193.

Rueda, David. 2005. 'Insider-Outsider Politics in Industrialized Democracies: The Challenge to Social Democratic Parties'. *American Political Science Review* 99(1):61–74.

Rueda, David. 2006. 'Social Democracy and Active Labour-Market Policies: Insiders, Outsiders and the Politics of Employment Promotion'. *British Journal of Political Science* 36(3):385–406.

Rueda, David. 2007. *Social Democracy Inside Out: Partisanship and Labor Market Policy in Industrialized Democracies*. Oxford University Press.

Rueda, David. 2008. 'Left Government, Policy, and Corporatism: Explaining the Influence of Partisanship on Inequality'. *World Politics* 60(3):349–389.

Ruggie, John Gerard. 1982. 'International Regimes, Transactions, and Change: Embedded Liberalism in the Postwar Economic Order'. *International Organization* 36(2):379–415.

Scharpf, Fritz W. 2000. Economic Changes, Vulnerabilities, and Institutional Capabilities. In *Welfare and Work in the Open Economy – From Vulnerability to*

*Competitiveness,* Vol. 1, eds. Fritz W. Scharpf and Vivien A. Schmidt. Oxford University Press, pp. 21–124.

Scheve, Kenneth and David Stasavage. 2009. 'Institutions, Partisanship, and Inequality in the Long Run'. *World Politics* 61(2):215–253.

Scheve, Kenneth and Matthew J. Slaughter. 2006. Public Opinion, International Economic Integration, and the Welfare State. In *Globalization and Egalitarian Redistribution*, eds. Pranab Bardhan, Samuel Bowles and Michael Wallerstein. Princeton University Press, pp. 217–260.

Schmidt, Manfred G. 1987. 'West Germany: The Policy of the Middle Way'. *Journal of Public Policy* 7(2):135–177.

Schmidt, Manfred G. 1996. 'When Parties Matter: A Review of the Possibilities and Limits of Partisan Influence on Public Policy'. *European Journal of Political Research* 30:155–183.

Schnabel, Claus and Joachim Wagner. 2005. 'Determinants of Trade Union Membership in West Germany: Evidence from Micro Data, 1980–2000'. *Socio-Economic Review* 3(1):1–24.

Schniewind, Aline, Markus Freitag and Adrian Vatter. 2009. 'Big Cabinets, Big Governments? Grand Coalitions and Public Policy in the German Laender'. *Journal of Public Policy* 29(3):327–345.

Schwartz, Herman. 2001. Round Up the Usual Suspects!: Globalization, Domestic Politics, and Welfare State Change. In *The New Politics of the Welfare State*, ed. Paul Pierson. Oxford University Press, pp. 17–44.

Scruggs, Lyle. 2005. 'Comparative Welfare Entitlement Dataset'. Downloadable data set. http//sp.uconn.edu/~scruggs/wp.htm

Seeleib-Kaiser, Martin, Silke van Dyk and Martin Roggenkamp. 2008. *Party Politics and Social Welfare – Comparing Christian and Social Democracy in Austria, Germany and the Netherlands*. Globalization and Welfare. Edward Elgar.

Shikano, Susumu and Eric Linhart. 2010. 'Coalition Formation as a Result of Policy and Office Motviations in the German Federal State'. *Party Politics* 16(1):111–130.

Sieberer, Ulrich. 2006. 'Agenda Setting in the German Bundestag: A Weak Government in a Consensus Democracy'. *German Politics* 15(1):49–72.

Sinnott, Richard. 1999. The Electoral System. In *Politics in the Republic of Ireland*, eds. John Coakley and Michael Gallagher. Routledge, Chapter 4, pp. 99–126.

Smith, Nicola Jo-Anne. 2005. *Showcasing Globalisation? The Political Economy of the Irish Republic*. Manchester University Press.

Solt, Frederick. 2016. 'The Standardized World Income Inequality Database'. *Social Science Quarterly* 97. SWIID Version 5.0, October 2014.

Spermann, Alexander. 2014. 'Zehn Jahre Hartz IV – Was hilft Langzeitarbeitslosen wirklich?' *IZA Standpunkte* (76):1–45.

Starke, Peter, Herbert Obinger and Francis G. Castles. 2008. 'Convergence towards Where: In *What Ways, If Any, Are Welfare States Becoming More Similar?*'. *Journal of European Public Policy* 15(7):975–1000.

Stephens, John D. 1980. *The Transition from Capitalism to Socialism*. Humanities Press.

Stephens, John D., Evelyne Huber and Leonard Ray. 1999. The Welfare State in Hard Times. In *Continuity and Change in Contemporary Capitalism*, eds. Herbert Kitschelt, Peter Lange, Gary Marks and John D. Stephens. Cambridge Studies in Comparative Politics. Cambridge: Cambridge University Press, pp. 164–193.

Stimson, James A. 1999. Party Government and Responsiveness. In *Democracy, Accountability, and Representation*, eds. Adam Przeworski, Susan C. Stokes and Bernard Manin. Cambridge Studies in the Theory of Democracy. Cambridge: Cambridge University Press, pp. 197–221.

Stone Sweet, Alec. 2000. *Governing with Judges – Constitutional Politics in Europe*. Oxford University Press.

Streeck, Wolfgang. 2003. 'From State Weakness as Strength to State Weakness as Weakness: Welfare Corporatism and the Private Use of the Public Interest'. *MPIfG Working Paper* (03/02):1–22.

Streeck, Wolfgang and Anke Hassel. 2003. 'The Crumbling Pillars of Social Partnership'. *West European Politics* 26(4):101–124.

Svallfors, Stefan. 1997. 'Worlds of Welfare and Attitudes to Redistribution: A Comparison of Eight Western Nations'. *European Sociological Review* 13(3):283–304.

Swank, Duane. 2001. Political Institutions and Welfare State Restructuring: The Impact of Institutions on Social Policy Change in Developed Democracies. In *The New Politics of the Welfare State*, ed. Paul Pierson. Oxford University Press, pp. 197–237.

Taylor-Gooby, Peter, ed. 2004. *New Risks, New Welfare – The Transformation of the European Welfare State*. Oxford University Press.

Thelen, Kathleen. 2001. Varieties of Labor Politics in the Developed Democracies. In *Varieties of Capitalism – The Institutional Foundations of Comparative Advantage*, eds. Peter A. Hall and David Soskice. Oxford University Press, pp. 71–103.

Thelen, Kathleen. 2004. *How Institutions Evolve: The Political Economy of Skills in Germany, Britain, the United States, and Japan*. Cambridge University Press.

Times, The Irish. 1995a. 'ICTU Wants 300m Tax Relief for PAYE Workers' in *The Irish Times*, November 30, Dublin.

Times, The Irish. 1995b. 'Tax Reform Should Help Job Creation, Says INOU' in *The Irish Times*, December 20, Dublin.

Times, The Irish. 1996a. 'Qualified Welcome by IBEC and ICTU Brings Hopes for New Pay Deal' in *The Irish Times*, January 24, Dublin.

Times, The Irish, 1996b. 'Quinn and SIPTU Clash over Merit of Budget' in *The Irish Times*, January 29, Dublin.

Times, The Irish. 2000a. 'CORI Calls for Social Welfare Increases in Budget' in *The Irish Times*, October 23, Dublin.

Times, The Irish. 2000b. 'ESRI Favours Incresed Social Spending' in *The Irish Times*, November 13, Dublin.

Times, The Irish. 2000c. 'Budget Will Show the Value the Coalition Puts on Children' in *The Irish Times*, November 28, Dublin.

Times, The Irish, 2000d. 'Key Unions Give Budget A Cautious Welcome' in *The Irish Times*, December 7, Dublin.

Times, The Irish, 2001a. 'CORI Says Tax Policy Unjust' in *The Irish Times*, March 2001, Dublin.

Times, The Irish, 2001b. 'CORI Assails Government on Poverty' in *The Irish Times*, July 23, Dublin.

Times, The Irish, 2001c. 'Unions Hostile to a Budget that Employers Find Good in Part', *The Irish Times*, 6 December, Dublin.

Trampusch, Christine. 2003. 'Ein Bündnis für die nachhaltige Finanzierung der Sozialversicherungssysteme: Interessenvermittlung in der bundesdeutschen Arbeitsmarkt- und Rentenpolitik'. *MPIfG Discussion Paper* (03/1):1–92.

Trampusch, Christine. 2005. Institutional Resettlement: The Case of Early Retirement in Germany. In *Beyond Continuity*, eds. Wolfgang Streeck and Kathleen Thelen. Oxford University Press, Chapter 8, pp. 203–228.

van Kersbergen, Kees. 1995. *Social Capitalism: Christian Democracy and the Welfare State*. Routledge.

van Kersbergen, Kees and Philip Manow, eds. 2009. *Religion, Class Coalitions and Welfare State Regimes*. Cambridge Studies in Social Theory, Religion and Politics. Cambridge: Cambridge University Press.

Vanberg, Georg. 1998. 'Abstract Judicial Review, Legislative Bargaining, and Policy Compromise'. *Journal of Theoretical Politics* 10(3):299–326.

Vis, Barbara. 2009a. 'Governments and Unpopular Social Policy Reform: Biting the Bullet or Steering Clear?'. *European Journal of Political Research* 48(1):31–57.

Vis, Barbara. 2009b. 'The Importance of Socio-Economic and Political Losses and Gains in Welfare State Reforms'. *Journal of European Social Policy* 19(5):395–407.

Vis, Barbara. 2010. *Politics of Risk-Taking: Welfare State Reform in Advanced Democracies*. Amsterdam University Press.

Vis, Barbara and Kees van Kersbergen. 2007. 'Why and How Do Political Actors Pursue Risky Reforms?'. *Journal of Theoretical Politics* 19(2):153–172.

Vis, Barbara and Kees van Kersbergen. 2013. 'Towards an Open Functional Approach to Welfare State Change: Pressure, Ideas, and Blame Avoidance'. *Public Administration* 91(4):840–854.

Volkens, Andrea, Pola Lehmann, Theres Matthiess, Nicolas Merz, Sven Regel and Annika Werner. 2016. 'The Manifesto Data Collection. Manifesto Project (MRG/CMP/MARPOR). Version 16a'. Electronic Database.

vom Berge, Philipp, Kerstin Bruckmeier, Jörg Heining, Barbara Hoffmann and Elke J. Jahn. 2015. 'Sanktionen im SGB II und die Situation von Leistungsbeziehern nach den Hartz-Reformen'. *IAB-Stellungnahme* (2/2015):1–67.

Wagschal, Uwe and Georg Wenzelburger. 2012. 'When Do Governments Consolidate? A Quantitative Comparative Analysis of 23 OECD Countries (1980–2005)'. *Journal of Comparative Policy Analysis* 14(1):45–71.

Walgrave, Stefaan, Frédéric Varone and Patrick Dumont. 2006. 'Policy with or without Parties? A Comparative Analysis of Policy Priorities and Policy Change in Belgium, 1991 to 2000'. *Journal of European Public Policy* 13(7):1021–1038.

Wallerstein, Michael. 1999. 'Wage-Setting Institutions and Pay Inequality in Advanced Industrial Societies'. *American Journal of Political Science* 43(3):649–680.

Wallerstein, Michael and Bruce Western. 2000. 'Unions in Decline? What Has Changed and Why'. *Annual Review of Political Science* 3:355–377.

Walsh, Brendan. 2003. 'When Unemployment Disappears: Ireland in the 1990s'. *CESifo Working Paper* (856). http//www.cesifo-group.de/portal/page/portal/ifoHome/b-publ

Walter, Stefanie. 2017. 'Globalization and the Demand-Side of Politics: How Globalization Shapes Labor Market Risk Perception and Policy Preferences'. *Political Science Research and Methods* 5(1):55–80.

Walter, Stefanie and Linda Maduz. 2009. 'How Globalization Shapes Individual Risk Perceptions and Policy Preferences: A Cross-National Analysis of Differences Between Globalization Winners and Losers'. *Weatherhead Center for International Affairs – Working Paper Series* (2009–2015):1–43.

Warwick, Paul V. 2006. *Policy Horizons and Parliamentary Government*. Palgrave Macmillan.

Wenzelburger, Georg. 2011. 'Political Strategies and Fiscal Retrenchment: Evidence from Four Countries'. *West European Politics* 34(6):1151–1184.

Wenzelburger, Georg. 2014. 'Blame Avoidance, Electoral Punishment and the Perceptions of Risk'. *Journal of European Social Policy* 24(1):80–91.

Whelan, Christopher T. and Bertrand Maître. 2014. 'The Great Recession and the Changing Distribution of Economic Vulnerability by Social Class: The Irish Case'. *Journal of European Social Policy* 24(5):470–485.

Wilson, Sven E. and Daniel M. Butler. 2007. 'A Lot More to Do: The Sensitivity of Time-Series Cross-Section Analyses to Simple Alternative Specifications'. *Political Analysis* 15(2):101–123.

Wolff, Joachim and Anton Nivorozhkin. 2008. 'Start Me Up: The Effectiveness of a Self-Employment Programme for Needy Unemployed People in Germany'. *IAB Discussion Paper* (20):1–49.

*The World Bank Data*. 2017. https//data.worldbank.org/.

Wright, Erik Olin. 2000. 'Working-Class Power, Capitalist-Class Interests, and Class Compromise'. *American Journal of Sociology* 105(4):957–1002.

# Index

*Note:* Page references for figures and tables are italicised.


activation, 102, 113, 115–16, 128, 133n25, 161
AfD (Alternative für Deutschland), 190
Agenda2010, 190
Ahern, Bertie (Fianna Fáil), 158, 160
Ahern, Dermot (Fianna Fáil), 163, 178
aircraft industry, 43
Alliance for Jobs (Bündnis für Arbeit, Ausbildung und Wettbewerbsfähigkeit), 114
ALMPs (active labour market policies), 12, 43, 65, 83, 85–86, 99, 101–2, 126, 149, 183–85, 193
ALMPs, ideal types, 185
Andres, Gerd (SPD), 105
Andrews, David (Fianna Fáil), 158
Anglo-Irish treaty, 138
Annual Social Welfare Bill, Ireland, 88, 158, 171–73
Arbeitsbeschaffungsmassnahme. *See* job creation scheme
Arbeitslosengeld. *See* unemployment insurance, benefits
Arbeitslosenhilfe. *See* unemployment assistance
ASU (Arbeitsgemeinschaft der selbständigen Unternehmer), 102, 107–8
Ausschuss für Arbeit und Soziales, 106, 108–11, 117–19
austerity, fiscal, 10–13, 64, 73–74, 182, 193
Austria, 33, 55, 60, 94
automatisation of production, 40

Babel, Gisela (FDP), 104
back-to-work allowance, Ireland, 149, 153, 161, 183
banking system, Irish, 173–74
bargaining, decentralisation of, 94
BDA (Bundesvereinigung Deutscher Arbeitgeberverbände), 102, 108, 117–18
Belgium, 33, 56, 76, 90
benefits: duration of, 59, 65, 85, 99, 104, 114, 122, 127, 154, 189; means-tested, 128, 136, 176n2
Beschäftigungsförderungsgesetz (employment promotion act), 100, *102–13*
bicameral system, 7, 50, 54, 80, 139, 159
Bismarckian welfare state, 90
Blair, Tony, 114
Blair/Schröder paper, 123
blame avoidance, 19–20

blue-collar worker, 40, 45, 90
Bretton Woods system, 38–39, 95–96
Britain, 90, 136, 141
Broughan, Tommy (Labour), 167
Bruton, John (Fine Gael), 178
Bruton, Richard (Fine Gael), 153
budgetary: cuts, 49, 173; pressure, 2, 7
budgetary constraints, 4–5, 12–13, 146
budgetary cuts, 49, 173
budget debate, 100
budget deficit, 48, 113
Bundesanstalt für Arbeit, 103
Bundesländer, German, 79–82, 92, 94, 110, 139
Bundesrat, German (second chamber), 11, 57, 79, 92, 110–14, 123
Bundestag, German, 79, 87, 93, 110
Bündnis90/Die Grünen (German Green party), 118, 132

capital flows. *See* financial flows
case selection, 79–82
cash benefits, 91
Catholic Church, Irish, 136, 137–38, 176
Catholic values, 136, 140
CDU/CSU (Christlich Demokratische Union/Christlich Soziale Union), 82–85
child care policy, 3, 20, 92, 134, 137, 147, 190
class scheme, 40–41
class structure, 4, 30
clientelistic patterns, 9–11, 53, 75, 181, 186
clientelistic policy-making, 38, 66, 79, 85, 187
clientelistic reform, 51, 78, 90, 189
coalition government, 94, 139, 141
coal mining, 43, 65
collective agreement, 94, 109
Commission on Social Welfare (Ireland), 137, 158
committee hearings, 99
committee stage, 87–88, 159
community employment, 152–53, 155–56
Comparative Manifesto Project, 17, 33, 80
Comparative Party Manifesto data, 60
compensation, 8–10, 20, 51, 71, 109, 153, 161, 188
conditioning effects. *See* interaction effects
conservative government, 20, 26, 52, 61, 69, 184–85, 192–93; Germany, 152; Ireland, 162–63, 170
conservative welfare state. *See* welfare state, conservative
consolidation: event (episode), 16–17, 20–22, 24, 26, 32; size, 16–17, 21, 24, 26, 32
constraints, 2; budgetary, 4–5, 12–13, 146; institutional, 6–9, 11–14, 23, 37, 49–50, 54, 59, 61, 66, 79, 114, 146, 159–60, 171–72, 181
constraints, political, 4, 6, 9–10, 12, 14, 36–55, 59, 62, 66–77, 186–89, 195–96; Germany, 79, 92, 110–11, 122–23; Ireland, 80, 159–60, 162, 169–70, 181, 183, 190–92
continental welfare state. *See* welfare state, continental
contractor. *See* fixed-term employee
convergence, of policy positions, 48
convergence, of welfare states, 4
core constituency, 6, 47, 51, 74, 120
core labour force. *See* core workforce
core social security programs (core welfare state programs) 10, 53, 59, 64–66, 75, 180, 186
core workforce, 6, 9, 11, 36–38, 51–53, 60, 66, 69–70, 107, 187; compensation of, 78, 120, 189; political preferences of, 12; protection of, 11, 75, 186
CORI (Conference of Religious of Ireland), 165, 168, 178n25
corporatism, 94

country dummies. *See* country fixed effects
country fixed effects, 59, 62–64, 70, 76n2, 76n3
credibility, 9, 37, 190
Croke Park agreement, 174
Cullen, Martin (Fianna Fáil), 154, 177n18

DAG (Deutsche Angestelltengewerkschaft), 102, 106–8, 132n19
Dáil Éirann. *See* Irish parliament
decommodification, 77n4, 91
decommodification index. *See* welfare state, generosity index
de-industrialization, 36, 65
democratic institutions, 3
Democratic Left, 82, 84, 141, 149–51, 157, 160, 177n15, 191
demographic ageing, 36
demographic change, 18, 23, 36, 61, 77n7
Department of Social and Family Affairs, Ireland, 147
de-politicisation, 34n8
deregulation, 82, 86, 101
De Rossa, Proinsias (Democratic Left), 150–51, 160
DGB (Deutscher Gewerkschaftsbund), 102, 107–9, 117–20, 132n19, 133n29
DIHT (Deutscher Industrie und Handelstag), 102, 108, 110
dismissal protection, 43
double movement. *See* embedded liberalism
dualisation, 42, 78, 174, 193–94

early retirement, 98, 174
economic: cleavage, 46; downturn, 24, 42–43, 98, 144–45, 163, 172, 174; interdependence, 2, 29, 64, 73–74, 78, 186; openness (open economy), 62, 64, 71, 73, 98, 144; pressure, 20, 23, 26
economic growth, 10, 18, 20, 28, 61, 64; in Germany, 95, *96*, 98, 128; in Ireland, 143, *144*, 146, 163
economy: German, 91, 95–96, 98, 111, 124, 129, 132n13; Irish, 135–36, 142–46, 151, 155–56, 163, 165–66, 168–69, 172–74, 178n31, 190
education, low degree of, 39, 108, 111, 115, 124, 129, 166, 194
EEC (European Economic Community), 144
egalitarian policy outcome. *See* egalitarian reform
egalitarian reform, 51, 75, 187, 193, 195
electoral cycle, 5, 17, 21, 23–24, *25*, 123, 163
electoral platform (ideological agenda), 2, 82, 201n6
electoral politics, 23
electoral punishment, 23–24
electoral risk, 5, 19, 23
electoral support, 6, 51, 82, 140, 162, 176n8, 190
eligibility, 59, 65, 84, 86, 90–91, 99–100, 104–5, 112, 127, 155, 182, 184
embedded liberalism, 39, 95, 142. *See also* double movement
emerging markets, 39
employee, unskilled (unskilled labour), 39, 41–42, 54
employer's organisation, 8, 54, 94–95, 98, 106, 108, 117–19, 124, 133n24; in Germany, 132n21, 144, 166, 189, 191; in Ireland, 147, 159, 169
employment: full-time, 36, 40, 56n5, 97, 103–6, 112; long-term, 60, 97; part-time (part-time job), 11, 36, 39–45, 51, 54, 99, 101–7, 112, 129, 148, 154–55, 161, 165, 191–94; protection, 98, 129, 183; temporary (temporary work), 100, 114, 120–21, 125–29
employment agency (placement or job centre), 103–4, 107–9, 114, 118–21, 127, 133n28

employment assistance, 183
employment contract, regular, 36, 40, 42, 97, 112, 121, 126
employment history, 41
employment relation, standard. *See* employment contract, regular
employment security, 39, 42, 85, 87, 121, 185
Engelen-Kefer, Ursula, 119, 133n29
ESRI (Economic and Social Research Institute), 178n28
Eurozone, 163
exchange rate, fixed, 38, 95–96
export market, 108

family policy, 20, 84, 137; expansion of, 190
FDP (Freie Demokratische Partei), 82, 84, 93–94, 99–104, 107–9, 112, 116, 118, 121, 123, 126
federalism, 50, 79, 97, 197
fertility, decreasing, 18
Fianna Fáil, 84, 139–43, 148–50, 154–55, 157–60, 162–63, 165
Fianna Fáil/Progressive Democrats coalition, 162–70, 172, 175
Financial Bill, 84, 88, 147, 150, 152–53, 159, 161–62, 164–65, 171, 183, 185, 192, 197
financial crisis, 146, 173–74
financial flows. *See* capital flows
financial market, 36, 82, 173
financial openness (capital flows), 18, 23, 28
Fine Gael, 82, 84, 137, 140–41, 166–68, 175, 178n31
Fine Gael/Labour/Democratic Left coalition. *See* rainbow coalition
first labour market (main labour market), 109, 116, 118, 121, 158, 191
fiscal adjustment, 16, 34n6
fiscal balance, 17, 24, 31
fiscal deficit, 16, 31, 49
fiscal year, 88
fixed-effect model, 59, 63–64, 77n9
fixed-term employee, 41–42, 174, 193
flat-rate benefit, 137
flat-rate contribution, 136
Fördern und Fordern, 101, 115
framing, 20, 24
France, 3, 33n2, 56n6, 76n1, 90, 178n27, 201n11
full-time job. *See* employment, full time
functionalist view on politics, 4, 15, 18

generosity index. *See* welfare state, generosity index
GDP: Germany, 35n13, 96; Ireland, 167, 173
GDR (German Democratic Republic), 81–82
global competition, 39
globalisation, economic, 2, 36, 52, 54, 61, 88n1
golden age (golden era), 4, 18, 30, 36, 40, 193
golden era. *See* golden age
government, left-wing, 8–9, 11, 26, 50–51, 53–54, 61, 63, 66–67, 69–72, 185; Germany, 84, 113–14, 123, 191; Ireland, 160, 163, 172
government, right-wing (conservative), 8, 12–13, 23, 26, 28–29, 47–48, 51, 54, 61, 63, 69–73, 187; Germany, 82, 84, 113; Ireland, 150, 163, 170–71
government expenditure, 43, 64, 167
government ideology, 17, 23–24, 26, 33, 58–63, 67–70, 77n9
government partisanship, 12–13, 28, 30, 46, 53, 64, 66, 180
grand coalition, Germany, 82, 93, 131n6, 190
Green Party: Germany, 81, 87, 93–94, 101, 105–10, 112–13, 121–23, 131n9, 189; Ireland, 141, 174
Gysi, Gregor (PDS/Linke), 109, 111, 132n21

Harney, Mary (Progressive Democrats), 160, 162, 164–65
Hartz Kommission, 133n26
Hartz, Peter, 133n26
Hartz Reforms, 101, 126–28, 189, 200n4
Heckman model. *See* selection model
Henisz's index of political constraints, 17, 33, 61, 77n5
Higgins, Joe (Socialist Party), 169
highly skilled employee, 39, 45, 132n16, 144
horizontal redistribution, 72

IBEC (Irish Business and Employers Confederation), 168
Ich-AG, 200n4
ICTU (Irish Congress of Trade Unions), 157–58, 168, 170, 174, 176n10, 170n32
ideological agenda. *See* electoral platform
IG Metall (Interessengemeinschaft Metall, German trade union), 121–22
ILO (International Labour Organisation), 56n6, 100, 177n14
IMF (International Monetary Fund), 173
IMF database, 34n2
incentive enforcement, 102, 104, 148, 152–56, 183–85
income inequality, 45; Germany, *130*; Ireland, 174, *175*, 179n34; means-tested, 121; tax, 122, 163–64, 166, 175, 179n33
industrial: accident, 103; production, 18, 38–39; relations, 94, 131, 139, 141, 176; revolution, 90
INOU (Irish National Organisation of the Unemployed), 154, 158–59, 167, 183
insider, 6, 8–10, 14, 42–44, 51, 54–56, 60, 70–71, 87, 180–82, 184–85, 187–89, 191–94; Germany, 111, 117, 124, 126, 129; Ireland, 135, 161–62, 170–71, 173–74
insider-outsider cleavage, 198
institutional: context (*see* institutional setting); factors, 5, 30; literature, 5, 188
institutional setting, 5, 7, 31, 49–50, 66, 79, 172, 198; Germany, 95; Ireland, 136, 139, 169, 189
interaction effects (conditional effects), 53, 62, 67–69, 79
interaction model, 66–67, 70, 77n10
interest groups, 7–8, 44, 50, 54, 71, 79–80, 83, 87–88, 116, 154, 159, 166, 192–93
internationalisation, 12, 36, 40, 48, 94, 195
international trade, 38–40
Irish parliament (Dáil Éirann), 87, 89n8, 139
*Irish Times*, 88
Italy, 33n2, 34n7, 76n1, 136

JobAQTIV, 84, 101, 113–26, 191
job centre. *See* employment agency
job creation, 96, 109, 152
job creation scheme (job creation programme), 110, 114, 155, 177n22, 184
job rotation, 114, 116, 118–20, 125–26, 200n2

Kauder, Volker (CDU), 106
Kemmy, Jim (Labour Party), 161
KOF index (globalisation index), 61
Kohl, Helmut (CDU), 84
Kohl government, 101, 113, 133n24
Kolb, Heinrich (FDP), 109

Labour Party (Ireland), 82, 84, 137, 140–41, 150–51, 156–57, 160–62, 165, 167, 175, 176n8
labour market: German, 90–92, 101, 190; flexibility, 39, 103, 114, 133n26; insider (*see* insider); Irish, 135–38,

174, 191; outsider (*see* outsiders); participants, 9, 38, 42–43, 87, 115–16, 125, 129; policies, 1, 6, 12, 40, 43, 85, 172; reform, 5, 11–12, 55, 78, 82–83, 85, 99–100, 113, 121, 123, 148–49, 181–82; risk, 42, 45, 85, 171; status, 45, 56n5, 42
labour union. *See* trade unions
Lafontaine, Oskar (SPD), 113–14, 123–24
lagged dependent variable, 76n2
Länder, German. *See* Bundesländer, German
Länderkammer. *See* Bundesrat, German
Laumann, Karl-Josef (CDU), 133n30, 134n34
left-wing government. *See* government, left-wing
legislative cycle, 35, 199
legislative process, 50–51, 61, 76, 199; Germany, 80, 87, 92–93, 110; Ireland, 80, 87–88, 146–47, 159
legislative term. *See* legislative cycle
Leiharbeit (temporary employment), *114, 125*
liberalisation: capital flows, 18, 39; labour market, 18, 121, 128, 190
liberal welfare state. *See* welfare state
long-term unemployment, 11; Germany, 114–20, 123, 125–26, 128, 191; Ireland, 149, 151–52, 154–57, 159–61, 163, 173–74, 183, 191
losers of globalisation (globalisation losers), 52, 66, 75, 188
low-skilled labour, 11, 39, 44, 54, 103, 129, 156, 165, 191, 195
low-tax and low-spend economy, 172
low-wage job, 44, 152, 156, 166
low-wage sector, 10, 36, 51; Germany, 96, 121–22, 128; Ireland, 155, 157, 161, 171, 175, 191

main labour market. *See* first labour market
marginal effects, 67, 73, *74*
marketable skills, 40–41, 43–44, 45
McDowell, Derek (Labour), 165, 167
McDowell, Michael (Progressive Democrats), 154–55
McManus, Liz (Democratic Left), 151
mediating effects: Germany, 110–11, 122–23; Ireland, 159–60, 169–70
middle-income: earners, 168; families, 153
mini-jobs (630 Mark job), 122, 127
Mitchell, Jim (Fine Gael), 166
mixed-methods design, 12
modifying effect. *See* interaction effects
monetary order, international, 38, 95
multi-dimensional policy space, 5–7, 11, 84, 181

Nahles, Andrea (SPD), 116
National Socialist regime, 91
Netherlands, 3, 33n2, 56n5, 76n1, 89n5
New Politics, 3, 5, 16, 18–20, 23–24, 30, 34n8, 73, 181
new social policies, 4, 30, 84, 198
nonlinear effects, 22

obfuscation, 20
occupational class, *46, 49*
O'Donoghue, John (Fianna Fáil), 160
OECD: average, 96, 143, 145; countries, 65, 98, 146
OECD Main Economic indicators, 77n7
OECD Social Expenditure database, 60
oil crisis, 107, 132n14, 143
old-age pensioners, 19, 149, 162
one-Euro Job, 127
on-the-job training, 117, 120, 124, 126, 200n3
open economy. *See* economic, openness
opposition party, 6, 8, 120, 199
organised labour, 10, 51–53, 75, 162, 170, 186
organised workforce. *See* organised labour

ÖTV (Gewerkschaft Oeffentlicher Dienste), Germany, 102, 106
outsiders (labour market outsiders), 36, 43–45, 51–52, 78, 83, 87; in Germany, 117; in Ireland, 135, 183
outsourcing, 18, 85–86

panel-specific heteroskedasticity, 58
paradox of redistribution, 75, 187
parliamentary minutes, 87, 147
Parteienstaat (party state, Germany), 93
partisan approach. *See* politics matter
partisan theory. *See* politics matter
part-time job. *See* employment, part-time
party competition, 2–3, 13, 18, 46, 93, 187, 200
party families, 29, 47–48, 56n8, 140
party government, 5, 7–8, 12, 20, 29, 31, 50, 54, 62, 78–79, 187; left-wing, 189; right-wing (conservative), 101; single, 139
party ideology, 23, 26, 28, 76, 81
Party Manifesto Research Group, 61
party politics, 1, 3, 6, 11–13, 18, 23, 36–57
party system: Germany, 92–94, 141, 190; Ireland, 82, 135, 139–41
path-dependence, 3, 19
PAYE (pay as you earn), 177n7
PAYE worker, 157, 183
PD (Progressive Democrats), 82, 141, 148–50, 153–55, 159, 162, 165, 168–73
PDS/Linke, 81–82, 89n3, 109–11
peak organisations, 196; Germany, 106; Ireland, 170
pension scheme, 98, 147, 182
placement centre. *See* employment agency
policy convergence, 4, 48
policy design, 74, 79, 142, 192, 200
policy preferences, 1, 87, 101; constituency, of, 4, 42–43, 50, 146; government, of, 38, 83, 167, 181, 190; interest groups, of, 88, 95, 102; political parties, of, 7, 30, 37, 61
political competition, 1–3, 60, 81, 180
political institutions, 3, 5, 66, 188; Ireland, 138–39
political spectrum: Germany, *81*; Ireland, *83*, 150
political strategy, 5
politics matter (partisan approach, partisan theory), 19, 15–16, 28, 30, 75, 85, 187, 195
pooled model, 64, 69, 77n8
poor law, 136
Poor Relief Act, 136
position, in the labour market. *See* labour market, status
post-industrial: democracies, 13, 39, 56n8, 76, 193; economies, 10, 58; societies, 96, 98, 196; welfare state, 15–16
poverty, 192; Germany, 129; Ireland, 136
professional: development, 118, 122; skills, 36, 111, 124, 128; training, 40, 43
profiling, 119, 128
Programme for Economic and Social Progress, 148, 177n13
Programme for Economic Expansion, 143, 177n13
Programme for National Recovery, 142, 145, 177n13
Programme for Prosperity and Fairness, 165–66, 170, 177n13
PRSI (payment-related social insurance), 148–49, 151, 155–56; ceiling, 153, 164–65, 167–69, 171; contributions (payments), 154, 156, 165, 169
PRSI-free allowance, 153–54
PRSI reduction, 157–58
public employment, 65, 109, 112, 118, 160, 185
public hearing, 102, 121
public spending, 16, 34n3, 85, 172, 178n27, 198
public support, of the welfare state, 16, 19

qualification scheme, 115–17
Quill, Mairin (Progressive Democrats), 157, 177n21

Rabbite, Pat (Labour), 157
rainbow coalition (Ireland), 11, 82, 84, 135, 150–62, 172, 183, 190–91
recruitment subsidy, 152–53, 156, 158, 160–61
redistribution, 8, 13, 45, 54, 71; horizontal, 60; preferences for, 46, 49, 56n6
redistributive: generosity of core welfare state programs, 6–8, 10, 12–14, 53, 59, 63–67, *69*, 70, 105–6, 123–24, 181, 188; justice, 9; policies, 24, 45–46, 56n7
reform: coalition, 26, 199; pressure, 37, 171; probability, 17, 20–24, *25*, 28, 31, 34n6
Reichsversicherungsordnung (National Insurance Code, Germany), 91
representative democracy, 2–3, 29
representative government, 3, 29
re-qualification, 117, 119
retrenchment (*see* welfare state, retrenchment); event (*see* consolidation, event); size (*see* consolidation, size)
re-unification, Germany, 110
revolving door, 128
RILE, 33, 61
room to manoeuvre, 2–3, 5–7, 13, 17–19, 29, 38, 48–49, 51, 64, 66, 73, 78, 80, 85, 102, 110, 113, 180–81, 187–89

salary cap, 116
Schröder, Gerhard (SPD), 84, 113, 123–24, 134n37
Schröder government, 101, 112–13, 119, 124, 126, 133n24, 190
Schulz, Werner (Green Party), 132n20
Schwaetzer, Irmgard (FDP), 123, 133n32, 134n36
Seanad, 80, 139, 159
second labour market, 104, 109–11, 118, 133n22
Second World War, 38, 91–92, 95, 137, 143
sectorial agreement, 94
Seehofer, Horst (CSU), 122
selection model. *See* Heckman model
self-employed, 45, 91, 156, 164, 171
self-employment, 106, 132n20; programmes, 107, 200n4
serial correlation, 59, 76n2
service industry. *See* service sector
service sector, 38–39, 41, 45, 96–97; expansion, of (growth of), 65, 129, 145
Shortall, Roisin (Labour), 156
sick pay, 12, 60, 65, 75, 90
single wage earner, 92
SIPTU (Services Industrial Professional and Technical Union), 158, 165, 170
630 Mark Job. *See* mini-jobs
skilled workers (skilled workforce), 36, 45, 71, 98; Germany, 103, 107, 109, 112, 115, 121, 126, 129; Ireland, 191
skill formation, 97
small government, 48
social assistance, 121–22, 125, 128, 147, 155, 189, 191; means-tested, 98, 130; payments, 123
social insurance contributions, *149*, 152, 154, *164*, 177n16
social insurance state. *See* Bismarckian Welfare State
social mobility, 128–29
social partnership, Germany, 109; Ireland, 142, 146, 167, 169–70, 174, 176n12
social policies, new. *See* new social policies
social protection, 40, 89n5, 106, 142, 148
social risk, 8

social security, 51
social spending, 8, 11, 17, 49, 52–54, 58–60, 62, 64–66, 71, 73, 75–76, 164, 186–87, 198–99
Social Welfare Act, Irish, 147
Social Welfare Bill, 84, 88, 147; 1996, 151–53, 158–59; 2001, 161–64, 168, 171. *See also* Annual Social Welfare Bill, Ireland
socio-economic factors, 17–18, 28; reforms, 78; systems, 91, 138, 147, 155
Soziale Marktwirtschaft (social market economy), 98
Sozialversicherungs Anpassungsgesetz (Social Insurance Adjustment Law), Germany, 91
Spain, 34n2, 56n6, 136
spending cuts (retrenchment), 8, 26, 29, 31, 51
spending dimension, 6–7, 10–12, 14, 38, 53, 85; Germany, 103, *108*, 109, 114, 119–20; Ireland, 152–53, 156–57, 164, 166–67, 171
status protection, 128
strategic behaviour, 5
strategic policy-making, 10–11, 18–20
strategic timing, 5, 13, 21, 24
structural change, 12, 94, 98
subsidiarity, 130n1
Sustaining Progress, 177n13
Sweden, 34n2, 56n6, 76n1, 94, 178n27
Switzerland, 3, 56n6, 57n10, 76n1, 140, 142, 176n8, 201n11

take-home pay, 152, 154, 191
Taoiseach (prime minister, Ireland), 80, 88, 139, 159
tax: breaks, 166, 171; cuts, 82, 159, 165–66, 169, 171–72, 178n28; payer, 107; reform, 162–63
taxation, regressive, 155
temporary contract, 121
temporary work agency, 129
Third Way, 113, 123, 126
time-series cross-section, 17, 21, 31, 58, 76n3, 79
Towards 2016, 177n13
trade openness, 76
trade unions. *See* labour union

unemployment assistance, 99
unemployment insurance, 10, 38, 43, 59, 62, 65, 75, 84; benefits, Germany, 99; benefits, Ireland, 136; contribution, 86, 91, 99, 103, 116–17, 136, 147; eligibility, 60
unemployment level, 23, 28, 34n3; Germany, 97–98, 102, 108, 113, 124; Ireland, 145, 163
union membership, 57n12, 94–95, 131n11, 196
United Kingdom, 34n2, 76n1, 136, 138–40, 144
United States, 34n2, 43, 76n1, 143, 166, 172, 201n10
unpopular reform, 5, 23–24, 26, 29, 199
unskilled labour. *See* employee, unskilled
up-skilling, 43, 85, *86*, 117–18

vertical redistribution, 60
veto point. *See* constraints, institutional
vocational training, 40, 43, 115–16, 119, 121, 132n17, 134n33
Volkspartei, 93

wage bargaining, 132n16, 133n31
wage inequality, 130, 192
wage pressure, 39
wage-setting mechanisms. *See* wage bargaining
welfare state: benefit, 19; conservative, 41, 55n1; continental, 3, 20, 55n1, 90, 92, 130n1, 182; development, 1, 4–5, 16, 29–30, 34n9, 75, 130n1, 175n1; expansion, 2; generosity index,

59–60, 70, 77n4; growth, 198; liberal, 136, 138, 175n2; policy-making, 2–4, 19, 48, 180–81; public support, of, 16, 19; reform, 2, 4, 20, 30, 48, 137, 180; retrenchment, 2, 15–35, 198
welfare trap, 152
Western democracies, 2, 16, 18, 31, 42, 48, 180
Westminster model, 138–39
white-collar worker, 45, 137
Wirtschaftswunder, German, 95
Woods, Michael J. (Fianna Fáil), 162
workforce: heterogeneous, 36–37; skilled (*see* skilled workers)
working-class, 4, 6, 29–30, 40, 140
work logic, 40–42, 44
Workmen's Compensation Act, 136

youth unemployment, 115

ZDH (Zentralverband Deutscher Handwerker), 102, 105

# About the Author

**Evelyne Hübscher** is associate professor at the Central European University's School of Public Policy in Budapest. She holds a PhD in political science from the European University Institute in Florence. Evelyne teaches courses related to public policy and policy analysis, welfare states and party politics at CEU and the University of Geneva. Her research interests lie at the intersection between party politics and public policy with a specific focus on the political determinants and costs of unpopular reforms on the one hand, and the impact of intra-coalition policy making processes on legislative output on the other hand. Her work has been published in the *European Journal of Political Research*, the *Journal of Legislative Studies* and the *Journal of Public Policy*, among others.

www.ingramcontent.com/pod-product-compliance
Lightning Source LLC
LaVergne TN
LVHW101501200926
848483LV00001B/188